SRI AUROBINDO

ALSO BY ROSHEN DALAL

Non-fiction

The Puffin History of India (two volumes)

The Religions of India: A Concise Guide to Nine Major Faiths

Hinduism: An Alphabetical Guide

The Compact Timeline History of the World

The Vedas: An Introduction to Hinduism's Sacred Texts

The Puffin History of the World (two volumes)

India at 70: Snapshots since Independence

The 108 Upanishads: An Introduction

J. Krishnamurti: A Life of Compassion Beyond Boundaries

A Complete History of India

Fiction

The Guru Who Came Down from the Mountain

SRI AUROBINDO

THE LIFE AND TEACHINGS OF A REVOLUTIONARY PHILOSOPHER

ROSHEN DALAL

MACMILLAN

First published 2023 by Macmillan
an imprint of Pan Macmillan Publishing India Private Limited
707 Kailash Building
26 K. G. Marg, New Delhi 110001
www.panmacmillan.co.in

Pan Macmillan, The Smithson, 6 Briset Street, Farringdon, London EC1M 5NR
Associated companies throughout the world
www.panmacmillan.com

ISBN: 978-93-90742-20-2

1 3 5 7 9 8 6 4 2

Typeset in Adobe Garamond Pro by Manmohan Kumar
Printed and bound in India by Thomson Press India Ltd.

FSC
www.fsc.org
MIX
Paper | Supporting responsible forestry
FSC® C116313

For Ardeshir

Contents

A Note on Place Names

In this book, we employ the old names of Calcutta, Pondicherry and other places, reflecting their usage during the lifetimes of Sri Aurobindo and the Mother.

Introduction

A Divine Vision

Sri Aurobindo is one of India's greatest philosophers. The breadth and depth of his intellect have few comparisons. The range of his readings was vast – from Greek, Latin and Sanskrit texts to books in English, French and other languages. His thinking and concepts went even further. His philosophy contains a blueprint of the whole world and everything within: its origin, present and future. His life, too, was extraordinary.

Aurobindo Ghose was born Aravinda Acroyd Ghose in Calcutta (now Kolkata), in British India, on 15 August 1872. At seven years of age, he moved to England with his two older brothers, studying first at St Paul's School, London, followed by Cambridge University. As a young man, he returned to India in 1893 and then worked in the princely state of Baroda until 1906. During this period, he became involved in the Freedom Movement against the British, who ruled most of India at the time. He had also begun certain yoga practices already, and it was while being imprisoned for his activities in the Indian freedom movement from 1908 to 1909 that he experienced a profound, divine vision. Less than a year after his release, he left British India for the small French-controlled territory of Pondicherry, present-day Puducherry, in South India. Away from the British authorities' reach, it was here he decided to give up politics and develop his own philosophy.

By 1920, Sri Aurobindo was joined by a Frenchwoman named Mirra Alfassa Richard, 'the Mother'. Together, they founded an ashram in 1926, where Sri Aurobindo blessed his followers by giving them 'darshan' three or four times a year. While the Mother was in charge of running the ashram, Aurobindo led a life of seclusion, immersing himself in extensive reading, the study of ancient texts and writing.

*

Sri Aurobindo's entire body of work is compiled in thirty-seven volumes entitled the *Collected Works*. Broadly, his writings can be categorized into poetry and drama, translations and commentaries of ancient texts, works relating to India, social and political analyses, autobiographical fragments and letters offering guidance. While all these feature aspects of his philosophy, *The Life Divine*, *The Synthesis of Yoga* and the 24,000-line epic poem, *Savitri*, are his primary philosophical works. His writings about historical and political developments are covered in *The Human Cycle* and related texts, as well as in his talks and discussions. These conversations, too, were recorded, and later compiled and published by his close associates like A. B. Purani, Nirodbaran and Champaklal.

The Mother's insights on Sri Aurobindo's works, as well as her answers to questions from her students, are captured in another seventeen volumes. Yet another thirteen volumes titled *The Mother's Agenda* feature her conversations with a key disciple, Satprem. Furthermore, numerous books by both close associates and others provide explorations into the lives and teachings of Sri Aurobindo and the Mother.

The philosophy of Sri Aurobindo encompasses two fundamental aspects: the theory of spiritual evolution and working to improve the world – in fact, to make it a veritable heaven on earth. While scientists assert human beings are the product of evolution, Sri Aurobindo further emphasizes that their evolution is ongoing and humans are continuously progressing towards a higher state of being. This process is not merely physical; it also involves the evolution of human life and mind towards an ultimate spirituality and a greater universality. He said that the light and power of the spirit, the 'Supermind', presiding over human evolution, can potentially transform human consciousness and remould life on earth. This evolution is bound to take place, but being aware of it and having a commitment to the Divine and spirituality would enhance the process.

In some Eastern religions, like Hinduism, Buddhism and Jainism, one of the key beliefs is to ultimately achieve moksha, or nirvana, meaning liberation from the cycle of life and death. Moksha, in many schools of thought, implies uniting with the Divine or living in the presence of the Divine. Sri Aurobindo's philosophy presents a different view, focusing on transforming both the world and individual consciousness. According to this view, the union or contact with the Divine is just the first step – the main aim is to bring the Divine to the earth. Therefore, the second key aspect of his thought is that the ultimate purpose of life is not moksha or nirvana but rather introducing divine consciousness on earth.

Expanding further, Sri Aurobindo explains that life, with its myriad experiences of sorrow and joy, beauty and ugliness, has a single aim – to achieve union with the Divine. How is such union then attained? Once united with divine consciousness, what happens to the individual? Does individuality disappear, merging into a universal consciousness, or does something else occur? Many religions and texts across the world have delved into this issue, seeking to find answers. Drawing from ancient texts such as the Vedas, Upanishads and Bhagavad Gita – while also going beyond them – Sri Aurobindo provides his own answers. The paths of *jnana* (knowledge), bhakti (devotion and surrender) and karma (action and work) are all mentioned in the Bhagavad Gita and combined in Sri Aurobindo's Integral Yoga, a unique and distinctive philosophy. While yoga generally refers to achieving union with the Divine, the goal of Integral Yoga is not only to connect with divine consciousness, which embodies Truth, Light and Bliss, but to bring down this consciousness into the whole being, so that it permeates every aspect of the person, including the body and mind.

Reaching such a state is not an easy task; it requires a long and devoted *sadhana* (spiritual practice), but even when it is reached, and a union with the divine consciousness is attained, there is more to be done. This union is only the first step; the next is to direct the divine light and truth towards the world. Sri Aurobindo did not believe that any religion of the past or present contained the whole truth. In his words:

> Truth cannot be shut up in a single book, Bible or Veda or Koran, or in a single religion. The divine being is eternal and universal … All religions have some truth in them, but none has the whole truth; all are created in time and finally decline and perish.[1]

On another occasion, writing about himself in the third person, he said: 'It is not his object to develop any one religion or to amalgamate the older religions or to found any new religion.'[2] The aim is 'inner self-development by which each one who follows it can in time discover the One Self in all and evolve a higher consciousness than the mental, a spiritual and Supramental consciousness, which will transform and divinize human nature'.[3]

Sri Aurobindo's spiritual awareness had begun to grow from his youngest days, further enriched upon his return to India. However, his mature philosophy developed only after he moved to Pondicherry, and his insights continued to evolve throughout his life. His goal was to unite with the Divine, and then bring the divine light and guidance into worldly activities. He attempted to explain to others how to achieve this.

To transcend both the world and the individual ego, one needed an understanding of both. Sri Aurobindo meticulously analysed in his works not only this and other worlds but also different levels of existence and the individual. While he did not prescribe fixed methods, he gave suggestions and hints on how to open up to a different way of life – one infused with a new transformative energy.

Following Sri Aurobindo's death on 5 December 1950, the Mother carried forth his work, running the ashram, establishing the international city of Auroville and continuing with her own sadhana of bodily transformation until her own death in 1973.

Despite the existence of several biographies and considerable literature on Sri Aurobindo's world-changing philosophy, his teachings have not received the recognition they deserve within India's intellectual thought. Perhaps this stems from the emphasis on his early political activities and vision for India. As he'd acknowledged himself, his mature philosophy had moved far beyond its roots in ancient Hindu texts. In fact, his philosophy can be seen as a unity of Eastern and Western streams of thought. Against the backdrop of Sri Aurobindo's life, this book aims to offer an understanding of the core principles underlying his universal ideas, thereby making them better known and accessible. As Sri Aurobindo himself had said, nothing he did was for himself or any group; his philosophy was for the whole of humanity.

Sri Aurobindo had said that no one could write his biography, since his life was not lived in the external world. Nevertheless, the first two chapters of this book provide a brief overview of his external life. To address discrepancies or variant accounts, Sri Aurobindo's own autobiographical notes have been referenced. The Mother, given her pivotal role during his lifetime, holds a prominent place in chapter 2 and a subsequent chapter about her. The book delves into Sri Aurobindo's philosophy as revealed through his writings to serve as an essential guide to understanding his philosophical concepts and his vision of the future.

1
The Early Years

Aravinda Acroyd Ghose, the third child and third son of Krishnadhan Ghose and Swarnalata, was born on 15 August 1872 in Calcutta.[1] By the nineteenth century, the East India Company, a trading company founded in 1600, had established control over parts of the subcontinent through a series of alliances and wars with the local rulers. Following a widespread revolt in 1857, however, the British crown assumed direct authority and Calcutta became the centre of British power and culture, which influenced the Indian middle class in many ways. Krishnadhan Ghose was no exception.

Born in 1844 to Kali Prasad Ghose and Kailaskamini, Krishnadhan had faced a difficult life. His father had died when he was twelve years old, and his mother, following tradition, left to live out her life as a widow in Benares (now Varanasi). Despite these circumstances, Krishnadhan and his brother studied at an English-medium school and somehow continued there, with the help of friends. After completing school, he joined Calcutta Medical College to study to become a doctor. In 1866, he took charge of the government dispensary in Bhagalpur, in present-day Bihar. His brother, Bhama Chandra Ghose, on the other hand, would be employed as a head clerk in Bhagalpur.

Later in life the two brothers would grow distant.[2] By 1864, he had married Swarnalata (born 1852), then twelve years old. While Ghose was from an orthodox family, Swarnalata was the daughter of Raj Narayan Bose, a prominent member of the Brahmo Samaj – a reformist group started by Ram Mohan Roy in 1828. She had been educated at home and was married young, as was customary in those times. Raj Narayan, although a Brahmo Samaji, also championed national or Bengali culture and language.[2] Krishnadhan, too, had been drawn to the ideology of Brahmo Samaj, one of his chief reasons to marry Swarnalata. Within a few years of marriage, two sons were born to the couple, Benoybhusan, in 1867, and Manmohan, in 1869. Manmohan was named after Manmohan Ghose, a good friend of Krishnadhan. Strangely, Manmohan Ghose's wife was also called Swarnalata.

Leaving his wife and two children behind, Krishnadhan went abroad for further studies in January 1870 and joined King's College in Aberdeen, Scotland, where he completed an MD in 1871. By this time in Great Britain, Darwinian ideas were gaining ground, and Krishnadhan was deeply influenced by them. He returned almost an atheist, having lost interest in the Brahmo Samaj, and with a fleeting belief in the superiority of the British. Another prominent member of the Brahmo Samaj, and a friend, Keshub Chandra Sen, had travelled to England at the same time, along with other Brahmo members. Later, Keshub would establish a different branch of the Brahmo Samaj, combining ideas of several religions and a belief in evolutionary spirituality drawn from Darwin's concepts.

Among their friends in England was Annette Akroyd, who came to India in December 1872 to pursue her mission to improve women's' education. Soon after, Krishnadhan and Swarnalata's third child and son, Aurobindo, was born.[3]

Krishnadhan, who admired Annette, added the name Akroyd, with a variation to the spelling, as a second name for his son.[4] The ideas of his father, grandfather and their friends also had a subtle influence on Sri Aurobindo.

Krishnadhan had violated the rules of the caste-dominated society in which he lived by going abroad and studying medicine. Refusing the *prayaschitta* or repentance rituals recommended for him, he ignored the requirements of his community, cutting himself off from it. He joined government service after returning by the end of 1871 and got posted as an assistant surgeon at Rangpur, in present-day Bangladesh. By February 1873, he'd become the civil surgeon for the district and grown popular for his hard work, organizational acumen and empathy. Outbreaks of malaria were frequent in the area at that time, and its causes unknown.[5] Krishnadhan, noticing a higher concentration of malaria patients in swampy areas, initiated the building of canals to drain the swamps. The first, completed in 1877, would later be called the 'Ghose canal'. Living alongside him in Rangpur, the beautiful and talented Swarnalata grew to be very well-liked, earning the moniker 'The Rose of Rangpur' from the locals. She comfortably socialized with the British residents, rode horses and also wrote short stories.

But Swarnalata's emotional and psychological difficulties had already begun to manifest around the time of her first child's birth, and unfortunately continued to gradually worsen. Due to diseases being rampant in Rangpur, she was sent to Calcutta to stay with Krishnadhan's friend Manmohan Ghose until the birth of her third child. In Rangpur Krishnadhan and Swarnalata had been good friends with the district collector, William Glazier, and the district judge, Henry Beveridge, who married Annette Akroyd in 1875. As there was no good school in Rangpur, in 1877, when Aurobindo was five years old, Krishnadhan sent his three sons to Loretto House, a boarding school in Darjeeling run by Irish nuns. The boys spent two years at the school before their father decided to send them to England. They were already fluent in English, since even at their home in Rangpur they only spoke in English, with some Hindustani thrown in while speaking to the servants. In October 1877 another child, a girl named Sarojini, was born and, before her, they had one child who did not survive. At the end of 1878, Krishnadhan and Swarnalata set off for England with their four children, arriving early in 1879. Krishnadhan wanted to leave his three sons there and also hoped to seek professional advice regarding Swarnalata's health. In January 1880, another son was born to them in England, Barindra Kumar, though he was initially named Emmanuel Matthew Ghose, after Swarnalata's doctor, Matthew.

Krishnadhan, and later Swarnalata, Sarojini and Barindra eventually returned to India, leaving the three boys in the care of William and Mary Drewitt in Manchester. William H. Drewitt, a pastor and relative of the Rangpur district collector Glazier, agreed to take care of the boys in exchange for £360 a year from Krishnadhan to cover their expenses. William's mother, Elizabeth, and Mary's sister, Edith Fishbourne, stayed with the couple.

It is said that Krishnadhan wanted his sons to grow up like English boys and have no contact with Indians, and also that he wanted them to join the Indian Civil Service (ICS), the administrative service through which the British ruled India. The Service was founded in 1853, and though theoretically open to Indians, it was extraordinarily difficult for them to qualify. The entrance examination was held in England, and the maximum age to sit for it was reduced to nineteen by 1876, down from the initial age of twenty-three.[6]

There must have been multiple reasons for Krishnadhan to

leave his sons in England, apart from his desire for them to qualify for the ICS. He wanted to do his best for them – provide them with the best possible education, free from the shackles of restricting traditions. It is possible that he also sought to remove them from Swarnalata's disturbing moods, which now ranged from unreasonable joy to fits of terrible anger. Perhaps influenced by Keshub's evolutionary spirituality, Krishnadhan, as he later explained to his brother-in-law, wanted to give the world 'children of a better breed', starting with his own, while also helping other less-advantaged children.[7]

The Drewitts seem to have been kind to the children, focusing on their education without trying to convert them to Christianity. To get them admission to school, William himself taught the boys for two years, his instruction including Latin, a necessary requirement. His wife also assisted in their education. In 1881 Benoy and Manmohan were enrolled in the Manchester Grammar School, while Aurobindo, then nine years old, continued to be taught at home. He studied Latin, French, history, geography and arithmetic.

But William resigned his pastorship in 1881 and emigrated to Australia by 1884, with his mother, Elizabeth Drewitt, staying back and moving to London with the three boys in her care. In September 1884 Manmohan and Aurobindo enrolled at St Paul's School in London, while Benoy completed school in Manchester. St Paul's focus was on academics over sports, which suited Aurobindo well, as he was never athletically inclined. His subjects included Greek, Latin, French and English literature, along with history, divinity and mathematics. Aurobindo received high praise from all his teachers due to his brilliant mind and ability to excel in any subject he put his mind to. In addition to what was required for his studies, he read widely. He joined the debating and the literary societies, though it would seem he did not make any good friends, being somewhat silent and also younger than his classmates. Manmohan, who later became a poet, started writing poetry, and Aurobindo emulated him. A poem he wrote at the age of ten was also published in a local magazine.

Upon completing school in 1887, Manmohan won a scholarship to Christchurch, Oxford, while Aurobindo, who graduated in 1889, was awarded a scholarship to King's College, Cambridge, after securing the first position in the scholarship exam. The last two years had been difficult for the brothers, as funds from home had almost dried up. Elizabeth Drewitt, who was a fervent Christian, had angrily moved out of the flat she shared with the boys when Manmohan made certain disparaging statements about Christianity. So, in 1887 Benoy and Aurobindo shifted into a room at the Kensington Branch of the Liberal Club, where Benoy worked for James Cotton, the club's secretary. James was the brother of Krishnadhan's friend Henry Cotton, an official in the ICS. The little money sent by Krishnadhan was needed by Manmohan at Oxford, even though he had a scholarship. Benoy and Aurobindo somehow managed on Benoy's meagre earnings of five shillings a week, enduring with inadequate warm clothing and almost a starvation diet. Aurobindo would describe the eating situation later, saying, 'During a whole year 1888–89 a slice or two of sandwich bread and butter and a cup of tea in the morning and in the evening a penny saveloy formed the only food'.[8] In these last two years, Aurobindo was more interested in extracurricular reading than his school subjects but worked hard in the final year.

In October 1890, Aurobindo joined Cambridge; the same year in June, he sat for the ICS entrance examination that lasted thirteen days, and ranked eleventh out of 250 candidates. This was only the entrance, and further steps were needed to actually qualify, including two years' undergraduate study at an English university. At Cambridge he had to study for both the ICS and the Bachelor of Arts exam, known as the Tripos. Fortunately, he received a scholarship that gave him a stipend of £80 a year, along with free accommodation and tuition. The ICS, too, granted him a stipend of £300, half during his course and half on completion. With these, he support his own needs as well as those of his brothers. The two courses ran parallel, and had different subjects, with law, political economy, Bengali and Sanskrit among those for the ICS, and classical and English literature studies for the Tripos. He did not make much headway in his own native language, Bengali, but was able to teach himself some Sanskrit by studying a passage from the Mahabharata.

Despite being financially constrained, Aurobindo was happy in his years at Cambridge, particularly with the intellectual stimulation that broadened his worldview. He enjoyed his studies and formed new friendships, despite his essentially solitary nature. One such friend was Keshav Ganesh Deshpande, who was studying at St John's College, and their friendship would continue in India. Even after his years in England, Aurobindo did not particularly like living there and instead felt inspired by France and the ideals of the French Revolution. He had already become interested in Indian independence and vowed to work for the cause, joining the Indian *majlis* (assembly) at Cambridge where he gave some nationalistic speeches. Founded on 1 January 1891, the Cambridge majlis was a forum where Indians aired their views,[9] and its other notable members would later include Jawaharlal Nehru, Muhammad Ali Jinnah and Subhas Chandra Bose.

Although Aurobindo had not met his father since the age of seven, somehow he was still deeply influenced by him. From being absolutely pro-British, his father had turned against their rule in India and begun sending his sons newspaper clippings detailing British atrocities, which likely played a role in leading Aurobindo's thoughts in the same direction. One of the reasons for Krishnadhan's changed feelings for British rule was that later in his career, he'd come into contact with some autocratic British officials. Apart from being the district surgeon of Rangpur, in 1876, Krishnadhan had become a member of the Rangpur Municipality, and by 1877, its vice-chairman. He was held in high regard by the British officials in Rangpur, and the British magistrate took no action without consulting him. But years of conflict ensued when the new magistrate did not like the influence Krishnadhan commanded. In June 1883 he was posted out of Rangpur, with short stints in different places, including Khulna, in present-day Bangladesh. From July 1885 until his death, he remained in Khulna. Through these conflicts, however, he gained a better understanding of British rule, giving rise to nationalistic ideas within him.[10]

Aurobindo performed well in his periodic exams but had to complete the three-year Tripos in two, as per the requirements for the ICS. Though he had a first class in the Tripos, he could not actually get the degree, as it would require him to stay on at Cambridge for another year. Now it was time for him to join the ICS. By nature, Aurobindo was a scholar, not an administrator, and he would have done well as an academic. English was his first language, and he was also proficient in French, Greek and Latin, with the ability to read German and Italian.

Krishnadhan no longer believed in the greatness of the British, so why did he still want Aurobindo to join the ICS? Was it so his son could do good as an administrator with India's interests at heart? And why did Aurobindo try to do what his father wanted? His two elder brothers had gone their own way.

If Aurobindo had dropped out of the ICS at this stage and continued at Cambridge, would his father have objected? And would such objection matter? Nevertheless, Aurobindo went ahead and passed the main ICS exam. The riding test remained, and for one reason or the other, this became a stumbling block. He had never learnt to ride, and riding lessons were expensive. In the first attempt, he failed the test and did not appear for it subsequently. A general view, which he also expressed in his own writing, is that he was looking for a way to avoid joining the ICS, as otherwise 'his family would not have allowed him to'. In 1940, in his evening talks noted by Nirodbaran, he echoed the same view.[11]

However, a newspaper interview from 1909 suggests he had mixed feelings about not being able to join. He said: 'If I was not actually glad, I was certainly not disappointed because the Civil Service was barred to me. I have never been fond of constraint of any sort and I was really not sorry to forego the service.'[12] Persuaded by James Cotton, he also wrote a letter dated 2 November 1892 to the Earl of Kimberley, the secretary of state for India, requesting another chance at the exam, explaining it was lack of money that prevented him from learning to ride and thus appearing for the test.[13] Nothing came of this and, as he was not able to join the ICS and not keen on doing so either, James Cotton set up a meeting between him and the ruler of the Indian state of Baroda, who was visiting England. The Gaekwar offered him a job with Rs 200 a month, and Aurobindo accepted.

Meanwhile, Krishnadhan had spent the months of September and October in Bombay waiting for his son's return before going back to Khulna, depressed.[14] Two months later, at the age of forty-eight, he fell ill and died sometime on 11 or 12 December. There are two conflicting explanations for his illness, both associated with a telegram he received regarding

Aurobindo. According to one account, he read a telegram conveying the news that the ship Aurobindo was travelling on had sunk. However, this seems unlikely because the *Roumania*, a steamer headed for Bombay, had actually sunk near Portugal on 28 October. This event could not have been the subject of the telegram since it reached him in December, and reports of the ship sinking had already been published in a Calcutta-based newspaper in November.[15] Another account comes from Brajendranath De, a Civil Service member and friend of Krishnadhan, providing a different version. Apparently, he invited Krishnadhan for dinner, but when he didn't arrive, Brajendranath grew concerned and sent someone to check on him. After the messenger reported that Krishnadhan was ill, Brajendranath went to see Krishnadhan and found him unconscious. He then discovered the telegram stating that Aurobindo's name was missing from the passenger list of the ship he was supposed to be on, which had left Krishnadhan devastated.

Years later, Aurobindo revealed that his father had specifically asked him to travel on that particular ship.[16] He believed that the false reports of his own death had tragically contributed to his father's passing. Pinning all his hopes and dreams on his third son, Krishnadhan had eagerly awaited his return. Aurobindo would also be informed that his father had passed away while calling out his name.

Krishnadhan Ghose had been an exceptional doctor and surgeon who had dedicated many years to practising in Khulna. He treated patients from neighbouring districts and played a role in the administration of Khulna. Due to his generosity and likeable nature, the local community held him in high regard. As a tribute, a school was later established in his name. While Krishnadhan did not leave behind much wealth, the brothers inherited a plot of land with a dilapidated small structure.

There are no accounts of Swarnalata's reaction to her husband's death. After returning from England in 1880, she stayed in Deogarh, Bihar, with her parents. She later moved to a house in Rohini, a nearby village, with Barin and Sarojini. During her periods of anger, she would beat up the children, so Krishnadhan removed them from her and placed them with a woman friend in Calcutta. Swarnalata's family did not appreciate his relationship with this woman, who, however, was kind to the children. After Krishnadhan's death, Swarnalata's brother adopted them, and they moved to Deogarh. By this time, Barin was thirteen years old, and Sarojini fifteen.

It was a month after his father's death that Aurobindo left for India on 11 January 1893, travelling by the *Carthage*, a mail-steamer that arrived in Bombay in February, and he proceeded to Baroda to take up his job. Under the rule of the Gaekwar, Baroda was one of the Indian states which was not directly under the British, with the city of Baroda as its capital. The local language was Gujarati, and the Gaekwar Sayajirao III was a Maratha, who was indirectly related to the previous ruler, and was fluent in English as well as Marathi and Gujarati.[17] In all the Indian states the British took care of defence and foreign affairs, and with the resulting safety and security, many of the rulers, with their vast wealth, indulged in luxurious and frivolous pastimes. The Gaekwar, though, was among those rulers who took governance seriously and did a lot for his state. Aurobindo's first appointment, on 18 February, was to work in the Settlement Department of the state. Other appointments in different departments followed. From this time onward, he never used his middle name; in Baroda, he became known as Aravind A. Ghose. It was almost a year after his arrival in January 1894 that Aurobindo went to Ajmer to meet Benoybhusan, before travelling to Deogarh and Rohini to meet his grandfather Raj

Narayan, his mother and other relatives.[18] He would continue to maintain relations with his family, particularly with Raj Narayan, Barin and Sarojini after this visit, but also with his uncles, aunts and cousins. Raj Narayan had nine children, six daughters and three sons. His eldest son, Jogendranath Bose, a journalist, sympathized with the national movement, and later started a revolutionary organization in Midnapore (now Medinipur in West Bengal) where he lived. Sarojini was keen that Aurobindo visit again, writing to him in Bengali. In response, Aurobindo wrote to her, 'If I only could, I would start tomorrow', but his circumstances and finances did not allow it. He also added that following his visit to their relatives, Baroda had become intolerable to him.[19]

Aurobindo had been deprived of parental love while he was growing up. Though his brothers were with him, there are no accounts of them pampering him like a younger sibling. This visit was perhaps the first time he had experienced family warmth, and despite his solitary nature, it appealed to him.

Back in Baroda, Aurobindo's work was greatly liked by the Gaekwar, and his salary steadily increased. As his abilities became known, the principal of the Baroda College requested his help as a teacher of French, and he began to teach part-time at the college; in January 1898, he was appointed as an acting professor of English literature. According to the official documents of the Baroda state, he taught there until 1901, and then he moved back to the revenue department before returning to teaching from 1904 to 1906. However, later he'd recount that after his appointment, he had continued to teach until he left.[20] Even while he was teaching, the Gaekwar would ask him to visit his palace in order to write letters or for some other work, sending a messenger to him on a horse with the request. Baroda College was affiliated to Bombay University, and Bombay was under the British; hence it had a British-oriented syllabus, and Aurobindo would teach according to it. Though he was very highly respected in Baroda, Aurobindo was generally considered too quiet and serious to be widely popular. But he had some good friends, including Madhavrao Jadhav and his brother Khesarao. Madhavrao was an officer in the Baroda army, and Khesarao a senior official, who was posted elsewhere in the state, but had built a house in Baroda, where Madhavrao and his family stayed. Aurobindo often stayed with them. K. G. Deshpande, whom he knew from their Cambridge days, and his brother Rajaram were among his other friends.

During his visits to Bengal, Sri Aurobindo would often go to the house of his aunt Lilavati, the fourth daughter of Raj Narayan Bose, in Calcutta. Lilawati had been married to the Brahmo leader, journalist, social reformer and nationalist Krishna Kumar Mitra in 1881, who started a Bengali journal called *Sanjibani* in 1883. On one of his visits, Aurobindo appointed a Bengali teacher, Dinendra Kumar Roy, recommended by his mother's elder brother, Jogindranath Bose. Dinendra returned to Baroda with him and stayed with him for two years.

Although Sri Aurobindo had already taught himself to read and write Bengali, he had problems with colloquial Bengali and needed practice in speaking the language. Dinendra wrote a short book about Aurobindo's nature and his own stay in Baroda. At first he was hesitant, wondering how this England-returned person would be, and whether he would be very arrogant. But that was not the case, he wrote. 'It goes without saying that I was very disappointed with my first meeting with Aurobindo. Old-fashioned slippers jutis with ends turned up on his feet; his clothes of coarse (*sic*), flounced Ahmedabad-mill khadi, the end of his dhoti hanging loose.' Aurobindo also wore a waistcoat and his hair was long and thin, 'parted in the middle and hanging down over the neck; tiny pockmarks on his face; his eyes with a gentle, dreamy look – who would have thought that this thin, dark-skinned young man was Sriman Aurobindo Ghose'.[21] Dinendra described Aurobindo as someone who cared little about clothes, food or any type of luxury. He slept on a cast-iron bed with a thin mattress and used an ordinary blanket on winter nights and a simple blue shawl in the cold. Aurobindo was always absorbed in reading, sensitive to the suffering of others and self-sacrificing. 'It seemed he had made a vow to devote himself to the acquisition of knowledge.' Aurobindo would often sit at a table, reading by lamplight late into the night. He was not particular about food and would eat whatever was placed before him. Sometimes, engrossed in a book, he would forget to eat. He never complained about heat or cold. Although his Bengali improved with Dinendra's help, English remained the language in which he could best think and write.

Dinendra commented that Aurobindo was so simple in worldly matters and unconcerned about money that everyone cheated him. He had no ambition and never aspired for position or praise. At one time they lived in an out-of-the-way dilapidated house, which according to Dinendra, would be considered worse than a cowshed for a member of the Bengali elite. But Aurobindo hardly seemed to notice the leaking tiles or the swarms of mosquitoes. 'I would see him with his eyes fixed on a book, sitting in the same spot with the same concentration for hours on end, oblivious of the outer world, like an ascetic rapt in yoga! He wouldn't have noticed if the house caught fire!' Dinendra would also recall that Aurobindo had books of all kinds in many European languages, including poetry, fiction, history and philosophy. Sanskrit classics were also piled up in corners of the rooms, in cupboards and trunks.[22] He constantly ordered books from Bombay and Calcutta, which arrived in enormous railway parcels and swiftly finished reading through all the books. Dinendra's account provides a glimpse of a man who would have made a good academician, living a simple ascetic life, finding joy in reading and studying.

In 1901, Aurobindo finally got married during his vacation in Calcutta, probably on 29 April. Both Benoy and Manmohan were already married and Aurobindo himself was keen on marriage. He admitted this in a later conversation, saying that at the time he had no inkling of the spiritual work he would undertake in the future.[23] There was also pressure from his family, and he placed an advertisement in the newspaper for this. In the manner of those days, he saw several girls and ultimately chose Mrinalini.

Born on 6 March 1887, Mrinalini was the daughter of Bhupalchandra Bose, a member of the Brahmo Samaj. She was fourteen years old, pretty, with a rosy complexion and black curly hair, though what attracted Aurobindo was her 'sweet innocence and childlike simplicity'.[24] Aurobindo was almost twenty-nine, but in those days, as in his father's time, girls were married off very young. It was Aurobindo's choice that they be married according to Hindu rituals instead of Brahmo rites, as he did not favour the Brahmo Samaj and its ideals.[25] But he was not orthodox, refusing to partake in the prayaschitta rituals required in those days for anyone who had crossed the seas, i.e., gone abroad, just as his father had refused before him. Unlike many girls of those days, Mrinalini had received some formal education, and even attended a boarding school for Brahmo girls.

The marriage took place in Calcutta and was arranged by Girish Chandra Bose, a friend of Mrinalini's father and the principal of Bangabasi College. Although Aurobindo's grandfather, Raj Narayan Bose, had passed away in 1899, he maintained good relations with other members of his mother's family, despite the fact that they did not attend the wedding. Aurobindo and Mrinalini stayed in Deogarh for a month after their marriage in the household now headed by Swarnalata's brother before proceeding to Nainital. The Gaekwar had gone to Nainital for the summer, and Aurobindo joined him there with both Mrinalini and his sister Sarojini. By this time, Aurobindo had learnt quite a bit of Bengali, which they likely communicated in. The newlyweds reached Baroda in July 1901, with Sarojini, as perhaps Aurobindo felt his young wife needed some company and help. He had rented a house prior to his marriage, and they lived there until April 1902, when Aurobindo visited Bengal again. Mrinalini went to stay with her parents in Assam, while Sarojini returned to Deogarh.

There were various aspects to Aurobindo's life between 1900 and 1910 when he moved to Pondicherry. He continued working for the Baroda state until 1906, although he often took leave. According to some accounts, he was appointed as *Huzur Kamdar* or private secretary to the Gaekwar in June 1904, but Sri Aurobindo denied this.[26] Records indicate his reappointment at the college in September 1904, but as mentioned earlier, Sri Aurobindo stated that he had never stopped teaching. During this period, his salary was raised to Rs 550, and he was promoted to vice principal. In March 1905, he assumed the role of acting principal when Clarke, the principal, took leave. Additionally, he received a separate allowance of Rs 160, bringing his salary to Rs 710, which was substantial for that time. Aurobindo used to send 80 rupees per month from his salary to support his mother, sister and grandmother (who resided in Varanasi). By then, he had acquired a basic understanding of Gujarati, Marathi and Hindi, and had become quite proficient in

Bengali. Simultaneously, Aurobindo was searching for ways to push for India's independence.[27] Soon after his return to India, he had started writing political articles for *Indu Prakash*, a bilingual weekly in Marathi and English edited by his friend K. G. Deshpande. One of Aurobindo's important series of articles was titled 'New lamps for Old', written between 1893 to 1894, pointing out ways in which India could move towards independence. The main organization in the struggle for independence was the Indian National Congress (INC), founded in 1885 with the encouragement of Allan Octavian Hume, a Theosophist and civil servant. In its early days, Congress leaders wrote petitions to the government, modestly aiming to increase Indian participation in the government and gain a few privileges. Soon another group arose, who came to be known as the Extremists, while the former was then termed the Moderates. Bal Gangadhar Tilak from Poona (now Pune) was among the main Extremist leaders, running two papers: *Kesari*, which had thousands of subscribers, and the other in English titled *Mahratta*. In 1894 Tilak started the public celebration of Ganesh puja, and by 1895, a festival celebrating Shivaji, intending to foster national sentiment among Indians. But even by 1900, the independence movement remained in its infancy.

Others targeted assassinations of select British officials, and secret societies began to crop up. Against this background, Aurobindo developed his own ideas to gain independence. At one time he thought there should be 'a secret revolutionary propaganda and organization of which the central object was the preparation of an armed insurrection', though later his views on this changed. In addition, he believed that the common people should be motivated to work for independence and to be involved in non-cooperation and passive resistance, which would then make British rule impossible.[28] Among the secret societies was the Anushilan Samiti, founded by the Calcutta-based lawyer Pramathanath Mitra and Satish Chandra Bose. Aurobindo managed to persuade a friend of his, Jatindranath Banerji, to join the society in March 1902. Jatindranath had long been keen on revolutionary activity and on getting some martial training. Aurobindo had helped him join the Baroda army, and he had been serving as the Gaekwar's bodyguard since 1897.[29] After a visit to Baroda, Barin, Aurobindo's younger brother, also joined the organization in January 1903. Around that time, Sister Nivedita,[30] part of another revolutionary organization, had visited Baroda in October 1902, where she met both Aurobindo and the Gaekwar. She hoped to draw the Gaekwar in anti-British activities, but although he was against the British, he refrained from taking an active part. Jatin and Barin did not get along, and Jatin left the Samiti after the Alipore Bomb case, in which Aurobindo and others were arrested in 1908. Jatin Banerji, not to be confused with the more famous Jatin Mukherjee, who was known as Bagha Jatin, in fact later became a swami.

There was a new impetus to the national movement with the British arbitrary partition of Bengal in 1905. It led to widespread protests and caused Aurobindo to step up efforts to work towards independence. He wrote an essay on the partition titled 'No compromise', which was distributed as a pamphlet. Inspired by *Anandamath*, Bankim Chandra Chattopadhyay's great historical novel, Barin thought of establishing a religious centre to serve as the source of inspiration in the struggle for independence.

Aurobindo and his friends often visited the sacred site of Chandod on the banks of the Narmada River. He and his friends admired Swami Brahmananda, who lived in Chandod, and was thought to be two to three hundred years old. Once, when Brahmananda looked into his eyes, Aurobindo felt something change within him. He was also inspired by the Kali temple at the nearby town of Karnali. There Deshpande, his old friend, had constructed a school where both Sanskrit and modern nationalist education was taught.

Following Barin's ideas, Aurobindo conceived of a temple to Goddess Bhavani, who reflected the spirit and Shakti of India. In fact, he wrote a pamphlet titled 'Bhawani Mandir'. The temple, he said, should be built far from any city and turned into a centre for karma yogis and sannyasis working for the nation. He also reiterated that the entire concept had come from Barin, not himself.[31]

Another aspect to Aurobindo's life was that in August 1905, he began to seriously practise *pranayama*, the yogic science of controlled breathing, combined with a focus on the Divine. Guided initially by a disciple of Brahmananda, he gradually increased his pranayama practice to six hours a day, dividing it into morning and evening sessions. He also switched to a purely vegetarian diet, with his dinner consisting of just bananas and milk. It yielded remarkable results: he put on weight, his skin became clear and radiant, his writing flowed effortlessly and he had more energy.[32]

His time with the Gaekwar would soon be over. There was a plan to set up a college for national education in Calcutta, and Aurobindo was keen on this. Subodh Chandra Mullick, son of a shipbuilder, financed this with an amount of Rs 100,000. In February 1906, Clarke, the principal of the Baroda College, returned from his long leave, enabling Sri Aurobindo to take leave himself and reach Calcutta in March. In Calcutta, the decision to set up the National College of Education was confirmed, and Aurobindo became one of the ninety-two founding members and one of the eight signatories of the Memorandum of Association for the college. It was at this time that he had begun signing his name 'Aurobindo Ghose'. By June, he returned to Baroda to apply for a full year's leave, after which he became the first principal of the Bengal National College, which opened in August in Calcutta. He received a modest salary of Rs 150, but he felt he was doing something worthwhile.

Bengal remained the epicentre of the national movement, and alongside his college work, Sri Aurobindo wrote articles providing guidelines for the movement, attended Congress sessions and gave speeches at various venues. In March 1906, a revolutionary Bengali weekly called *Yugantar*, also spelt *Jugantar*, was launched, and Aurobindo contributed articles to it. In August of the same year, the weekly *Bande Mataram* was founded by Bipin Chandra Pal, another Extremist leader, with Aurobindo serving as the assistant editor. Due to financial problems, *Bande Mataram* was made into a joint-stock company in October, and Bipin Chandra Pal was gradually edged out. Many of Aurobindo's ideas were first expressed in these journals.

In 1906, Aurobindo stayed for some time with the Mullicks before moving to a house on Chhuku Khansama Lane. Barin, Abinash, Sarojini and Mrinalini joined him there. Later, they moved to 23 Scott's Lane, while Barin shifted to their father's property at Murari Pukur Bagan, in the Manicktola suburb of Calcutta. In November of that year, Aurobindo fell ill with a protracted bout of influenza. He moved to his father-in-law's house and then went to to Deogarh to recover. He also felt he'd became prone to infection after discontinuing the intensive pranayama that he had started a year earlier.[33]

Between 11 to 23 April 1907, Sri Aurobindo wrote a series of seven articles titled 'The New Thought: The Doctrine of Passive Resistance', published in *Bande Mataram*, which led the British to keep a close watch on him. In these writings, he examined Congress's early attempts to gain minor concessions from the British, how passive resistance was used after the 1905 partition of Bengal and how they were now planning to resist the British rule to achieve freedom for India. Passive resistance, he explained, was not 'meek submission to illegal outrage' but as far as possible, violence was not to be used.[34] By 28 May 1907, Sri Aurobindo formally assumed the editorship and, by June, they started a weekly edition, which enjoyed a wider reach, consisting of a selection of articles from the daily edition. In August, he was arrested for his work in *Bande Mataram*, though released on bail and acquitted after a month. Once he was acquitted, he rejoined the National College as a professor, having resigned from *Bande Mataram* after his arrest. By December, he was recognized as a leader of the Bengal nationalists, and even delivered public speeches in Calcutta. In the previous two years, the Moderates and Extremists in the INC had increasing difficulties in reconciling their starkly different approaches to the national movement, but at the annual Congress sessions in 1905 and 1906 in Benaras and Calcutta, these differences were patched up. Then, at the Surat session of the INC in December 1907, the two groups parted ways. On the side of the Extremists, Aurobindo played a major role in this split due to his uncompromising approach. After the Congress fiasco he briefly returned to Baroda, and in the following year gave several speeches on the national movement in Baroda, as well as in various places in present-day Maharashtra and Calcutta. In his speeches and writings, he spoke of how nationalism had to be viewed as a religion and how faith, self-sacrifice and courage were required to free the nation. One had to deny one's separate self and find that universal self of the 300 million people of India, 'in whom God himself lives'.[35]

Though conflicts between Hindus and Muslims had begun, Sri Aurobindo felt they were the result of faulty and divisive British policies. After the Partition of Bengal in 1905, the British feared the effects of the Swadeshi and Boycott movements on their trade and industry, and therefore encouraged these conflicts.[36] He asserted: 'Regional and communal individualities and activities cannot be blotted out from this vast country, but they can be harmonized into a dominating unity.' He also pointed out that the fight was not between Muslims and Hindus, despite the recent disturbances, rather between 'the bureaucrats and swadeshists'.[37] This early understanding would be further emphasized in his later writings.

In early May 1908, just a few days after he'd joined the office of the Bengali weekly *Naba Shakti* on Grey Street and moved in with Mrinalini and Sarojini, Aurobindo was arrested again. Barin had been picked up too from the centre of his revolutionary activities – the Maniktola suburb – at the plot they'd inherited from their father. Thirty-four others got arrested with him, among whom were Nolini Kanta Gupta and Bejoy Nag. The reason for the arrests was the attempted assassination of Mr Kingsford, the district magistrate of Muzaffarpur in April 1908. The primary accused were Prafulla Chaki and Khudiram Bose, who had thrown a bomb at what they thought was Kingsford's carriage but had turned out to be of one Mrs Kennedy and her daughter, leaving both dead. Not only this incident, there were also other acts of violence that were linked to the Maniktola group.

Initially, there was a plan to deport Aurobindo, though this was set aside and he was sent to Alipore Jail instead. As the trial was held in the Alipore Sessions Court, this came to be known as the Alipore Bomb Case. Khudiram Bose was hanged in August 1908 before his nineteenth birthday, while Prafulla Chaki shot himself upon finding that he was on the verge of arrest. Barin was to be executed; however, his sentence was commuted, and he was sent to Andaman Jail, where he was to remain until 1920. Many of the others who were arrested received jail terms. Aurobindo was imprisoned for a year until his acquittal on 6 May 1909. Some others, such as Nolini Kanta Gupta and Bejoy Nag, were also acquitted at this time.

After his release, Aurobindo went to his uncle Krishna Kumar Mitra's house at 6 College Square in Calcutta. Since Krishna Kumar had also been arrested, Aurobindo ended up living at the house for about ten months with his aunt Lilavati and cousins Kumudini, Basanti and Sukumar, until he left for Chandernagore. Mrinalini continued to stay with Girish Bose, her father's friend and the principal of Bangabasi College.

During his stay at College Square, he was visited by many, including Rabindranath Tagore and Ramsay Macdonald, who thought of Aurobindo as a mystic, not a politician.[38] Macdonald, a British politician of the Labour Party, would go on to become the prime minister of the UK in 1924 and from 1929 to 1931.

During the period when Sri Aurobindo was imprisoned, the national movement had lost its momentum. *Bande Mataram* and *Yugantar* had shut down and most of the Extremists, including Tilak, had been arrested. After his deep spiritual experiences in jail, Sri Aurobindo's focus, too, had changed. Soon he also started two new publications, *Karmayogin* in English, founded on 19 June, and *Dharma* in Bengali, on 23 August 1909. He contributed articles to both, but wrote more in *Karmayogin*, as he felt most comfortable in English. His articles were now no longer purely political and featured a strong spiritual element. He wrote about *sanatana dharma*, the eternal religion, a term often used to refer to Hinduism, explaining that this was something far wider than outer forms or rituals. He saw the world moving towards a synthesis of religious thought, as he said, a 'religion which embraces Science and faith, Theism, Christianity, Mahomedanism, Buddhism, and yet is none of these, is that to which the World-spirit moves'. Aurobindo believed that Hinduism was closest to the world spirit, but not in the narrow form as it was commonly practised. He explained that he referred to a 'wider Hinduism which is not a dogma or combination of dogmas' and further added, 'This sanatana dharma has many scriptures, Veda, Vedanta, Gita, Upanishad, Darshan, Purana, Tantra, nor could it reject the Bible or Koran; but its real, most authoritative scripture is in the heart in which the Eternal has its Dwelling'. Aurobindo envisioned a spiritual revolution that would be reflected in the material world through this wide religion based on sanatana dharma. He believed it would not be confined to Hinduism and include other religions.[39] He emphasized that Muslims had a role in India as much as Hindus, and that understanding had to be created deep in the heart and mind, for which 'we must strive to remove the causes of misunderstanding by a better mutual knowledge and sympathy'. He added that they needed to 'make it a main part of our work to place Mahomed and Islam in a new light before our readers, to spread juster views of Mahomedan history and civilisation, to appreciate the Musalman's place in our national development and the means of harmonizing his communal life with our own'.[40]

He also continued to write and speak about Swaraj or independence and autonomy from foreign rule as well as on spirituality, politics, society, art, education and other topics. *Karmayogin* had a large circulation and soon there were Bengali, Hindi and Tamil versions.

With Barin still in jail, the members of the Maniktola group who had been released saw Aurobindo as their leader, and became his close associates, among them Nolini Kanta Gupta, Bejoy Kumar Nag, Suresh Chakravarti and Saurin Bose, who was a cousin of Mrinalini.

Sometime later, in February 1910, Aurobindo came to know he was likely to be arrested again. He received an *aadesh* or inner command, to leave British India and move to French India. Immediately, and with great secrecy, he left Calcutta by boat and went to Chandernagore, which was in French territory. After spending a couple of months there, he left Chandernagore by ship on 1 April and reached Pondicherry on 4 April.

Giving up active politics, he never again returned to British India and embarked on an intense spiritual path until 1910. In the meantime, there were even other aspects of his life.

From Politics to Spirituality

Among the rest of his family members, Benoybhusan, Aurobindo's eldest brother, was practical and pragmatic. In England, he had been the first of the brothers to take up a job and help to support Aurobindo and himself. He worked hard for the free accommodation they received and the small sum of five shillings a week. Benoy returned to India in September 1893, and initially stayed with his father's friend in Calcutta, Manmohan Ghose. Soon, he found a job as a tutor to the young prince of the state of Coochbehar, in the north of Bengal. Aurobindo met him in Ajmer in 1894, where Benoy had gone with his pupil. Well respected by the Raja, Benoy had been also given the position of auditor and finance secretary. Aurobindo held Benoy in high regard and respected him, but they hardly met after their return to India.[41]

Manmohan had a romantic and poetic nature, and in England, he was often out of sync with his more serious brothers. He became known as a poet, and his poetic venture served as inspiration for Aurobindo. Unlike Aurobindo, Manmohan loved England and wanted to remain there. Since this wasn't possible, Benoy had to send him money for his return to India. Upon his return, he taught at Patna, Bankipur and Calcutta. In 1897, Manmohan joined Dacca College as an assistant professor and later became a full professor in 1901. He continued to write poetry, and married Malati. After her death in 1918, however, he became depressed, and his health deteriorated. He wanted to return to England and had tickets booked for his daughter and himself, but he died in Calcutta on 4 January 1924 before they could leave. When Aurobindo was teaching at the National College in Calcutta, he'd met Manmohan a few times, and they used to enjoy discussing poetry. Though Manmohan was not involved in politics, he admired the role of both Barin and Aurobindo.[42]

Yet, Aurobindo was closer to his younger siblings, Sarojini and Barin, whom he got to know after returning to India. Soon after his marriage, Sarojini accompanied him and Mrinalini to Nainital, and also to Baroda. He regularly sent money to support her. Although Sarojini and Mrinalini did not get along, Aurobindo always urged Mrinalini to overlook their differences and to be patient and tolerant.

Barin was the closest one to Aurobindo, sharing his passion to free India from British rule. After Barin's arrest, however, he would have to remain in the Andaman jail until 1920. As for their mother, Swarnalata, Aurobindo met her after his return and sent money to support her but was never close to her. He shared a good relationship with his grandfather Raj Narayan and engaged in several discussions with him. He was not influenced by his Brahmo Samaj philosophy, though, and did not think much of it.

Involved with his work in Baroda state, followed by politics and then his spiritual journey, he could never spend much time with his wife. Nevertheless, he often corresponded with her. Mrinalini had stayed with him when they were first married, and again came to stay in Baroda for a few months at the end of 1904. She was shy and found it difficult to mix with his friends. While she was away, he wrote affectionate letters to her. For instance, on 25 June 1902, he urged her to stay warm and take some medicine, when she told him she had a fever.[43] There were a few more letters exchanged that year, with the early ones being in English.

A letter he wrote to her on 30 August 1905, in response to hers, is indicative of their relationship. 'Priyatama Mrinalini', Aurobindo began, and then empathized with her on the death of one of her brothers. Next, he wrote about himself. 'I think you have understood by now that the man with whose fate yours is linked is a man of a very unusual kind. My field of action, purpose of life and mental attitude are not the same as those of people of today in this country. I am in every respect different from them and out of the ordinary.' Many people, he said, would call such a person a 'madman', but if the madman succeeded in his endeavours, he would be called a genius. According to the Hindu scriptures, he said, the husband was to be revered as God and the guru. She must help him, counsel him, encourage him in whatever work he accepts as his Dharma. Would she do this, he asked, would she 'choose the path of the Hindu religion or follow the ideal of the new culture?' Despite her Brahmo education, he said, she was 'a woman from a Hindu home', with Hindu ancestors, and he had no doubt she would follow the Hindu dharma. He went on to explain that everything he had – his learning, accomplishments and wealth – were given to him by God, and he felt he had a right to spend for essentials for him and his family, but not for pleasures and luxuries, as that would make him a thief. So far, he had not spent enough on others. 'The money I gave to Usha or to Sarojini causes me no regret. To help others is a sacred duty; to give protection to those who seek refuge is a yet greater sacred duty. But the account is not settled by giving only to one's brothers and sisters. In these dark days the whole country is seeking refuge at my door. I have three hundred million brothers and sisters in this country. Many of them are dying of starvation and the majority just manage to live, racked by sorrow and suffering. They too must be helped.' He asked if she would share his ideal, to eat and live simply, and offer the rest to God, i.e., to the suffering people.

Further, he asked Mrinalini to 'try to be the mad wife of this madman', meaning she should follow him in all respects. He also had resolved, he wrote, to have 'a direct vision of god' – this was his second madness. He was not satisfied with prayers and public displays. The Hindu religion said God exists within one, and he was discovering the truth of this. Perhaps she could not be in step with him, but certainly she could follow him. His third madness, he explained, was that he loved his country like a mother, and he was going to free her, not with a sword, but with 'the strength of knowledge'. If she would support and encourage him, his strength would increase, as the wife was the shakti of the husband.

He wanted her to be out of the ordinary, and wrote 'Will you remain like this for ever: "I shall put on fine clothes, have nice things to eat, laugh and dance and enjoy all the pleasures?" Such an attitude cannot be called progress. At the present time the life of women in this country has taken this narrow and contemptible form. Give up all this and follow after me. We have come to this world to do God's work; let us begin it.' He added, 'You have a natural turn towards doing good for others and towards self-sacrifice. The one thing you lack is strength of mind. You will get that through worship of God. This is the secret of mine I wanted to tell you. Do not divulge it to anybody.' He asked her to meditate and pray to the Divine, that she may be a helper on her husband's path, in his attempt to realize God.[44]

On 6 December 1907, he wrote to her: 'I received your letter the day before yesterday. The shawl was sent the very same day. I do not understand why you did not get it ...' Further in the letter, he wrote that he was very busy with Congress work, the *Bande Mataram* problems and his own work, and finding it difficult to manage everything. It was a time of great anxiety, of pulls and pressures from all sides. If she could write 'encouraging and comforting letters', that would give him great strength, and enable him to 'overcome all fears and dangers with a cheerful heart.' He said separations and sorrows could not be avoided as 'I cannot make the happiness of family and relatives my primary aim in life'.[45]

In a letter written on 17 February 1908, that he had wrongly dated 1907, he said: 'I have not written to you for a long time. This is my eternal failing; if you do not pardon me out of your own goodness, what shall I do?' He explained that he could no longer make his own decisions. 'Like a puppet I must go wherever God takes me; like a puppet I must do whatever He makes me do. It will be difficult for you to grasp the meaning of these words just now. But it is necessary to inform you, otherwise my movements may cause you regret and sorrow.' He wanted her to understand that he was not neglecting her, but his will was no longer his own. He had given himself to God and did everything according to his *aadesh* or command. He hoped that God would reveal the path to her too. He added further: 'Do not let anyone see this letter, for what I have said is extremely secret. I have not spoken about this to anyone but you; I am forbidden to do so. This much for today.'[46]

Aurobindo confided his innermost thoughts and emotions to Mrinalini, seeking her companionship on the spiritual path. While Mrinalini supported him, she also desired to be physically close to him. She spent considerable time with her parents in Assam and, at Aurobindo's request, with his family in Deogarh. During his illness in Calcutta, she cared for him. Mrinalini stood by his side during his arrest, which deeply shook her. Seeking solace, she found peace through her association with Sarada Ma, the spiritual companion and widow of Sri Ramakrishna. She visited Aurobindo in jail and maintained composure despite adverse circumstances. However, after Aurobindo's departure to Pondicherry, they did not meet again.

As for his spiritual path, Aurobindo had intimations of spirituality in his younger days. Then, when he stood on the Indian shore in 1893 for the first time after he left India as a child of seven, he felt a great sense of peace. As seen earlier, he was inspired by the sannyasis he later met, and by his concept of the divine mother, that he expressed in his pamphlet on the proposed Bhawani Mandir.[47] In 1905 he began a dedicated practice of pranayama, which brought about changes in his body and mind. He shared his spiritual path and his unwavering determination to realize God with Mrinalini. In January 1908, during a visit to Baroda arranged by Barin, Aurobindo had the opportunity to meet Guru Vishnu Bhaskar Lele. Under Lele's guidance, he experienced the profound silence of *Brahman*.

While Aurobindo had already read parts of the Upanishads and the Mahabharata, it was when he was imprisoned from May 1908 to May 1909 that he dived deeper into his reading of the Gita and Upanishads, and also his yoga practice. He received an inner divine message indicating that he had earlier been asked to step back from his political work, but he had not done so and, therefore, prison would free him from it. During his confinement, Aurobindo had profound experiences of the Divine and cosmic consciousness. He had a vision of the god Krishna as the universal soul, present in all beings and everything that existed. At times during the trial, everything became divine in his eyes. Even the magistrate and prosecuting counsel took the on the form of Krishna.[48] After his release the following year, he felt a divine command to leave British India.

His political writings were numerous, as were his writings on other topics. Among his many apolitical works, only a few are mentioned here. He started writing poetry at a young age, and in 1898, he published a collection of his poems titled *Songs to Myrtilla*, some of which were composed during his time in Cambridge. One poem on Charles Stewart Parnell was written in 1891, after Parnell's death, while another poem, 'The Lost Deliverer' explores the death of German socialist leader Ferdinand Lasalle. Many of his poems revolve around themes of love and the appreciation of beauty. Also intriguing is a dialogue on the Harmony of Virtue, in which an Indian character instructs his English companions and explains the distinction between virtue and morality. Throughout his entire stay in Baroda, he devoted long hours to reading and writing, amassing a vast collection of books. His interest in the Mahabharata and Hinduism deepened, and he wrote, 'When I speak of Hinduism I do not refer to the ignorant and customary Hinduism of today … but the purer form of Vedanta which under the pressure of Science is now reasserting its empire over the Hindu mind'.[49] He began to translate the Bhagavad Gita and selected works of Kalidasa, including 'Meghduta' and *Vikramorvashiyam*. He also started writing a study on Kalidasa, although this remains unfinished.[50] His works *Baji Prabhu* and *Chitrangada* were published in *Karmayogin*.[51] Other early works comprise a play, *The Viziers of Bassora*, based on a story from the *Arabian Nights*; a verse tragedy, *Rodogune*; *The Prince of Edur*, a dramatic romance; and *Perseus the Deliverer*, a drama.[52]

The multifaceted nature of Aurobindo's life did not fade away upon his arrival in Pondicherry. Rather, there was a consistent continuity in his thoughts and approach to life. But gradually, everything assumed a subsidiary role to his grand spiritual vision – a vision encompassing the whole world, along with its past, present and future.

2

Pondicherry (1910–50)

'I look across the world and no horizon walls my gaze;
I see Paris and Tokyo and New York,
I see the bombs bursting on Barcelona and on Canton streets.
Man's numberless misdeeds and rare good deeds take place within
my single self.
I am the beast he slays, the bird he feeds and saves.
The thought of unknown minds exalt me with their thrill,
I carry the sorrow of millions in my lonely breast.'

Collected Poems, 120

Sri Aurobindo's arrival on 4 April 1910 in Pondicherry marked a major change in his life. Until then he had travelled to different places and had numerous experiences, meeting people from all walks of life. He had lived in England, studied in Cambridge, worked in Baroda and Calcutta and been involved in national politics. After reaching Pondicherry, he moved his residence a few times, but he never left, remaining there till the end of his life. Though he did not give up his interest in Indian and world events and continued to comment on them, his focus was on the spiritual world.

Pondicherry was one of the few remaining French territories in India. In the seventeenth century, France was one of the European countries struggling to gain a commercial and political foothold in India. The French were the last of the European entrants, after the Portuguese, British and Dutch. They set up a trading centre and factory in Surat in Gujarat in 1668, followed by another at Masulipatnam, which was then under the kingdom of Golconda in central India. Pondicherry was settled in 1673, and Chandernagore near Calcutta in 1674. At first the French were only involved in trade and commerce, but gradually they allied with Indian rulers, in an attempt to acquire territory. There were conflicts between the Dutch, French and British, both in Europe and India, and the French lost most of their Indian territories. At end of the Napoleonic Wars in 1815, a few small territories were returned to them in 1816: Chandernagore in Bengal; Yanam, Pondicherry and Karikal on the Coromandel Coast; and Mahe on the Malabar Coast. These places were run by a form of local government but were also represented in the French Parliament at the time of the Second Republic and later the Second Empire of France. The local people spoke Tamil, which Sri Aurobindo had been learning even before he reached there, while the officials spoke French, a language known by many of the elite. Sri Aurobindo, of course, was fluent in French.

Aurobindo's earlier political career followed him to Pondicherry. In fact, the very day he reached, a warrant was issued by the British for his arrest under the charge of sedition, for an article he had written titled 'To My Countrymen' that had been published in the *Karmayogin* on 25 December 1909. The case was even discussed in England and Ramsay Macdonald, who had earlier met and been impressed with him, raised a discussion in the House of Commons in which he supported Aurobindo. He said that Aurobindo's writings criticized terrorism, and people like him should be cultivated by the British government rather than being persecuted.[1] Finally, in November, the case came before the Calcutta High Court, which did not find anything seditious in the article, and the warrant was withdrawn.

Barin's old friends, who had become close to Sri Aurobindo after the former's imprisonment in the Andamans, became his first companions in Pondicherry. Of them, Suresh Chakravarti, known as Moni, reached Pondicherry before him and informed associates there about his arrival. Bijoy Kumar Nag came along with Sri Aurobindo, both travelling under invented names. In Pondicherry, Aurobindo along with Moni and Bijoy, first stayed in the house of Shankar Chettiar on Comty Chetty Street. They did not want their presence to be known but were soon discovered and plainsclothes detectives were posted across the street to keep a watch on their activities.[2] Aurobindo did not meet too many people, but Subramania Bharati and Srinivasacharya were regular visitors. Both had been involved in the national movement and in the foundation of the nationalist Tamil journal *India* that was published from Pondicherry. With a towering intellect, Bharati was also a poet. Rangaswami Iyengar, a landowner and nationalist, and Ramaswami Iyengar, a friend of Bharati, were other visitors. Rangaswami was also convinced that Aurobindo was 'the yogi from the North', whom his grandfather's guru, Sri Vasudeva, had predicted would come down to the south. In 1911 *Yogic Sadhan*, a book compiled by Sri Aurobindo based on 'automatic writing', was printed by Rangaswami through Vani Vilas Press. It was later revised and republished, but Sri Aurobindo did not really believe in automatic writing, and did not acknowledge this work as his own.

In April soon after their arrival, the elections to the French chamber were taking place. Srinivas and Bharati persuaded Sri Aurobindo to meet the Frenchman Paul Richard, who had come to India, possibly to assist one of the candidates, Paul Bluysun, or according to some accounts to stand for election himself.[3] Elections took place on 24 April, and in the run-up to them, there was much violence amongst rival supporters, but Bluysun won.

Born in Marsillargues, France, on 21 June 1874, Richard was an extraordinary individual with a varied career, and he shared various aspects of his life with Sri Aurobindo. He joined the army straight out of school to serve in North Africa. Upon his return, Richard studied theology and theological philosophy, going on to preach in Montauban in Southwest France for two years.

In 1900, Richard became a pastor after joining the Reformed Church of France in Lille. During the same year, he published a book on Christ after the resurrection and married Wilhelmine from Amsterdam. By 1905, he was sent to French Guiana, where he conducted an examination of the lives of convicts in South America. Following this, he pursued the study of law and successfully obtained his degree in 1908, becoming a barrister at the Paris Court of Appeals.

Richard's explorations extended into the realm of the occult, but his understanding of it deepened due to his association with Mirra Alfassa. It was through this connection that Mirra would soon become the most significant person in Sri Aurobindo's life.

*

Born in Paris on 21 February 1878, Blanche Rachel Mirra Alfassa was the third child of an Egyptian mother and a Turkish father, who had recently settled in France. Their first child had died, while their second, Matteo, was born in 1876. Mirra had spiritual and occult experiences even in childhood.[4] In around 1908, after a divorce ended her first marriage, she became close to Paul Richard, who was fascinated by her and began to write books on the occult with Mirra's help. At this time Sri Aurobindo was impressed with Richard, who in turn looked on him as a great yogi. It was also helpful for him to have Richard on his side, as the latter knew several of the French officials.

In October Aurobindo and his companions moved to another house belonging to Sunder Chetty on Rue de la Pavilion Rue Suffren, where they paid a rent of Rs 20 per month. Two more early associates joined them that year, Saurin Bose in September and Nolini Kanta Gupta in November. Moni, Bijoy, Saurin and Nolini all stayed with Aurobindo. Meanwhile in October Rangaswami helped him out with finances which were low. A servant was appointed to assist them, while a wandering dog was adopted, whom they named Yogini. Aurobindo was fond of her and the pups she gave birth to.

By now Sri Aurobindo and his revolutionary and spiritual past were well known, and many people attempted to visit or just to see him, coming even from different parts of India including from Punjab and Karachi. On the whole, Aurobindo lived a quiet life, continuing his meditation and focus on inner spirituality and also writing on philosophy, yoga and different themes. Among his varied writings was a long poem, *Illion*, combining ideas from the Greek classics with his inner vision, a play named *Eric* set in Viking times and a revision of his earlier work, Rodogune. His study of Tamil led him to compare the root words of Tamil and Sanskrit.

In April 1911, they moved to a house on Rue St Louis known as Raghavan House. Though Aurobindo was immersed in his reading and writing, political events still followed him. Some of the Indian revolutionaries continued with sporadic assassinations, and Robert Ashe, the acting collector of Tirunelvelli was shot dead on 17 June 1911. Vanchi Aiyar, the shooter, killed himself but there were links to Srinivas, Bharati and some others in Pondicherry, and thus indirectly to Sri Aurobindo. There was a threat of extradition, and Sri Aurobindo wrote to Paul Richard about it. It was Matteo Alfassa, the brother of Mirra, who worked in the Paris colonial office and, upon seeing the letter requesting Sri Aurobindo's extradition, squashed it. The *Madras Times* published articles against political activists taking refuge in Pondicherry, and even referred to 'Arabindo Ghosh' as a criminal and assassin. Aurobindo wrote letters to the *Madras Times* and the *Hindu*, refuting this. His letter to the *Hindu* was published on 20 and 21 July 1911.[5] There was also an attempt to plant evidence to convict Sri Aurobindo of anti-India crimes, but this was discovered and removed in time. He himself repeatedly reiterated that he had come to Pondicherry for his spiritual practices, and he was not interested in active politics. Gradually the government interest in him diminished, though the police still kept an eye on him.

In the initial years after coming to Pondicherry, Aurobindo continued to keep in touch with the revolutionary movement in Bengal, exchanging letters with Motilal Roy in Chandernagore and with other early friends and contacts. As there were financial problems, Motilal Roy gathered funds to send to them. What is interesting is that their requirements amounted to a paltry Rs 50 a month! In one letter to Motilal he remarked that his birthday, 15 August 1912, marked a new phase, a turning point in his yoga. Birthdays were often significant, and this time, he had a profound realization and 'dwelt in Parabrahman for many hours'.[6] As he continued his research, spiritual practices, translation and writing on various topics, his companions studied some languages with him, and were subtly influenced by him.[7] During these early years, he met a few distinguished people, including Alexandra David Neel in November 1911, later known for her travels in Tibet.

In 1913 there were two more moves, in April to a residence to Rue des Missions Étrangères (Mission Street), and in October they shifted to a house on Rue François Martin. Aravamudachari Iyengar, very young at the time, joined the small group of men at Rue des Missions Étrangères, and came to be known as Amrita.

He was later sent by Sri Aurobindo to college to acquire an education. He was a traditional Vaishnava *brahmana* and his family were against his association with Sri Aurobindo, but one night, Nolini cut off his *shikha* or the tuft at the back of his head. Somehow, after facing the anger of his family for this, he became closer to Sri Aurobindo and was later appointed the secretary of the ashram. Nagen Nag, related to Bijoy, was another addition, and as he was ill with tuberculosis and needed some assistance, his helper Biren joined them. Sometime later, Biren Roy was bribed by the police to report on the group, but soon he stopped doing this and confessed to Aurobindo about what he had done.[8]

It was with Nagen's money that they were able to move to a larger house on Rue Francis Martin. Sri Aurobindo and others continued to live in this house for several years. He believed in living a normal life and incorporating his yoga into all aspects of it. His reading and writing were not confined to spiritual subjects. There were no special practices or fixed times for meditation or anything else, nor any restrictions on food. In those days, he also smoked and occasionally drank wine.[9] In the evenings, there were discussions and talks. His yoga at this time was based on what he defined as the seven *chatusthiyas*, or steps, beginning with a state of equanimity or *samata*. Each of these steps is explained in detail. For instance, in its passive aspect, samata includes *titiksha*, *udasinata* and *nati*, which means to be calm in pleasure or pain, to be indifferent to dualities and to submit to the will of God. In its active aspect, samata has *rasa*, *priti* and *ananda*, that is, to derive pleasure and joy by perceiving God in all aspects of life.[10] This path included raising all aspects of the individual to the highest state possible before moving further in the evolution towards a 'Supramental' being. He kept notes on his daily sadhana and his progress from 1912–27. Published much later in two volumes as *Record of Yoga*, these have a historical, rather than a spiritual importance, as his sadhana in later years was far deeper.[11]

Very soon, a significant intervention would occur in his life. In 1914, Paul Richard returned to Pondicherry, this time accompanied by Mirra. Paul had divorced his first wife and married Mirra on 5 May 1911. But their marriage was platonic, and Mirra insisted on maintaining a purely intellectual and spiritual relationship with him. She had heard of Sri Aurobindo, and upon seeing him in 1914, recognized him as the guru she had seen in her dreams.

During this visit, Paul Richard had the intention of running for election to the French chamber, and Sri Aurobindo supported his decision. However, their visit became notable for other reasons as well. They proposed the idea of publishing a newspaper or journal, which led to the establishment of *Arya: A Philosophical Review*. This publication primarily featured articles written by Sri Aurobindo himself and was edited by Paul and Mirra. He held both Paul and Mirra in high regard. In a letter to Motilal Roy in April 1914, he referred to Paul as both 'a personal friend' and 'a brother in yoga', expressing their shared aspiration to contribute to the world's rejuvenation from a spiritual perspective. Sri Aurobindo also noted that Richard embraced Indian beliefs and culture to a great extent, suggesting that if a Bengali translation of his manifesto could be made, and there were votes for him in Chandernagore, it would be a good start.[12] But once again the election was marred by tremendous fraud and violence, and Paul Richard lost.

In September 1914, the First World War began. Sri Aurobindo realized that a British defeat would not be beneficial, as the Axis powers could then invade India. Around the end of September, the German ship, *Emden*, attacked British ships on the coast and even reached Pondicherry, but the Germans left without causing significant harm. As France and Britain were allies in the war, there was a concern that refugees from British India could be extradited. The Bengal government themselves did not want Aurobindo sent back, though, and felt it was better for them if he remained in Pondicherry, far away from any political activity.

So, Sri Aurobindo continued to read, write and meditate. Walking up and down in his room and veranda, his steps wore out a pathway in the floor. One of the favourite pastimes of his companions was playing football, which they became well known for. Local young men joined them and also became influenced by Sri Aurobindo. In 1914, Mirra started a group called '*L'Idee Nouvelle*' and some of these young men became part of it. Meanwhile, Bejoy Nag, who had left Pondicherry in October 1914, was captured by the British and remained interned till the end of the war.

Paul and Mirra left Pondicherry on 22 February 1915. Paul, in fact, had been ordered to leave by the French government, partly because of his association with Sri Aurobindo and 'political refugees'. Mirra, who had recognized Aurobindo as the Supreme Lord as soon as she saw him, wanted to stay in his presence, but had to leave with Paul. On 3 March 1915, on board the *Kama Maru*, she wrote that she felt an immense solitude, as if she had been plunged into darkness. On 4 March the same sense of isolation persisted. 'Each turn of the propeller seems to drag me farther away from my true destiny', she noted. This melancholic sense of being pushed away from the one she saw as the Lord continued for quite some time.[13] At this time Sri Aurobindo was still married to Mrinalini and must have expected her to join him. He may not have been aware of the depths of Mirra's devotion to him. *Arya* continued to be published till 1921, with most of Sri Aurobindo's major works being written and published in it, although many were revised later. A French edition of the magazine, with translations by Mirra, was published until February 1915. Paul had owned *Arya*, but when the two left, its ownership was transferred to Sri Aurobindo.

Upon their arrival in Paris on 18 March 1915, Paul and Mirra soon travelled to Lunel in southern France. Mirra had fallen ill during the voyage, and her illness continued for some time.[14] She believed there was an occult reason for this illness, and said it was because she had left her soul with Sri Aurobindo.[15] After a brief visit to Paul's birthplace, Marsillargues, where he had been called for conscription into the army, they returned to Paris in November 1915, as he was exempted on medical grounds. From Paris they embarked on a long ship journey to Japan, reaching Yokohama on 18 May 1916 through London, Capetown and Shanghai as the Suez Canal was closed due to the war. Paul had a commission to sell French products to China and Japan from the National Union for the Export of French Products. Dorothy Hodgson, who held Mirra in high regard, almost viewing her as divine, accompanied them. Dorothy (1884–1949), was Irish, though born in England.

After her fiancé's death, she had dropped all ideas of getting married.[16] The three of them lived in Japan for four years. Mirra deeply appreciated the Japanese way of life and sense of beauty, meeting interesting mystics and spiritual people.

A major event during this period was the death of Mrinalini, Sri Aurobindo's wife in Calcutta on 17 December 1918. Mrinalini had been just a child, but as she grew older, she began to appreciate Aurobindo, and wanted to be with him and follow his path. Unfortunately, after he left for Pondicherry, she was not able to meet him. According to one account, Sri Aurobindo had asked Sauren Bose to bring her to Pondicherry in 1914, but when the war broke out, it was no longer possible. Her father, after his retirement in 1916, had attempted to take her to Pondicherry; however, he was denied permission by the British government. Finally, in 1918, when they began the journey, Mrinalini fell ill upon reaching Calcutta and could not travel further. She passed away there after contracting a virulent strain of influenza, the Spanish flu, which was spreading across the country.

There are poignant accounts of how Mrinalini lived during the intervening years. While Aurobindo was in prison, Mrinalini's friend Sudhira, whom she had known since her school days, took her to see Sarada Ma, the spiritual companion of Sri Ramakrishna Paramahamsa. Sarada Ma assured her that Aurobindo would be found innocent and released from prison. Mrinalini found great solace in her association with Sarada Ma and continued to meet her whenever possible. When Sri Aurobindo moved to Pondicherry, Mrinalini stayed with her parents in Shillong, living like an ascetic, sleeping on a mat on the floor, wearing plain saris and performing puja, meditation and reading sacred books, particularly those of Sri Ramakrishna and Swami Vivekananda. She received occasional letters from

Aurobindo, which have unfortunately not survived, as she asked while on her deathbed for the letters to be thrown in the ocean. According to one account, she received a letter from Sri Aurobindo urging her to join him, but her own father's version written after her death suggests differently:

> After Sri Aurobindo left Bengal, the two never met again, but all who knew her could see how deeply she was attached to her husband and how she longed to join him at Pondicherry. The fates however decreed it otherwise. During the first 3 or 4 years of his exile, Sri Aurobindo lulled her with the hope that some day which we thought could not be very distant he would return to Bengal. His letters to his wife as well as to the writer were few and far between, but they gave ample grounds for such a hope. At last Sri Aurobindo ceased to write at all, possibly because of his exclusive preoccupation with Yoga, but to the last day of her life Mrinalini never ceased to hope.

In reply to another query, he wrote 'Sri Aurobindo never called his wife to Pondicherry for Sadhana.'[17]

A telegram was sent to Sri Aurobindo regarding Mrinalini's death. Her younger sister, writing an account of her life, recorded: 'On reading it, Sri Aurobindo said, "Too late!" My cousin who was there at the time wrote to my mother: "Today I saw tears in the eyes of your stone-hearted son-in-law. With the telegram in one hand, he sat still and tears were in his eyes."'[18] On 19 February 1919, Sri Aurobindo wrote a letter to Mrinalini's father.

> I have not written to you with regard to this fatal event in both our lives; words are useless in face of the feelings it has caused, if even they can ever express our deepest emotions. God has seen good to lay upon me the one sorrow that could still touch

> me to the centre. He knows better than ourselves what is best for each of us, and now that the first sense of the irreparable has passed, I can bow with submission to His divine purpose. The physical tie between us is, as you say, severed; but the tie of affection subsists for me. Where I have once loved, I do not cease from loving. Besides she who was the cause of it, still is near though not visible to our physical vision … It is needless to say much about the matters of which you write in your letter. I approve of everything that you propose. Whatever Mrinalini would have desired, should be done, and I have no doubt this is what she would have approved of. I consent to the *chudis* gold bangles being kept by her mother; but I should be glad if you would send me two or three of her books, especially if there are any in which her name is written. I have only of her letters and a photograph.[19]

After the war, travel became possible again. Nolini Kanta and Saurin Bose, who were living with Sri Aurobindo, made a trip to Bengal in mid-1919 and even got married there to suitable young women. The same year, Amrita returned to the household after completing college. Aurobindo's notebooks record the continuous progress of his spirituality.

In 1920, Barin was finally released from Andaman jail and planned to visit Pondicherry. Before his arrival Sri Aurobindo updated him on the changes in the political landscape and described the developments in his yoga.[20] He was still, at this time, thinking of returning to Bengal. In his letters, he had shared how his perspectives had transformed, realizing that political and social transformation could only occur through the transformation of the individual. Aurobindo believed that just a hundred such individuals could bring about a transformation that would be free and fluid, rather than following a rigid form resembling the old 'Aryan society'. He said after fifteen years of yoga, he was now reaching the lowest level of the Supermind. He was not impatient, further progress depended entirely on God. Then he wrote about India, explaining that its weakness was not because of subjection, poverty or lack of spirituality, but because people had stopped thinking. The civilization in India had become stagnant, he lamented, and 'our religion a bigotry of externals.'[21]

On his first visit to Pondicherry, Barin stayed for one week. Nolini and Suresh were back, Amrita had returned, and Paul Richard and Mirra Alfassa had arrived in India on 24 April 1920. Along with them was their friend Dorothy Hodgson. The three stayed elsewhere but visited Sri Aurobindo regularly, while he went over on Sundays for dinner, usually cooked by Mirra. Describing the Richards in his book on Sri Aurobindo, Barin remarked that Paul was an imposing figure, with a flowing beard and luminous eyes, while Mirra had the sweetest smile.[22]

A conflict between Paul and Mirra soon arose, as Mirra desired to stay in India with Sri Aurobindo, while Paul, despite deeply admiring Aurobindo, wanted Mirra to follow him. The crisis reached a breaking point, and Paul left Pondicherry. Mirra believed that Paul was an *Asura* (see chapter 9) and Sri Aurobindo was aware of the problems that could arise from Asuric forces. He recounted a dream, or rather a vision, the Mother had about Paul Richard, which indicated that he, too, believed that Paul was a negative force, though it is clear from his letters in 1914 that he had not felt so earlier. He said about her vision: 'The Mother, Richard and I were going someplace. We saw Richard going down to a place from which rising was impossible.' In the vision, he and the Mother were then in a carriage going up and down a hill, but finally settled at the highest point. 'The significance was quite clear to us', he remarked, in one of his discussions with Nirodbaran. It was during the Second World War that Sri Aurobindo made it clear he believed in the powerful, negative, Asuric force of Paul, who was in communication with the Lord of the Nations, the Asura-guiding Hitler.[23] However, there is no indication of this in Paul's life.

Leaving Pondicherry in November 1920, Paul travelled to the Himalaya. He later returned to France, remarried, and eventually moved to the US to become a professor. He wrote several books on spirituality during his life.[24] In an interview in 1927 he told Dilip Roy, one of Sri Aurobindo's disciples, 'I have not met his peer in the whole world. To me he is the Lord Shiva incarnate.' Later he regretted not working with Sri Aurobindo. 'I was too self-willed to be a mere contributor of *His Book of Life*. I had no humility.' He said that Sri Aurobindo was the person he held above all others, yet he chose to leave him.[25]

After a storm damaged their building, Mirra and Dorothy Hodgson joined Sri Aurobindo and his companions in the house on Rue François Martin. Until they moved in, Aurobindo and his friends had lived in a slightly disorganized way and Mirra, with the assistance of Dorothy (renamed Vasavadatta by Aurobindo and known as Datta), set about bringing some order to the household. From January 1922, Mirra's role in supervising and organizing the household grew, as Sri Aurobindo asked her to take over its management. He held morning and evening sessions with the residents of the house and a few others. During the evening meetings, there were discussions on various topics, informal talks, and at times, he conveyed his spiritual ideas. Initially, everything operated in an informal manner, as Sri Aurobindo did not believe in asserting his superiority and considered all as equals. But as the numbers of people around him increased and things became chaotic, he accepted a more central role. Nolini explains that it was the Mother's reverential attitude towards Sri Aurobindo that prompted them to change theirs. He says, 'The Mother came and installed him on his high pedestal as Master and Lord of Yoga.'[26] They had always known in their hearts that he was a guru, to them he was also 'a dear friend and close companion', who did not like the term guru. Their experience was like that of Arjuna, who saw Krishna as a friend but then realized his divinity.[27] Although Sri Aurobindo believed sadhana, or spiritual practice, did not require any restrictions on what one ate or drank, he now ate only vegetarian food. Celibacy was deemed essential for the *sadhaks* (spiritual seekers), but apart from that, there were no fixed rules. The emphasis was on making efforts to surrender to the Divine.

The house they were staying in was in bad shape, and Barin found another for them all. In October 1922, Sri Aurobindo and the Mother, along with Dorothy and five others, moved to a house on 9 Rue de la Marine. The previous residence was maintained as a guest house and over time, more people joined the group, reaching a total of fifteen by August 1923.

A few cats too were part of the household, and there are interesting accounts of these. The Mother was known for her fondness for cats, and there are records of two cats often sitting on her shoulders. Cats were never popular in India, and many found the care she took over their food, mashing fish and mixing milk pudding, quite astounding. Nolini Kanta Gupta describes how one day a wild-looking cat turned up, but soon became quite tame. The Mother looked after some kittens, and Sri Aurobindo named the first, pure white one, Sundari. More cats descended from them. Nolini recalls that they were fed with special food as if they were 'children of some royal family'.[28] Sri Aurobindo himself was also fond of the cats. Known for his profound poems, he wrote one on a cat, observing it standing alone on top of a staircase.

It ended with the lines: 'A charm and miracle of fur-footed Brahman, / Whether she is spirit, woman or cat, / Is now the problem I am wondering at.'[29] There are various stories involving these cats, including one where a cat named Kiki was bitten by a scorpion and healed by Sri Aurobindo. Pujalal recalls that Sri Aurobindo would not disturb a cat if it was sitting on his chair, choosing instead to sit on the edge himself.[30] The Mother also had an occult reason for caring for the cats (see chapter 9).

Meanwhile, Sri Aurobindo continued with his sadhana and attempts to bring the Supramental into the physical plane but faced difficulties. He explained that it was when the sadhana descended into the physical and Subconscient, a lot of problems arose. It was something even previous yogis had not explored, an undoubtedly 'Herculean labour'.[31] Both Sri Aurobindo and the Mother had progressed far in their spirituality and surrendered to the Divine. Sri Aurobindo mentioned that he no longer had thoughts of his own; they came to him from the Divine. The Mother indicated the degree of her surrender in 'Meditations and Prayers'.[32] Most of the Indians did not understand or easily accept the presence of Mirra and Dorothy in the same house as Sri Aurobindo. Many resented it. Even as Mirra increasingly took on a larger role, during the early years, she remained in the background while Sri Aurobindo met residents and visitors. It was known that Sri Aurobindo thought of her highly, and therefore, she was respected. But Sri Aurobindo affirmed that she was essential to his work, and that, in fact, they were one – two aspects of the same energy.

Initially Sri Aurobindo wanted to set up spiritual centres in other parts of India. Motilal Roy in Chandernagore was encouraged to start spiritual activities, and he set up the Prabartak Sangha. In August 1920, a monthly called *Standard Bearer* began to be published from Chandernagore, inspired by Sri Aurobindo.

Barin again came to Pondicherry in 1921, this time accompanied by Motilal Roy. Returning to Chandernagore, Roy continued with the Sangha, and Aurobindo soon dropped all involvement in it, as he felt it was not propagating his yoga. Barin settled in Pondicherry, though he visited Calcutta on occasion. But Sri Aurobindo still held the idea of establishing spiritual centres and sent Barin to Bengal in 1922 to set up the centres as well as gather more funds. In a letter to Barin on 18 November 1922, he explained that outer work would proceed from the spiritual basis of his yoga, and 'It is therefore necessary to establish a number of centres small and few at first but enlarging and increasing in numbers as I go on, for training in this sadhana.'[33] At the same time, he wrote to Chittaranjan Das that he had achieved some success in his spiritual venture, and while there was still far to go, he was ready to start training others.[34] In December 1922, Barin started a centre in Bhowanipore, Calcutta, to spread Aurobindo's yoga. Some genuine spiritual aspirants joined, and Aurobindo provided guidance after seeing their photographs. The centre continued to function for a couple of years, though Barin returned to Pondicherry in 1923. Aurobindo's sister Sarojini visited in 1922. He was happy to meet her and even went to fetch her from the station. As she was struggling financially, he gave her the rights to one of the editions of his book *War and Self-determination*. She visited once more in 1923, and after that their connection faded away.

After his stint in jail, and particularly after moving to Pondicherry, Sri Aurobindo had always asked the revolutionaries to stop their violent activities whenever they requested his advice. M. K. Gandhi returned to India in early 1915, and would soon take over the leadership of the freedom movement, gaining the title of 'Mahatma'. At one point he wanted Sri Aurobindo to join him and sent his son Devdas to Pondicherry to meet him.

Though Aurobindo was not in favour of violence, he did not favour Gandhi's concept of ahimsa. He believed that if attacked, one should defend oneself.[35] The very day Gandhi began the Non-cooperation Movement, 1 August 1920, Balgangadhar Tilak died, whom Sri Aurobindo had deeply admired. Once again, a request was made to Aurobindo by former Extremists to rejoin politics, but he refused. He knew Indian independence would be achieved without his intervention, and he had a far greater task before him. In 1920, he was invited to be the president of the Nagpur Congress. He declined and wrote to Balkrishna Shivaram Moonje, then a leader of the Congress, that he was no longer primarily involved in politics, engaged instead in a spiritual mission. He also added that no one could ever take Tilak's place.[36] Soon after this, Moonje left the Congress and joined the Hindu Mahasabha. Other political leaders persisted in their efforts to convince Aurobindo to reengage in politics. Chittaranjan Das, popularly known as Deshbandhu, was able to meet Sri Aurobindo in 1923. Das had been a prominent figure in the Congress and had defended Sri Aurobindo in the Alipore Bomb case. However, he eventually broke away from the Congress and founded the Swaraj Party in 1923. While Aurobindo appreciated C. R. Das' political ideas, he maintained that there was no existing programme that he could fully endorse or support.[37] In 1925, he would also be visited by Lala Lajpat Rai and Purushottam Das Tandon.

Many of the early versions of Aurobindo's major works were published in *Arya*, the last issue of which dates to 15 January 1921. The first issue, dated 15 August 1914, contained the first instalments of *The Life Divine*, *The Synthesis of Yoga*, *The Secret of the Veda*, and *The Isha Upanishad*. Later years saw instalments of *The Ideal of Human Unity, Essays on the Gita*, *The Psychology of Social Development* later renamed *The Human*

Cycle, *The Future Poetry*, *The Indian Renaissance* and other essays on India, as well as translations of some Sanskrit texts and miscellaneous poems. The foundations of his philosophy belong to these years, though these works were revised and expanded later. Even before reaching there, he had extraordinary spiritual experiences, but in Pondicherry he worked out an entire scheme for the transformation and future of mankind. Apart from these profound spiritual experiments, he continued to write poetry on other themes too. He explained: 'I myself never gave up poetry or other human creative activities out of tapasya; they fell into a subordinate position because the inner life became stronger and stronger slowly'.[38] It was noted that as Sri Aurobindo's sadhana progressed, his skin colour lightened and took on a glowing, luminous tone. He was only five feet four though he looked taller. His voice is described as soft and melodious, with a British accent.

Initially, Mirra lived in the house on equal footing with the others, without any special status. She embraced the Indian culture and way of life, setting aside her western clothes and opting to wear cotton saris. Due to financial constraints, she would sew her own blouses from patches of cloth. As time passed, her role in Sri Aurobindo's work increased, and she became known as the Mother. Sri Aurobindo recognized that she possessed the same essence as him, and their inner worlds were in alignment, even though their external activities may have differed. He emphasized that the divine, universal Mother and the Mother who lived with them in the ashram were one and the same.[39]

To spread spirituality in the world, the presence of Shakti, the feminine power, was necessary. The Mother fulfilled this role and, as she took on responsibilities in worldly matters, Sri Aurobindo was able to delve deeper into the spiritual realm. It is important to note that their spiritual union transcended any sexual component, as both had surpassed the influence of sex. Sri Aurobindo clarified that the sexual act itself is neither inherently good nor bad, as it is simply a natural movement. However, for a yogi, engaging in sexual activity posed a significant obstacle. He stated that 'the ordinary sexual act destroys the psychic possibilities of the man' and declared that sex was completely incompatible with the path of Yoga.[40] He often spoke in the same way. The Mother's significance lay in her shared vision with Sri Aurobindo. She not only understood his vision but also provided him with the practical form for his work. Sri Aurobindo expressed this in his writings about her. She had felt above the human aspect even in her childhood.[41]

By 1926, the number of sadhaks grew. Two more houses were rented to accommodate them. Sri Aurobindo, as he focused more on his own spiritual practice, became more reclusive. However, a significant breakthrough occurred on November 24, 1926. Through the joint meditations of Sri Aurobindo and Mirra, the Overmind descended into the physical world. The Overmind, a level above the ordinary mind but below the Supermind, had been previously only been described in Sri Aurobindo's other works.

On that day all the residents were requested to come to their house, and when all had assembled, Mirra came out followed by Sri Aurobindo. Everyone felt some presence and divine energy. Sri Aurobindo and Mirra blessed the sadhaks and then returned to the room.[42] After this descent of the Overmind, Sri Aurobindo temporarily dropped political writing and commentary and went into seclusion, focusing only on the Divine. Mirra became Mira, and her spirituality was recognized in her other name, the Mother. Sri Aurobindo equated her with the divine mother, the supreme shakti.

His name was now standardized as Sri Aurobindo, and he communicated to everyone that the Mother would represent him and his work. She would take care of everything based on his inner guidance and her own spiritual practice. The descent of the Overmind brought the opportunity to establish a connection with the gods or their divine attributes. Sri Krishna was believed to have united with Sri Aurobindo at this stage. In fact, Sri Aurobindo affirmed that the god Krishna, who had earlier been his guide, had become part of him.[43] Nolini recounted that the Mother had also placed some of the close disciples in touch with the inner godhead and, following this, they were asked to realize this divinity within them, through focused sadhana.[44] Most of the disciples were unable to progress further on this path, but the Mother and a few others experienced remarkable and miraculous developments for a certain period of time. Sri Aurobindo explained that this was not the ultimate goal at present. The aim was to go beyond this and establish the Supermind on earth; therefore, the creation of the Overmind gods had to be renounced, and this was immediately done.[45]

The Years of Seclusion

On 8 February 1927, Sri Aurobindo and the Mother, along with the sadhaks moved again, this time to a much larger house on 28 Rue François Martin, which they had managed to buy. Sri Aurobindo briefly emerged from his seclusion in July to sign the sale deed. Within this house, he resided in a series of interconnected rooms on the second floor. Following this move, there were no further changes in residence. This house remains a part of the ashram to this day.

As he continued sadhana, he pointed out that the aim to bring down the Supermind was for the benefit of the whole world. Truth, Light, Harmony and Peace would then descend into the earth-consciousness.[46]

After this, Sri Aurobindo came out in public only thrice a year to give 'darshan' to the hundreds of people who came to seek his blessings on these occasions. The first darshan took place on his birthday on 15 August 1927. Additional darshan days were 24 November and 21 February, the latter being the birthday of the Mother. Apart from this, he hardly met anyone except for the Mother and his attendants, though he guided many through his letters. There were some exceptions, such as Rabindranath Tagore, whom he met in February 1928. After meeting him, Tagore commented that Aurobindo's 'face was radiant with an inner light'.[47] Tagore was his great admirer, saying that Sri Aurobindo was the greatest person he knew and that he had for him not just admiration but reverence.[48] Sri Aurobindo also met Sylvain Lévi in August that year, and Olive Maitland Match in 1929. Sylvain Lévi, a French scholar and Indologist, an expert in Sanskrit and Buddhism, had founded a school of oriental studies in Hanoi, Vietnam, and was for some time a visiting professor at Visvabharati. Olive was a resident of Aurobindo's ashram, known to be influential in Britain. In subsequent years, Aurobindo refused meetings with all others, even with Mahatma Gandhi. His writing continued, and his innumerable letters provide guidelines not only on spirituality, but on literature and other aspects of his life.[49] Aurobindo meanwhile continued with his meditations as he sat on his bed or in his chair. These were not exactly meditations in the usual sense of the term, rather an exploration of different states of being, leading to his understanding of the past, present and future. He sat still for hours every day, entering different worlds through his consciousness. At night, too, he sat reading and writing until late, rising late in the morning. There were also times when he worked all night till six in the morning, answering letters from sadhaks.[50] Letters were written and left near the main door any time before 11 p.m., and though most were addressed to the Mother, it was usually Sri Aurobindo who answered them after a discussion with her. At times he would provide replies to up to 100 queries in a day, which were written either in notebooks or on paper.

In those days before the advent of computers, Sri Aurobindo received letters from the disciples and seekers written in their own handwriting, which required extra effort to read and decipher. Sri Aurobindo dedicated eight hours or more each day to replying to these letters, which could range from short notes to lengthy ten-page missives. He considered this correspondence worthwhile, as it allowed individuals to share their genuine difficulties and seek guidance while walking the path of Integral Yoga. Sri Aurobindo believed that a few individuals in the ashram had already attained the consciousness of Brahman, and he was keen to support and guide them further in their spiritual evolution. At the same time, he remained aware of all that was happening in the world and exerted his spiritual influence there too. However, his main focus was to bring the Supramental down to earth and into the material realm. This endeavour saw many ups and downs along the way.

After 1934, his sadhana progressed slowly for a while, as the subconscious seemed to reemerge and pose difficulties. Even as he explored this, he could still feel the Supermind above. He explained that the Supermind was above the Overmind, which had already descended, but it was possible to mistake the Overmind for what was above it, and acknowledged that he had also made such errors.[51]

The Mother and Sri Aurobindo were helped by a number of key disciples. Among their notable disciples was A. B. Purani, a former freedom fighter. When he first met Aurobindo in December 1918, the latter had assured him that India would be free. Purani visited again in 1921 and eventually settled in Pondicherry in 1923, taking care of the guest house.

Champaklal, from Gujarat, along with eleven others, had walked all the way from Gujarat to Pondicherry to meet Sri Aurobindo. Only three would make it on 1 April 1921, covering the last portion of their journey by train.[52] They met Sri Aurobindo the same evening thanks to Amrita, who was now in charge of scheduling appointments. Champaklal settled in Pondicherry in 1923, and his brother Bansidhar joined him four years later.

Dilip Kumar Roy from Bengal, another disciple, had studied mathematics and music at Cambridge and was known for his soulful songs on the god Krishna and other deities. He knew English, French and German and also several Indian languages, and composed a number of books during his lifetime. It was Sri Krishna Prem, the name adopted by Ronald Nixon of the Mirtola ashram in Almora, who suggested he meet Sri Aurobindo. Roy first met him in 1924, and then joined the ashram in 1928. Despite Sri Aurobindo's seclusion from 1928 onwards, he continued to receive guidance from him through an extensive exchange of over 4,000 letters![53]

Philippe Barbier Saint-Hilaire, a French engineer with an interest in spirituality, fought in the First World War. In 1920, he travelled to Japan to study Zen Buddhism and explored various aspects of Japanese, Indian, and Chinese religions. After travelling in Mongolia, he arrived in Pondicherry in 1924 and settled there, receiving the name Pavitra from Sri Aurobindo.

Among others who joined were K. D. Sethna and his wife Daulat in 1927, who were renamed Amal Kiran and Lalita. Sethna wrote a number of valuable books on Sri Aurobindo, along with other scholarly works. Chunnibhai Patel, a former freedom fighter, also joined that year and was known as Dyuman. Chandulal Shah and his younger sister Vasudha arrived in 1928. Shah became the ashram engineer, and Vasudha became the Mother's assistant. Sahana Devi, a musician, came to the ashram with Dilip K. Roy. John A. Chadwick, an Englishman who had studied at Cambridge, was a talented poet and took the name Arjava. Nirodbaran Talukdar, a doctor who had studied in Edinburgh, first visited in 1930 and later joined the ashram. Nishikanto, a resident of the ashram, was a highly regarded poet in Bengali. Mridu, born in 1901, became Sri Aurobindo's cook. She was known for her excellent cooking skills, especially her specialty of delicious *luchis*. Sri Aurobindo had to eat whatever she cooked for him, as she would become upset otherwise!

While many sadhaks wholeheartedly accepted the Mother and her guidance, there were others who did not appreciate or accept her as the Mother of the ashram, and even less as the divine mother. Sri Aurobindo, however, emphasized that she was the same as him and represented his force, and all work was to be done through her. The number of residents in the ashram increased from twenty-five in 1926 to eighty in 1928, indicating the growth of the community.[54] To take care of so many people involved considerable organization, in order to provide for accommodation, food, and other activities. With such a large group there were conflicts and different opinions, and many wanted a return to the old days when there was more freedom. Barin, who had been there since 1923, resented not having access to his brother, and eventually left on 25 December 1929, and never to return.[55] He wrote several books in both Bengali and

English, documenting his experiences, including an account of his time spent in the Andaman Jail and an unpublished account of Sri Aurobindo. Bejoy Nag, who had also been a part of the ashram, left around the same time as Barin.

The Mother believed that many of the ashramites had been with them in previous lives. They themselves, she said, had many previous lives helping in evolution. Now the mother and Aurobindo were considered avatars, but as avatars, they had to limit themselves in order to understand humanity and facilitate the progress of the entire collective. Avatars, as per stories of Vishnu, could even take the form of animals or fish.

Sri Aurobindo's Integral Yoga was not bound by any fixed path or system. While it may have drawn inspiration from previous systems, it was fundamentally different. Each aspirant or sadhak was at a unique stage of development, and therefore, a single method or path could not be universally prescribed. However, from that point forward, Sri Aurobindo emphasized the importance of focusing on the Mother as a divine force and seeking her assistance, as she provided both psychic and spiritual guidance. A spiritual connection existed between the Mother and those who accepted her, similar to the relationship between gurus and their disciples. She had a close relationship with some and was there for them whenever they needed her help. It was believed that an emanation of the Mother, an aspect of herself, resided within each sadhak. All knowledge resided within the Mother, but she accessed only what was necessary for the given circumstances.

In the ashram, each sadhak was assigned various duties and responsibilities. In the early years, the ashram followed a disciplined routine. The day would begin with the sadhaks lining up to meet the Mother for darshan in the morning. They would offer their respects, and she would bless each individual, often presenting them with a flower or flower petals infused with her spiritual power. Throughout the day, the sadhaks would engage in their assigned tasks and responsibilities. In the evening, they would gather once again for the soup ceremony. At 8 p.m., they would line up to receive the Mother's darshan. During this ceremony, the Mother would present each sadhak with a bowl of soup from a large vessel. Before handing it to them, she would taste the soup, infusing it with her power.

Though there were no uniform rules for spiritual progress, these were some of the common aspects of life in the ashram. All surrendered their property to the ashram when they joined, and then were taken care of for life, with everything provided for them. The auras of Sri Aurobindo and the Mother were believed to protect the ashram from occult hostile forces which are always present when there is spiritual progress. The Mother and Sri Aurobindo had to confront and overcome the negative aspects of the sadhaks, dealing with their shortcomings and helping them in their individual processes of transformation. Jealousies and rivalries sometimes arose among the sadhaks, resulting in demands for the Mother's time and energy.

Managing the ashram involved numerous responsibilities and tasks. Houses had to be rented, repaired and maintained, adequate furniture had to be placed in the rooms, and innumerable visitors had to be met, apart from the regular sadhaks. This there were different departments, for building maintenance, cooking, gardening, tailoring, library, etc. There were also paid workers, local individuals employed to assist with various tasks required for the functioning of the ashram.[56] The Mother provided accounts of the expansion to her son André. In a letter of August 1930, she reported that there were twenty-one houses, eighty-five to a hundred residents, sixty to sixty-five paid workers, five cars, twelve bicycles, four sewing machines, several typewriters and a reading room with thousands of books.[57] By this time the Mother had transcended sleep; she would rest, but was always conscious.

One of the key changes made by the Mother was to organize sports and games for everyone and encourage physical fitness. She believed there was no reason why girls and women should not have the same activities as boys and men, and soon young women started playing in shorts and shirts, much to the consternation of some older residents, as this was hardly acceptable in Indian traditions of those times.

Towards the end of 1931, there was a change in the routine. The Mother fell ill on 18 October but was somewhat better by darshan day on 24 November. She and Aurobindo explained this illness as a result of an attack by adverse forces. After she recovered, the face-to-face darshans of the morning were replaced by balcony darshans. The Mother stood on the balcony at the back of the main ashram building and blessed the many people gathered below to greet her. As she stood there, she looked at each person in turn and was able to gauge their problems and concerns, providing solace through her inner power. No words were required, as she could see into their depths and understand their inner selves.

Birthdays were special days for the sadhaks, and the three darshan days – 15 August, 24 November and 21 February – were full of activities that had to be meticulously organized. These were the days when Sri Aurobindo emerged from his room, and he and the Mother sat together as the disciples filed past to receive their blessings. A list was made, beginning with the ashram residents, with one and a half minutes allotted to each person.

By 1934, numbers in the ashram rose to 150, including Indians and some foreigners. Among the Indians, there were people from all backgrounds – Hindus, Muslims, Parsis and Christians. A few years later, Sri Aurobindo commented that there were people from Bengal, Gujarat, Madras Presidency, Central Provinces, Punjab and Bihar. As they were given new names in the ashram, their origin became unimportant. Guidance from Sri Aurobindo was constant, and he warned against false visions of other worlds and beings, which were usually a product of the imagination. As he commented on one sadhak, 'He could not distinguish between what was true and what came to him from the vital and lower worlds.'[58] In their desire for spiritual progress, people often start imagining things.

The French government kept a watch on their activities, and at times, raised questions about their aims. Once again, Mirra's brother Matteo Alfassa, came to their aid, but the French government banned them from renting more buildings, asking them to build their own properties. The number of sadhaks stayed stable till 1937, as no expansion was possible, money had to be raised.

That year, Hyder Ali, diwan of the nizam of Hyderabad, provided a donation for a new building which gradually took shape and was known as Golconde.[59]

In 1938, Margaret Wilson, daughter of former US president Woodrow Wilson, arrived at the ashram and remained there till her death in 1944. She was given the name Nishta.

On the night of 23 November 1938, while everyone was resting after making all the preparations for the darshan on the 24th, a disaster took place. At 2 a.m., Sri Aurobindo tripped over the head of a tiger skin while on his way to the bathroom. (In those days, before wildlife protection laws, tiger skins were frequently offered to gurus as traditionally they used to sit on the skins of deer or tigers during meditation. Sri Aurobindo probably never sat on them but had accepted some as gifts.

Evidently, several tiger and leopard skins presented by devotees were kept in his suite of rooms). The Mother realized the fall telepathically and rushed to help. She then called Dr Manilal at night, and later a doctor and radiologist from Madras were also summoned. The radiologist arrived with an X-ray machine, and X-rays showed an impacted fracture of the right thigh bone above the knee. The position of the bone fragments being close to the blood vessels, posed a danger, and the doctors decided that the best course of action was a plaster, with gradual traction. Meanwhile, the Mother gave darshan alone in the evening of 24 November. Both were aware of occult dangers during the time of darshan, and by focusing on the Mother, Sri Aurobindo had not adequately protected himself.

Treatment was initiated, but a change occurred in Sri Aurobindo's way of life. He ceased corresponding with sadhaks and instead formed a closer association, engaging in daily dialogues, with those who took care of him. Some of these conversations were recorded and provide insights into his life during the following years. Nirodbaran documented these talks until 1941 when Sri Aurobindo grew increasingly silent. Nirodbaran also wrote *Twelve Years with Sri Aurobindo*, a valuable account of the various aspects of Sri Aurobindo's life. Initially, it was only the Mother and Champaklal who attended to him, but now there was a whole team involved. Manilal was a visiting doctor, while Nirodbaran, Becharlal, and Satyendra Thakore played roles in his care. Nirodbaran and Becharlal were doctors and Satyendra was a dentist. Mulshankar, who possessed some medical knowledge, and Purani also provided assistance, while Champaklal remained a constant presence. The Mother spent more time with Sri Aurobindo, tending to his grooming, combing and plaiting his hair, and ensuring that he ate by personally bringing him his food every day. During this period, the Mother would often enter trances herself, becoming completely absorbed and unaware of her surroundings. After some time, her consciousness would return, and she would be present once again.[60]

In 1939, as Sri Aurobindo's health improved, there was an increasing demand for darshan, leading to the establishment of a fourth darshan day on 24 April, which marked the anniversary of the day the Mother first arrived in Pondicherry in 1920. Sri Aurobindo made a relatively shorter appearance on that day. Despite his health, Sri Aurobindo continued to dedicate long hours to reading, writing and revising his earlier works. During this time, he focused on revising *The Life Divine*, which serves as a comprehensive exposition of his philosophy. The first part of *The Life Divine* was published in 1939, followed by the publication of the second part in July 1940. Notably, *The Life Divine* was nominated for the Nobel Prize in Literature in 1943, although no prize was ultimately awarded that year.

The Second World War started in September 1939. According to the Mother and Sri Aurobindo, the world war would have started by the end of 1938, but Sri Aurobindo used his occult forces to push it forward by almost a year. Though he was not an active participant in any event after reaching Pondicherry, he had not withdrawn totally from the world. He and the Mother keenly followed the stages of the war and quickly realized Hitler was a disaster for the world. They also recognized that Hitler and Nazism were 'dark Asuric forces' and, if they succeeded, there would be a setback to spiritual evolution and even an enslavement of India. He repeatedly warned against Hitler, saying, 'Hitler stands for diabolic values or for human values exaggerated in the wrong way until they become diabolical'. His victory would be a disaster for humanity. Hitler, too, believed that the Superman was being created, but his conception of it was very different from that of Sri Aurobindo's. He and the Mother and Sri Aurobindo felt that the world war was directly connected to the division between the divine powers and the asuras, and Sri Aurobindo explained that the Allies' fight was the struggle for an ideal.[61] If the Axis powers won, 'there would be a reign of falsehood and darkness'. In the early stages of the war, not all world leaders, including Mahatma Gandhi and many in India, had a clear understanding of the nature of the conflict. However, on 19 September 1940, Sri Aurobindo and the Mother publicly declared their support for the Allies. They sent a telegram to the secretary of the Viceroy expressing their support, contributed Rs 1,000 to the War Fund and also sent a letter to the governor of the Madras Presidency conveying their stance.[62] This led to a backlash against them, as India was still struggling for independence against the British. Many ashramites also supported Germany, and were against Aurobindo's support for the Allies. Dilip Roy was among those who opposed this stance. In fact, it appeared that about half of the ashram supported Hitler, which could have prompted the French government to close down the ashram. However, the friendship with Governor Bonvin helped prevent this. Sri Aurobindo also pointed out that if Hitler were to win, it was unlikely that he would grant India its freedom. Among the ashramites, Udar had a radio set, and every night, Pavitra and Pavita would listen to the *BBC News* at 9:30 p.m. and report everything back to Sri Aurobindo. Pavita, whose real name was Margaret Aldwinckle, was an Englishwoman and had been Paul Brunton's secretary. Eventually, a radio was installed in the ashram so that Sri Aurobindo could directly listen to the news. According to some accounts, Sri Aurobindo also exerted his spiritual force in support of the Allies during certain battles, particularly at Dunkirk in late May 1940, as the fall of Britain would have had dire consequences.[63] Sri Aurobindo and the Mother were also against Stalin, well aware of the destruction he was causing within Russia.[64] Sri Aurobindo had been in favour of the rise of Asian powers, but after 1942 and the Japanese threat to India, he no longer supported Japan. He believed Subhas Chandra Bose's National Army was ill-conceived, and if it succeeded, they would bring ruin to India through Japanese or German occupation.[65] The Mother and Sri Aurobindo are also said to have intervened through their occult powers to get the USA to join the war, and to stop the Japanese from entering India. This took place in March 1944, when 230,000 Japanese troops, along with Subhas Chandra's INA crossed into India and reached Imphal, but excessive rain prevented them from proceeding further. Nirodbaran observed that, 'rain during that season had never been heard of before',[66] suggesting that it was caused by Sri Aurobindo, although it was just a natural weather occurrence as rain is common in the area during March.

Sri Aurobindo was no less focused on independence and kept in touch with the events in India too. When the Cripps Mission proposals were made in 1942, Sri Aurobindo supported the offer and believed it should be accepted, but other Indian leaders rejected it. The Cripps Mission, so-called as it was headed by Sir Stafford Cripps, was a term for the proposals made in March 1942 to gain the unstinting support of Indian leaders for the British war effort. In return for this, the British promised to include more Indians in the government, even in the Executive Council, except for the sphere of defence. Dominion Status was promised after the war. A plan was also worked out for the Indian states. The proposal was broadcast over the radio, and Sri Aurobindo sent Cripps a telegram expressing his support for it. He wrote that as someone who was once a nationalist, he hoped the offer would be accepted so that there would be friendly relations between Britain and India in the future. He also sent telegrams to C. Rajagopalachari of the Congress Working Committee and B. S. Moonje of the Hindu Mahasabha, and additionally sent the lawyer Duraiswamy Iyer to meet the Congress leaders.[67] But despite all his efforts, the offer was rejected. He later said that he knew his attempts would fail; nevertheless, it was important to try. Spiritual forces had to be understood, and these acted only under certain conditions.

Even during the war years, the ashram was steadily growing. Some families reached there with their children, and considering the conditions, they could not be rejected. On 2 December 1943, a school for the children was opened. The children provided a new and broader dimension to life in the ashram. Teachers in the school included Sisir Kumar Mitra, who had been a professor at Visvabharati, Pranab Kumar Bhattacharya, who was also close to the Mother and the Mother herself. Pranab joined in 1945 along with his four brothers; he was put in charge of physical education, which started at that time with just fourteen students. A new ground for sports and games was acquired, and adults too began to participate in these. A publication division with a printing press was set up. On 21 February 1944, a quarterly magazine was started in Madras, called *Advent*, for the 'Exposition of Sri Aurobindo's Vision of the Future'. Similar magazines were started in Bombay and Calcutta. These were not ashram publications, though they included some of Sri Aurobindo's works along with those of his followers. Donations for all these activities came both from within and outside the ashram. During these years after his accident, his life had a different routine. He rose early and did a few recommended exercises before the Mother came in to greet him at 6:30 a.m. Parts of various newspapers were read to him, including the *Hindu* and the *Madras Mail.* The Mother came again after 9 a.m. and discussed ashram affairs while she combed and plaited his hair. His attendants helped him wash, after which he pursued his inner sadhana for a few hours. His main meal was served to him by the Mother between 3 and 4 p.m., with an array of vegetarian dishes, including something sweet. He ate what was put before him; even during his earliest days, he had never really been interested in food. Then, after he was sufficiently recovered, he would walk for a short time, using his stick for support, following which his attendants would help him with a bath. For quite some time, only a sponge bath was possible, as there was no attached bathroom. As before, he usually wore a simple white dhoti, one end thrown over his shoulder, with the addition of a shawl if it was cold. The Mother would come in to talk to him, and he discussed various issues for some time in the evening with his attendants. As his leg healed, he worked on *Savitri* and on revising his other books. He started dictating his work, as his eyesight had also deteriorated.[68]

The war ended, and the new viceroy, Lord Wavell, put forward another plan for dominion status, but this too was refused, though once again Sri Aurobindo was in favour of it. Then, with the fall of the Conservative government in Britain and the election of a Labour government, India finally gained independence on 15 August 1947. The day marked Sri Aurobindo's seventy-fifth birthday, and a message from him was requested by the Trichinopoly station of All India Radio and read out on 14 August. He had predicted long ago that independence was inevitable, but along with independence came the unforeseen partition into two countries, India and Pakistan, accompanied by murder and mayhem. Around one million people were killed, and around ten million migrated across the newly created borders. Though Sri Aurobindo had been against the Partition, he was unable to stop the tide of events. He found it significant that independence was proclaimed on his own birthday.

In his independence message, Sri Aurobindo put forward his five dreams for the world and India: the freedom and unity of India, of which only the first was attained; the rise of Asia; a world union to maintain peace; the spiritual gift of India to the world; and the rise of humans to a higher consciousness. But he was not happy with the division into India and Pakistan; he hoped they would be reunited. If it lasts, he said, India would be seriously weakened, with a constant possibility of civil strife. Even internal development and prosperity would be affected. He emphasized, 'The partition must go,' though the manner in which this happened was not important. Perhaps it would be through 'an increasing recognition of the necessity not only of peace and concord but of common action'. Unity was necessary for India's future greatness; therefore, it must be achieved.

After independence, the Mother drew a map of what she believed was the true India, including West and East Pakistan, Burma, and Ceylon. However, on that very day, some hooligans also attacked the ashram and one ashramite, Mulshankar Jain, was killed. Mulshankar had been a close attendant of Sri Aurobindo. This happened a day after a successful Darshan earlier that day. Even after India gained independence from Britain, Pondicherry remained under French control. He wanted the French territories to merge with India while retaining some autonomy. In September 1947, he came out of isolation to meet the governor of French territories in India, François Baron von Trott, as well as a representative of a French cultural delegation. However, the transfer of French territories to India occurred well after Aurobindo's death. There was considerable confusion at the time regarding the conditions in Pondicherry with the new Indian government. There was even a temporary blockade against goods entering French territories.[70]

In the aftermath of independence and partition, a further tragedy took place when Mahatma Gandhi was assassinated on 30 January 1948. Jawaharlal Nehru, spoke over the radio, 'The light has gone out of our lives'. Sri Aurobindo was asked for a message and, in his message too, he said, '… the light that led us to freedom, though not yet to unity, still burns and will burn till it conquers …'[71] Once again, Aurobindo was requested to rejoin political activity, and he refused. But he would comment on politics in *Mother India*, a newspaper started by his disciple K. D. Sethna.

Sri Aurobindo continued his work, delving deep into other worlds through *Savitri*. He dictated passages of the book to Nirodbaran, who would read them back to him the next day, after which he made revisions and additions.[72] Once it was typed out, further amendments were made. In 1950, the first part of *Savitri* was published.

Sri Aurobindo had not left the ashram for many years. Yet, he was known and widely respected, not only in India but also in the West. Scholars such as the Russian-born American sociologist Pitirim Sorokin (1889–1968), as well as other American, English, and French academics, who were impressed with Aurobindo's work, recognized his colossal intellect and spiritual depths. Aldous Huxley, Madam Montessori, Albert Schweitzer, W. Somerset Maugham, Paul Brunton, Mircea Eliade were among others who found his work important. In 1945, he was again nominated for the Nobel Prize in literature, though it was eventually awarded to Chilean poet Gabriela Mistral.

After 1947, a few people were allowed to visit him, including the photographer Cartier-Bresson, whose photographs provide an important record of this late stage of his life. S. Radhakrishnan asked him for an essay on philosophy through one of his disciples, but he refused. At no time did Sri Aurobindo want publicity or fame, or to create a sect or school, or a movement. 'It means that hundreds or thousands of useless people join in and corrupt the work or reduce it to a pompous farce from which the Truth that was coming down recedes into secrecy and silence. It is what has happened to the "religions" and it is the reason for their failure.'[74]

And yet, without any effort, he became known to prominent people in the western world.

From 1949 onwards, Sri Aurobindo was not keeping well. He had an enlarged prostate and urinary problems, as well as mild diabetes, but made a temporary recovery. He felt the need to complete his work soon.[75] By mid-1950, his prostate symptoms surged again, and he spoke less and less. Finally, surgery seemed like the only solution, as suggested by a visiting surgeon, Dr. Satyabrata Sen, but neither Sri Aurobindo nor the Mother could agree to this. On 24 November that year, the darshan took place as usual. Due to Sri Aurobindo's discomfort, less time was given to each person, and it concluded at 5 p.m. Soon after this, he was diagnosed with a kidney infection, and despite temporary improvements, it persisted. He did not want to be administered strong medicines. On one of his good days, he was asked whether he was using yogic powers to heal himself, but he denied this, though he would not explain why. On 2 December, they celebrated the foundation day of the school; Sri Aurobindo had a high fever, so the Mother did not attend the festivities either. She remarked that he was losing interest, withdrawing from the world.[76] He also had difficulty breathing and the condition deteriorated over the next few days. Always undemonstrative, he was half unconscious or in a trance, but each time he temporarily revived, he hugged Champaklal.[77]

At 11 p.m. on the fourth night, he drank half a cup of tomato juice given to him by the Mother, and not long after that, he left his body between 1:20 and 1:26 a.m. on 5 December. The Mother asserted that he was not compelled to leave the body, but actually chose to do so. Soon after he left his body, the tremendous Supramental force within him entered the Mother, and she felt it in a concrete way.[78]

Later, he was dressed in a white silk dhoti, and people were allowed to view him. At least 60,000 people filed past, and it is said that he looked as if he was in a peaceful sleep, with a light emanating from him for a few days. Despite the disapproval of the French government, on 9 December, Sri Aurobindo was buried in the ashram compound, following the tradition of Indian gurus who are placed in Samadhi. His death was reported not only in India but also in newspapers across the world, and his intellectual and philosophical achievements were universally lauded.

The Mother continued his work after his death.

3

A New Analysis of Ancient Texts

Sri Aurobindo commented on Vedic literature and translated and analysed parts of the Rig Veda, several Upanishads, and the Bhagavad Gita. These are the most sacred texts of Hinduism, said to be '*shruti*', that is, 'heard' by or divinely revealed to the ancient rishis and sages. Sri Aurobindo, with the belief that these texts must also support and confirm his philosophy, took a fresh look at them. He concluded that they had been misinterpreted in the past and then used these texts to elaborate on and explain aspects of his philosophy.

The Vedas

The term Veda is a generic term for a group of Sanskrit texts, which are the most sacred texts of the Hindus. Veda comes from the Sanskrit root '*Vid*', meaning 'to know', and the word Veda implies 'divine knowledge'. Vedic literature encompasses the four Vedic Samhitas, the closely related texts of the Brahmanas, Aranyakas, Upanishads and many more texts that explain, comment on and elucidate various aspects of these.

The Samhitas consist of the Rig Veda, Sama Veda, Yajur Veda and Atharva Veda, and are considered the most sacred texts among them. The Rig Veda has 1,028 *suktas*, or hymns, containing 10,552 *riks*, or verses. It is the earliest available text in India, composed in archaic Sanskrit. Some composers of the hymns are mentioned in the text, while others are listed in later sources. These composers include *rishis* and *rishikas*, male and female sages, kings and even the gods themselves. The Rig Veda contains prayers to various deities such as Indra, the god of thunder, rain, and war; Surya, the god of the Sun; Agni, the god of fire and many more. It also includes accounts of battles and conflicts, providing names of several clans and tribes along with those of their kings or leaders. The text also mentions rivers, mountains, animals and plants, helping to locate the composers of this text and their socioeconomic background.

The Sama Veda selects, rearranges and adds to some of the Rig Vedic riks in a manner appropriate for singing and chanting. The Yajur Veda describes rituals and provides specific mantras to be used in them, while the Atharva Veda contains prayers to deities, chants, spells to aid healing, and other miscellaneous hymns. Over time, the mantras and prayers in these four *samhitas* came to be used in elaborate and complex sacrificial rituals or yajnas, conducted by sixteen or more priests.

The Brahmanas are texts attached to each of the samhitas, describing the rituals in more detail, while the aranyakas contain some unique rituals along with the beginnings of a symbolic interpretation. The Upanishads are philosophical texts that form the basis for the philosophy of Vedanta. Numerous other texts form part of Vedic literature, including Padapathas or word texts, three categories of Kalpa Sutras comprising Dharma Sutras, Grihya Sutras and Shrauta Sutras, along with auxiliary texts categorized as Vedangas.

The accepted date for the Rig Veda is between 1500 and 1000 BCE, and the three later Vedas are dated between approximately 1000 and 600 BCE. Some of the attached texts also belong to this latter date, while others are later. Despite the accepted dates, all these texts could be earlier, and a broader time frame of between 4000 BCE and 1000 BCE would be more appropriate for the Rig Veda.[1]

Focusing on the Rig Veda, Sri Aurobindo sought to discover its essential spiritual meaning. Although the Rig Veda is a small part of the vast corpus of Vedic literature, it holds significant importance, and Sri Aurobindo's work on the text showcases the depth and scope of his knowledge and understanding. His writings on the Rig Veda mainly took place before 1920, with a few later additions. His primary works on the subject culminated in two books: *The Secret of the Veda* and *Hymns to the Mystic Fire*.[2] Some additional translations and essays on the Vedas, which were not published during his lifetime, were later compiled in *Vedic and Philological Studies*.

The Secret of the Veda, first published in *Arya* from 1914 to 1916, consists of a series of essays exploring various aspects of the Rig Veda, including its origin, composition and, most importantly, its meaning. Sri Aurobindo rejects the notion that it was primarily a ritual text but acknowledges the difficulties in understanding it. He explains that the text is written in an ancient language, and many of its words and forms were unknown in later Sanskrit. Even when known, their meanings could be entirely different, as every Sanskrit word has multiple interpretations. Sri Aurobindo lists three main attempts made to understand these ancient hymns.

The first attempt was the elaboration on the Rig Veda and other Samhitas in the Brahmanas and Upanishads, but this is fragmentary and incomplete. The second attempt was the work of Sayana, who lived in the fouteenth century, and the third was the work of the Europeans in the nineteenth century, who based their translations on Sayana's work. While many scholars trace the beginning of Indian philosophy to the Upanishads, Sri Aurobindo finds the roots of Upanishadic philosophy and spirituality in the Rig Veda. He explains that the truths of the Rig Veda were concealed behind apparent material forms because these highest truths were meant only for the select few. Although outwardly they may seem to explain rituals and ceremonies for pantheistic nature worship, they were actually 'symbols of a spiritual experience and knowledge'.[5] These outer rituals and ceremonies were for the common people, whereas for the initiate, there were inner mysteries concealed in the same words. As he explains, 'The ritual system recognised by Sayana, may in its externalities, stand; the naturalistic sense discovered by Europeans may, in its general conceptions, be accepted; but behind them there is always the true and still hidden secret of the Veda.'[6] If the Rig Veda could be reinterpreted in this way, it would shed new light on several other religious texts, including the Upanishads, Puranas and Tantras, and even on the history of religion.

In this book, Sri Aurobindo explained why he attempted this reinterpretation. He said:

> In the fixed tradition of thousands of years, they have been revered as the origin and standard of all that can be held as authoritative and true in Brahmana and Upanishad, in Tantra and Purana, in the doctrines of great philosophical schools and in the teachings of famous saints and sages. The name borne by them was Veda, the knowledge – the received name for the highest spiritual truth of which the human is capable. But if

we accept the current interpretations, whether Sayana's or the modern theory, the whole of this sublime and sacred reputation is a colossal fiction.[7]

Sri Aurobindo believed that the profound philosophy of the Upanishads must have originated in the Rig Veda. However, he observed that even by the time of the Brahmanas and Upanishads, the great truths had become obscured, and 'the material aspects of Vedic worship had grown like a thick crust over the inner knowledge and were stifling what they had once served to protect'.

Sri Aurobindo also comments on the rishis who composed the Vedic texts, and his understanding is relevant to his own philosophy. He explains that the rishis did not attain their understanding or powers through miracles or supernatural means. Instead, they achieved their wisdom through their own diligent efforts and 'progressive self-culture'.[8] Despite the different composers and different deities referred to, Sri Aurobindo finds the same truths and the same themes revealed in even apparently disparate hymns.[9] He explains that there is just one Truth, one Light, that is revealed 'through the sameness of experience'.[10] The hymns of the Rig Veda have a 'finished metrical form,' yet they all share 'the same framework,' with the aim of expressing the Divine that was revealed to the rishis. However, over time, only the material aspects of the hymns were known, and the universal divine aspects were forgotten. Sri Aurobindo views the Brahmanas and Upanishads as a revival of Vedic thought. The Brahmanas fixed the form, while the Upanishads revealed the soul. However, even the Upanishads do not greatly assist in 'determining the accurate sense of the texts which they quote. Their true purpose was to establish

Vedanta rather than to interpret the Veda'.[11] Through Vedanta, the importance of outer ritual was diminished, and symbolic and mysterious aspects were expressed in clear language. Sri Aurobindo fittingly relates this development to his theory of different ages, seeing it as a transition from the age of Intuition to the age of Reason (see chapter 4). He then traces the rise of Buddhism, which opposed Vedic rituals, and discusses the composition of the Puranas, which introduced new elements.

Sri Aurobindo also acknowledges the precise preservation of the Vedic hymns and commends the contribution of auxiliary texts such as the Padapathas in preserving them. He highlights the work of the ancient Indian linguist Yaska in explaining the terms used in the hymns. However, he notes that Sayana's work represents the last significant contribution of the classical tradition.[12] While Sayana's commentary has many aspects, it predominantly emphasizes the material and ritualistic aspects of the text. Sri Aurobindo states, 'It is the final and authoritative binding of the Veda to this lowest of all its possible senses that has been the most unfortunate result of Sayana's commentary.' Additionally, Sayana's work 'became, in the European mind, the source of fresh errors'.[13]

However, the extensive scholarship Sayana brought to his analysis and commentary made his work invaluable. He said, 'At every step we are obliged to differ from it, but at every step we are obliged to use it.'[14] He examined aspects of European scholarship of the nineteenth and early twentieth centuries that were based on Sayana. They developed their ideas in light of modern knowledge in the fields of history, mythology and philology, and went into great depth and detail, building theories of Vedic mythology, civilization and history, but he feels most of these were pure conjecture.

> What it found in Sayana and in the Brahmanas it has developed in the light of modern theories and modern knowledge; by ingenious deductions from the comparative method applied to philology, mythology and history, by large amplifications of the existing data with the aid of ingenious speculation, by unification of the scattered indications available it has built up a complete theory of Vedic mythology, Vedic history, Vedic civilisation which fascinates by its detail and thoroughness and conceals by its apparent sureness of method the fact that this imposing edifice has been founded ... on the sands of conjecture.[15]

Who were the people who wrote the Rig Veda? The prevalent theory at the time that Sri Aurobindo wrote was that they were invaders, perhaps from Central Asia or elsewhere, or else migrants. Sri Aurobindo points out that in the texts there is little or no evidence of an 'Aryan invasion',[16] and supposing there was a migration, there is no evidence that it took place at the time of the composition of the Rig Veda. The theory of Sanskrit being part of the family of Indo-European languages led to comparisons with other ancient peoples from the same language group. Sri Aurobindo suggested that if the Vedic people were to be compared with Greek and Celtic peoples, they too had high philosophical conceptions. He also pointed out that there must have been antecedents to the development of these philosophies, whether of Plato or of the Upanishads, as they could not have suddenly emerged and must have developed over a long period of time.[17] For the Upanishads, therefore, the origin must be in the Rig Veda.

He also looked at the work of scholars closer to his time, particularly that of Balgangadhar Tilak, T. Paramasiva Aiyar and Swami Dayananda. Tilak postulated an Arctic home for the Vedic people in distant times. Aiyar's work is little known today, but he felt aspects of the Rig Veda represented geological phenomena. Swami Dayananda's views are more important and still influential today. Dayananda's most important work is Satyartha Prakasha, which is a comprehensive exposition of his philosophy. He wrote other books too, including *Rigvedadi-bhashya-bhumika*, a nine-volume commentary on the Rig Veda. Sri Aurobindo commends Swami Dayananda's efforts at reinterpretation but does not agree with them:

> Dayananda's interpretation of the hymns is governed by the idea that the Vedas are a plenary revelation of religious, ethical and scientific truth. Its religious teaching is monotheistic and the Vedic gods are different descriptive names of the one Deity; they are at the same time indications of His powers as we see them working in Nature and by a true understanding of the sense of the Vedas we could arrive at all the scientific truths which have been discovered by modern research. Such a theory is, obviously, difficult to establish.[18]

The key to understanding the Rig Veda, said Sri Aurobindo, is to view it as a spiritual text and reinterpret it accordingly. *The Secret of the Veda* has over 600 pages on the origin and meaning of the Vedas, with many pointers on the spiritual interpretations behind what seems to be material descriptions and, though Aurobindo could not find time to pursue a total reinterpretation, his ideas on this text are significant.

His main theme is that the Rig Veda has deep spiritual insights pointing the way to Truth and symbolically explains the conflict between the powers of Light and Darkness. As mentioned earlier, he also sees the same truths repeated in all the hymns, even though they were composed by different people and apparently refer to different deities.[19] Each deity and each aspect of nature, thus, has a double meaning, and its hidden or secret meaning reveals ultimate truths. Analysing Goddess Sarasvati, he sees her as the goddess of shruti and the divine word.[20] A correct understanding even reveals psychological states, and the flow of her waters represents the inspiration of truth-consciousness. The many rivers, the herds of cows, the waters, are similarly analysed to reveal their inner, divine meaning.[21] For instance, quoting various passages on the *go*, or cow, he observes: 'The Vedic cow was an exceedingly enigmatic animal that came from no earthly herd.'[22] *Ashva*, or horse, was also symbolic to Sri Aurobindo. To him, go and ashva symbolized Light and Energy, Consciousness and Force. Thus, wealth in terms of cows and horses signified mental illumination and energy.[23] The entire symbolism of the Vedas reveals their focus on the inner divine light and divine word. Even the seven rishis can be understood as symbolic forces of light and other divine powers,[24] and further mysteries can be revealed through an analysis of the *pitris* or ancestors.[25]

Even for the average reader, *soma*, the intoxicating drink which occupies almost the entire ninth mandala in the Rig Veda, appears to be more than just a drink. It is seen as a representation of something divine. In Sri Aurobindo's words, 'The wine of soma is the intoxication of the Ananda, the divine delight of being.' He further explains that the different deities mentioned, such as Indra, Agni and Vayu, are not individual gods but rather aspects of the Divine. This understanding is clearly conveyed in one of the hymns.[26] Agni, meaning not only fire but also force and brilliance, represents the 'illumined energy which builds up the worlds'.[27] Every word in Sanskrit has numerous possible interpretations and Sri Aurobindo tries to understand the spiritual meaning, which had long been forgotten.

Sri Aurobindo offers his own interpretation of many stories from the Rig Veda, and one such story is that of Sarama and the Panis. In conventional translations, Sarama is described as the dog of the god Indra who leads the way to the Panis, a group that has captured some cows, and retrieves the cows from them. Sarama even engages in a dialogue with them, where they ask her to stay with them, but she remains loyal to Indra. To Aurobindo, Sarama symbolizes the seeker, the traveller on the path to Truth. The struggle between Indra and the Panis represents the struggle between Light and Darkness. Sarama, guided by her intuition, seeks that which is lost. She embodies the power of Truth, while the cows represent the rays of divine illumination. In a late hymn, 10.14, the Sarameyas, the two dogs of the god Yama, are mentioned. Sri Aurobindo explains that Yama was originally the Sun and the two four-eyed dogs serve as guardians who protect the person on the path to heaven.[28]

Sri Aurobindo acknowledges that there may have been physical battles, which the rishis metaphorically represented to convey profound truths. The theory of conflicts between *aryas* and *dasas*, understood as conflicts between two different groups, holds a deeper meaning as a conflict between Light and Darkness. The aryas represent Light, while the dasas and *dasyus* represent Darkness.

He states, 'The Dasyus stand in opposition to both the Aryan gods and the Aryan seers. The Gods are born from Aditi in the Supreme Truth of things, the Dasyus or Danavas from Diti in the nether darkness; they are the Lords of Light and the Lords of Night fronting each other across the triple world of earth, heaven, and mid-air, body, mind, and the connecting breath of life.'[29]

Sri Aurobindo has attempted to uncover the symbolism behind the material aspects of the Veda, but he acknowledges that there is still more to be explored, as these are only 'the leading clues'.[30] There are few who have delved deeply into his interpretations of the Rig Veda, and even fewer who have questioned them. In the spiritual realm, his stature as a philosopher and scholar makes such questioning unlikely, while historians may see little value in his endeavours.

To approach the Veda comprehensively, one must consider it at two levels: there are historical elements that can be analysed and interpreted. The mention of cows, horses and dogs would not exist if these did not exist during that time. The numerous clans mentioned likely had some basis in reality, as did the battles described. Rituals, sacrificial fires, and soma were not purely symbolic but had tangible manifestations. Alongside these outer forms, there may also be deeper messages, and it is these that Sri Aurobindo attempts to explain. However, it remains unclear why and how the ritualistic elements became crystallized in the later Vedic texts and the Brahmanas if they were meant to be symbolic. Furthermore, if each deity represents not only an element of nature but also an aspect of Light and Truth, would this hold true for nature deities in other traditions as well?

In the second part of the book, Sri Aurobindo provides translations and commentaries on selected hymns, further elucidating his ideas. In his analysis, he offers specific interpretations of each deity. For example, he suggests that the Maruts 'are the Purushas of separate thought energies, with Indra being the one Purusha encompassing all thought energies'.[31] Agni is not just fire, but 'the divine Will at work in the world'.[32] There are detailed explanations of what these and other deities signify. As for the rishis who were the composers, he says they see the world first as an aspect of consciousness, and only secondly in its concrete form.[33] Solar energy is the physical form of Surya, Lord of light and truth.[34] In this way

Aurobindo, along with his translations, reinterprets the nature of the deities praised in the hymns.

In the foreword to part three, containing the hymns of the Atris, who were a family of rishis, Sri Aurobindo says it is almost impossible to translate the Veda. A literal rendering misses their sense and spirit, while to reveal the concealed thought would be an interpretation, rather than a translation. He says he has taken a middle path that includes interpretative devices[35] and explains how he has tried to understand the true sense of the hymns. Yet, so much time has passed. 'The rishis attempted to conceal their knowledge from the unfit',[36] and now it is difficult to understand all its secrets. As he says, 'The secret of the Veda, even when it has been unveiled, remains a secret.'[37] The Vedas portray 'the ancient psychological science and the art of spiritual living of which the Upanishads are the philosophical outcome and modification, and Vedanta, Sankhya and Yoga, the late intellectual result and logical dogma'.[38] He also links Puranic concepts with the deeper spiritual ideas in the Veda. To him, the Vedic sacrifice represents a journey, the end being the ocean of light and infinity; the wars and battles against dasas, dasyus and others reflect the battles against evil and ignorance. The Vedic deities represent aspects of the universal godhead.[39] They call man to a divine alliance against the sons of darkness and division. In return man calls him to the sacrifice, in which the sacrificial objects also have a symbolic significance.[40] There is a struggle between cosmic powers, and the gods are various energies. *Agni*, outwardly fire, is the force and will of the Divine, and the other gods can be related to this force.[41] He has translated several hymns to Agni, Surya and other deities. Surya Savitri is the creator, as in the Gayatri mantra. The concept of 'Total Night' in the Vedic hymns represents the Inconscient, while the notion of the 'lesser night' symbolizes ignorance.

Through their beautiful hymns, the Vedic rishis offer divine hints and insights. Sri Aurobindo unveils the inner meaning of each deity, shedding light on their significance.

It is obvious to any translator that all the references in the Vedas to material items – cows, horses, wealth – are not always literal. It has often been pointed out that cows represent clouds at times, and *ashva* has different meanings, including knowledge. Soma, probably also had two different meanings, of an actual drink and the divine *amrita*. At the same time, it does not seem possible to deny all material and historical references, as even Sri Aurobindo said that it had two levels, one for the ordinary person and the other for the spiritually advanced. He himself believed that a lot more work was required on it, and he wanted to rewrite and expand his work on the Veda.[42]

Some aspects of Sri Aurobindo's later thoughts on the Vedas are captured in *Hymns to the Mystic Fire*, a compilation of translations and writings by Sri Aurobindo centred around the god Agni. The book includes an enlightening foreword and introduction. It is divided into three parts, with the first part published separately during his lifetime, and the latter two added later.

In the foreword, Sri Aurobindo once again elucidates the mystical tradition of the Vedas, a tradition that was alluded to by Sayana but largely overlooked by European scholars.[43] He says originally there was the worship of powers of nature, though both in India and elsewhere these nature deities soon gained different, psychological dimensions. As they retained their external character, the new Puranic deities developed with a wider cosmological base. He affirms that the mystical understanding of India's ancient rishis had its counterpart in Egypt, Greece, Persia and elsewhere. In the following essay, 'The Doctrine of the Mystics',[44] he also explains why battles were necessary, for instance between dasa/dasyu and arya, and the true nature of the sacrificial ritual – all that it represents and the essential nature of each deity. These gods, or rather what they represent, form part of each individual, and have to be perfected within us. As he says, 'The soul of man is a world full of beings, a kingdom in which armies clash, to help or hinder a supreme conquest, a house where the gods are our guests and which the demons strive to possess.'[45] Much of the rest of the book brings out the true meaning of Agni, through translations of Rig Vedic hymns devoted to this deity. His translations reflect his views of how the numerous hymns with many different authors, all present the same theme, the same mystical understanding.

In the *Secret of the Veda* and *Hymns to the Mystic Fire*, Sri Aurobindo focused only on the Rig Veda. He did not analyse the three Later Vedic texts, the Sama Veda, Yajur Veda and Atharva Veda, and also largely ignored the Brahmanas and the Aranyakas, though there is a progression and connection of all these texts with the Upanishads. In the latter half of the twentieth century and in the twenty-first, there have been innumerable works on the Vedas, the related Avestan texts and the Indo-Europeans. Recent research does not see a major contrast between arya and dasa/dasyu. Later Avestan sources also see the *ahuras*/Sanskrit asuras as good, and the devas as evil. Research on the Indo-Europeans is immense, and the Vedic texts need to be reviewed in this context. In addition, there is DNA analysis that has to be added to the mix, along with an understanding of the archaeological context. The Harappan Civilization was discovered during Sri Aurobindo's lifetime but was analysed and described after he wrote these works.[46]

But none of this has relevance to his spiritual interpretation, which has to be placed in the context of his spiritual philosophy, as explained in *The Life Divine* and other works. He had understood the divine forces of *sat-chit-ananda*, representing True Being, Consciousness and Bliss. As the Vedas are traditionally shruti, revealing the divine word, they must also reveal and describe these forces, even if the descriptions are concealed behind mundane words and events. His approach could also be applied to Avestan and Indo-European sources, leading to a new understanding.

The Upanishads

Sri Aurobindo commented on and translated some of the Upanishads, which belong to the fourth category of Vedic texts. The term *upanishad* has been interpreted in different ways. It is often explained as 'sitting near the feet of a master,' derived from *upa* meaning near, and *nishad* meaning sitting down. Another interpretation suggests *shad* as destruction, and 'upanishad' as 'that which destroys ignorance'. However, the original meaning was 'secret doctrine'.

These texts are connected to or sometimes form the latter part of the Brahmanas or Aranyakas and are associated with one of the Vedic Samhitas. They are referred to as Vedanta, which means 'the end of the Vedas', both because they form the concluding part of the Vedas and because they represent the ultimate or highest philosophy contained within the Vedas. In the seventeenth century, a total of 108 Upanishads were recorded in the texts, but the early Upanishads hold the greatest significance. The earliest ones are believed to date back to the sixth or seventh century BCE, while at least fourteen have been dated to before the third century BCE. The Aitareya, Kaushitaki, Taittiriya, Brihadaranyaka, Chhandogya and Kena are among the earliest Upanishads, while slightly later ones include the Kathaka, Shvetashvatara, Mahanarayana, Isha, Mundaka, Prashna, Maitrayaniya and Mandukya.

These early Upanishads primarily focus on attaining the supreme goal of Brahman, the One Reality. Discrimination and reason are employed to understand and merge with Brahman. Some of the later Upanishads advocate the worship of deities as a means to reach this goal. Brahman and *Atman*, the soul often identified with Brahman, are the main concepts explored in the Upanishads. Additionally, the Upanishads discuss theories about the nature and origin of the world, the symbolism of sacrifice, worship, asceticism, karma, reincarnation, the nature of the body and mind, and include prayers aimed at achieving specific ends. However, the underlying theme in most Upanishads revolves around the exploration of Brahman. It is assumed that true knowledge is the ultimate attainment and through it, all else can be attained. The Upanishads mention various teachers, including Prajapati, Brahma, Sanat Kumara, as well as different rishis and kings. Women also actively participated in discussions, with Gargi and Maitreyi being well-known figures.

Sri Aurobindo translated and commented on several Upanishads.[47] From early philosophers such as Gaudapada of the eighth century and Shankara of the ninth century, up to the present, there have been innumerable translations of the major or early Upanishads. However, Sri Aurobindo differs from other commentators and interpreters. He links the Upanishads to the concepts and deities in the Rig Veda, and sees in them a life-affirming philosophy, one that is not just about attaining moksha, as is generally presumed, but about action in the world. In his interpretation, spiritual goals are connected to the concept of world transformation. The third difference is his deep analysis of the Upanishads to reveal stages of spiritual growth.

Sri Aurobindo began translating the Upanishads even before he reached Pondicherry in 1910. The early translations included those of the Taittiriya, Aitareya, Prashna and Mandukya Upanishads. Once in Pondicherry, he provided further commentary on the Taittiriya, along with translations and commentaries on the Isha, Kena, Mundaka and Katha Upanishads. There are also partial translations and commentaries done at various times. Among them are those on the Brihadaranyaka, Chhandogya, Shvetashvatara, Kaivalya and Nilarudra Upanishads.

He also looked at Gaudapada's commentary and the work of Sadananda. Sri Aurobindo begins his introduction to these texts with, 'The Upanishads are the supreme work of the Indian mind'.[48] He says that the intuitive and psychological experiences of the Vedic rishis, culminates in the Upanishads, which is not a revelation only to the intellect, but to the soul. As he points out, their ideas are found in other philosophies – in the thoughts of Pythagoras and Plato, in Neo-Platonism and Gnosticism and in much of German metaphysics. The ideas are repeated in Sufism, the only difference being that Sufism 'uses another religious language'.[49] He explains: 'The Upanishads are Vedanta, a book of knowledge of a higher degree even than the Vedas, but knowledge in the profounder Indian sense of the word, jnana.'[50] The Upanishads combine poetry with spiritual philosophy and form the soul of later literature and thought.

Though it is not possible to delve into all of Sri Aurobindo's translations here, we can provide an overview of his translation and analysis of the Upanishads. Among them, his most extensive work is on the Isha Upanishad. This Upanishad is part of one of the recensions of the Yajur Veda, which primarily describes various Vedic rituals and sacrifices, while also encompassing other aspects.

The Yajur Veda consists of two main recensions: *Shukla* (white) and *Krishna* (black). The Isha Upanishad is the fortieth and final chapter of the Vajasaneyi Samhita, which belongs to the Shukla Yajur Veda. The dating of this Upanishad varies, with some placing it between approximately 600 and 300 BCE. However, scholars like S. Radhakrishnan suggest that it is one of the earliest Upanishads, originating in the eighth to seventh century BCE, predating the advent of Buddhism. This Upanishad, consisting of eighteen verses, encapsulates the essence of Upanishadic philosophy and is frequently translated and interpreted. It contains passages that are challenging to interpret, leading to diverse explanations from different philosophical schools. The introduction by the philosopher Shankara, from the ninth century, indicates that only those seeking to dispel ignorance, alleviate sorrow and attain supreme Bliss are in the right state of mind to study this Upanishad.[51]

Sri Aurobindo wrote ten incomplete versions of his commentary and translation before finalizing it in 1914. The opening word of the text, '*Ishavasyam*', is usually translated as 'covered by god', but Sri Aurobindo interprets it as 'All this is for habitation of the Lord'. He provides a word-by-word translation and commentary, often differing with Shankara's interpretations. Sri Aurobindo further analyses the Upanishad, revealing the implicit and profound aspects within each verse. The first three verses explain the foundation of cosmic existence, emphasizing that the entire world is inhabited by the divine spirit. Verses 4 and 5 delve into the analysis of Brahman, the eternal reality, teaching us how to perceive Brahman in the universe and within our own existence.[52] The next two verses indicate how to attain Brahman, through the atman, that is essentially the same, and here Sri Aurobindo also explains the three-fold *Purusha*, and sat-chit-ananda, true being, consciousness and bliss – that is the true nature of the universe.[53] Continuing his explanations in succeeding verses, he shows how this single short Upanishad reveals the essential divine truth.[54] Sri Aurobindo undertook many more translations and commentaries of the Upanishads, some partial and fragmentary, and some which he perfected and completed. Among the latter are the Kena, Katha, Mundaka and Taittiriya Upanishads.[55] He also commented on Gaudapada's Karika and wrote several essays on the Vedanta. Gaudapada, who lived in the seventh or eighth century CE, was the teacher of Govinda, who was the teacher of Shankara, the most notable Upanishadic philosopher. The Karika is a commentary on the Mandukya Upanishad, which along with Shankara's commentary on it, provides the basis for the philosophy of Advaita Vedanta.

Sri Aurobindo also suggests how to study Indian philosophy. Beginning with the Upanishads, one could go on to Gaudapada and Shankara, along with Paul Deussen's *System of the Vedanta*. Once the monism by Gaudapada, Shankara and Anandagiri, is understood, one could look at modified monism, and dualistic monism. Simultaneously, one should look at the six classical systems of Indian philosophy, of which Vedanta is only one; the others are *Mimamsa*, *Samkhya*, Yoga, *Nyaya* and *Vaisheshika*. This should be followed by Vijnanabhikshu's work 'and the great synthesis of the Bhagavad Gita to crown the whole structure'.[56]

The Bhagavad Gita

Sri Aurobindo laid great emphasis on the Bhagavad Gita, translating and commenting on it. He explored its depths while in prison and began to see the whole world as a manifestation of Vasudeva-Krishna.

The Bhagavad Gita, the 'Lord's Song' or Divine Song', is an early Sanskrit text revered as one of the most sacred. Though usually published as a separate text, it forms part of the Bhishma Parva of the Mahabharata. It has eighteen chapters with 700 verses, though the number of verses differs in different recensions. Most of it is in the form of a dialogue between the Pandava Arjuna and the god Krishna, which takes place just before the great Mahabharata War begins. On the battlefield, where the two armies of the Kauravas and Pandavas are arrayed against each other, Arjuna's courage fails him as he thinks of fighting against his friends and kinsmen. Surely, he says, it would be better if he left the battlefield and became an ascetic? Krishna encourages him to throw off his weakness and fight, for that is the duty of a *Kshatriya*. In a much-quoted passage, he assures Arjuna that no one ever dies. The Spirit in every living being is immortal and beyond change. After death, the Spirit takes on a new body, just as a person changes clothes.

Further chapters describe the various paths through which God, either as the formless One or as Krishna, can be reached. The path of action of karma yoga is described, with particular emphasis on Nishkama Karma, or work done without focusing on rewards gained through it. Another path is that of jnana yoga, the path of knowledge, where union with God is achieved through true knowledge and understanding. A third way is that of bhakti, or devotion. The Gita also explains the concepts of Purusha and *Prakriti*, which form part of the philosophical system of Samkhya, and the nature of the three *gunas*, or characteristics, inherent in every person. Its date is uncertain, though many scholars feel it probably acquired its present form between the second century BCE and the second century CE. However, several others place it much earlier. Among them, S. N. Dasgupta, the noted writer on philosophy, placed it in the eighth or ninth century BCE and believed that it predates the Mahabharata and may have been added to the epic later.[57]

The profound philosophical content of the Gita had been recognized from early days, and there are, therefore, innumerable commentaries on this text as well as translations in all regional languages, and in English. Modern translators and commentators also include B. G. Tilak, Sri Rajagopalachari, Vinoba Bhave and Mahatma Gandhi.

Sri Aurobindo not only translated and commented on the Bhagavad Gita, but also wrote a series of essays on the text. With his consent, his disciple Anilbaran rearranged the essays as a commentary on the verses, thus making his ideas easier to access. This version was published in 1938, with Sri Aurobindo's approval, and is used here.[58]

In his introduction to the text, Sri Aurobindo makes some significant points. Before analysing any ancient scripture, it would be good, he says, to indicate how one plans to approach it. Such texts do contain an eternal truth, but this truth 'is not likely to be found in its entirety or in all its bearings in any single philosophy or scripture', nor has it been totally explained by any avatar or teacher. This eternal truth is conveyed within time through the mind of a person, and therefore every text or teacher has two aspects: one represents the circumstances under which it was composed, and the second the eternal truth. But even this truth has more relevance for the time in which it was composed. To understand the Gita, or any other text, in the same way as it was understood at the time of its composition would not be possible, as people's minds too have changed over time, along with the understanding of symbols and even words. But still, the living truths of the Gita can be sought, even if 'in this attempt we may mix a good deal of error born of our own individuality and of the ideas in which we live.'[59] If we try to live that truth, to whatever extent it is possible, we will begin to get a deeper understanding. Every truth in an ancient text, must be relived and 'reshaped and developed in the inner thought and spiritual experience of a developing humanity'.[60] Without this, they have no force.

Explaining the Gita, he says, it is not pure monism, even though the concept of the one, unchanging, eternal self is prominent in it. Nor can it be categorized as qualified monism, Mayavada, or Vaishnava Theism. Instead, it is a synthesis, both spiritual and intellectual that avoids any rigidity. As he points out, some commentators classified this as 'one of the three highest Vedantic authorities and attempted to turn it into a weapon of offence and defence against other schools and systems.'[61] This was never its purpose. On the contrary, the Gita provides a gate to the entire world of spirituality and spiritual experience. There were earlier syntheses too; for instance, the Vedic texts provide the psychological heights of knowledge, power and joy behind what is apparently concrete, while the Upanishads provide a synthesis of spiritual knowledge. Based on the Vedantic synthesis, the Gita 'builds another harmony of the three great means and powers, Love, Knowledge and Works, through which the soul of man can directly approach and cast itself into the eternal.'[62] He then comments that the Tantric is another spiritual synthesis that 'is even more bold and forceful than that of the Gita'. It includes not only love, knowledge and works but also hatha and raja yoga and the use of the body and mind to attain divine perfection.[63] But now, he says, there must be a new development, a new synthesis. 'We do not belong to the past dawns, but to the noons of the future.'[64] The starting point for this grand new synthesis is the texts of the past, particularly the Gita.

His translation more or less follows the pattern of other translations, with some divergences, but his commentary provides new insights. He explains that the Gita is not just a text for a spiritual life but also has practical guidelines on how to apply ethics and spirituality in daily life. Arjuna's dilemma as he stands on the battlefield is personal; at the same time, it raises the question of human life and action. His dejection is that of every human when they see life as it really is. Kurukshetra represents the battle of life, and the message here is to acknowledge Kurukshetra and 'submit to the law of Life by Death before we can find our way to the life immortal'.[65]

Commenting on chapter 2 of the Gita, Sri Aurobindo points out that Arjuna's pity for those assembled against him on the battlefield is one of weakness, not the higher element of compassion. Arjuna is a man of action, not of knowledge[66] and he asks for guidance to know his dharma, not the secrets of the universe. But Krishna's response takes him to a higher level, as he tells Arjuna to abandon all dharmas, except that of living consciously in the Divine. Sri Aurobindo also points out that it is a mistake to interpret the term '*nishkama* karma' as the disinterested performance of duties, as Krishna is actually speaking of abandoning all duties, and following the divine life.

Death is a part of existence and there is no reason to mourn when someone dies, as 'every creature born with a mind' survives death and is reborn. Immortality is something beyond this; it is living 'as a spirit and in the spirit.' The person fit for immortality is one who has transcended the joy, sorrow, grief and attraction or aversion to the transient things of the world and retains a tranquil spirit in all circumstances.[67] The soul is eternal; it can never cease to be and is the one reality beyond change.[68] As he explains, 'Our sorrow for the death of men is an ignorant grieving for those for whom there is no cause to grieve, since they have neither gone out of existence nor suffered any painful or terrible change of condition, but are beyond death no less in being and no more unhappy in circumstance than in life.'[69] Sri Aurobindo raises the important point that, though the Gita is a Vedantic work, it has in it elements of the main principles of Sankhya and Yoga before they crystallized into elaborate systems. These two linked philosophies are among the six classical philosophical systems of India. (For more on this, see chapter 5.) The early Sankhya, Sri Aurobindo explains, was basically dualistic, with the principles of a passive Purusha and a dynamic Prakriti. Purusha is pure consciousness, immobile and self-luminous. It is the soul, but not in the ordinary sense. Prakriti is energy, which has a mechanical process, but when reflected in Purusha, it appears to be conscious. Its three gunas, *sattva*, *rajas* and *tamas*, are inactive when in equilibrium, but when disturbed, they act, and thus creation, preservation and dissolution begin. Intelligence and will are properties of *Buddhi* (higher intelligence), the first of the twenty-four tattva, or elements, but not of the soul. In these philosophical systems, there are many Purushas, just as there are many souls, but at the same time, there is one universal Purusha beyond these, and this is mentioned in the Gita. In chapter 13 of the Gita, the Purusha is also the lord of nature and knowledge; he is Ishvara, or God, and the cause of action of Prakriti. At a different level, there are two or even three Purushas, but only one is supreme. The Upanishads refer to two Purushas, the silent witness and the one who acts; the Gita refers to three Purushas: the *kshara*, the one that becomes, the *akshara*, the unmanifest, and the *uttama*, *purushottama*, or unchanging. This last is Brahman.[70]

Sri Aurobindo further explains that in the first six chapters, the Gita lays out a synthesis of works and knowledge from

Sankhya, Yoga and Vedanta. For the Vedantin, he says, karma, or works, refers to the Vedic *yajnas*, or sacrifices. For instance, Krishna says (v. 45) that the action of the three gunas is the matter of the Veda, and Arjuna must go beyond these.[71] When a person reaches a higher level, he is no longer subject to his work. In this context, Aurobindo translates (v. 2.51) thus: 'The sages who have united their reason and will with the Divine renounce the fruit which action yields, and, liberated from the bondage of birth, they reach the status beyond misery.'[72]

Throughout his translation and commentary, Sri Aurobindo emphasizes that the Gita puts forward the goal of union with the Divine. And it is this and only this that frees oneself from the bonds of the world.

In chapter 6, he points out how action without attachment to the results leads to the conquest of the lower self and attainment of the higher self, the akshara or *kutastha.*[73] It is not easy to do this; therefore, in this chapter, a special process of Raja Yogic meditation is described as sitting erect and focusing on the divine (verses from 11 to 14), which the text says will lead to nirvana (v.15). This is not a nirvana beyond action, but one in which action is in harmony with the Divine. The sixth chapter ends with verse 47, which states that the yogi who is devoted to Krishna is the highest. Sri Aurobindo explains that this element brings in 'bhakti as the climax of the Yoga'.[74] The seventh chapter continues with the theme of yoga and bhakti and also refers to knowledge. Sri Aurobindo explains that unifying knowledge has two aspects: the essential, or jnana, and the comprehensive, or *vijnana*, which is the direct awareness of the supreme Being and also contains within it the knowledge of Purusha, Prakriti, and other components of existence.[75] Thus the Gita reveals Integral Knowledge as well as how to synthesize devotion, knowledge and action. The person has to reach his spiritual personality and then perform actions through that, which will always be in accordance with the divine law.

The Gita thus provides a unity of different philosophies of yoga, Samkhya and Vedanta, as well as a method of uniting the paths of bhakti, knowledge and work, leading to an integral approach to the Divine. Arjuna is 'the chosen human soul', whose doubts are removed by the god Krishna and, therefore, can perform actions in the world according to the divine law.[76]

Sri Aurobindo's interpretation of these texts is in line with his own philosophy, in which he affirmed that the purpose of each human life was to be in touch with the Divine, to understand the essential divine nature of Truth, Consciousness and Bliss, and to use this understanding to transform life on earth.

Sri Aurobindo's reinterpretation of these texts indicates that they confirmed and supported his ideas that had come to him through a direct connection with the Divine. He often used these texts to explain or elucidate aspects of his philosophy.

4

Early Historical and Political Works

Sri Aurobindo did not confine himself to writing on spirituality, and there are numerous works by him on other themes. There are also early pieces focused on historical and political subjects. While these writings may not overtly address spiritual matters, they still embody Sri Aurobindo's comprehension of life and the universe. His unique philosophy serves as a backdrop against which he analysed and interpreted the world.

The Human Cycle

The Human Cycle was first serialized in *Arya* between August 1916 and July 1918 and was at that time titled *The Psychology of Social Development*. It was revised in the 1930s and next in 1949, and published as a book under its present name.

The Human Cycle examines how society should and will ultimately evolve.[1] Sri Aurobindo begins by examining the materialists' view of the world and their belief that there are economic causes for historical change. He points out there are other reasons for change, including psychological aspects. For this, he provides the example of Karl Lamprecht, a German historian. Lamprecht analysed the psychological stages through which a nation or civilization passes, classifying them as symbolic, typal or conventional, individualist and subjective. Using this framework, Sri Aurobindo sees the elaborate Vedic ritual as wholly symbolic, not something used to propitiate the gods of nature. Even the social institutions of those days were symbolic. He comments on the marriage hymn in the Rig Veda, where Suryaa, the daughter of the sun god Surya, gets married. Though this hymn is used later in human marriages, Sri Aurobindo says that it reflected something divine and mystic. Early symbolism is reflected in the Purusha–Prakriti concept and the Vedic *Nri* and *Gna*, the early representation of the idea of masculine and feminine, which was reflected in society and in the social position of women. He points out that the first stage is predominantly religious and spiritual, while the second is psychological and ethical. The second stage, known as the typal, creates the great ideals but then passes into the conventional stage. Here, the external and outer supports become more important than the person, establishing rigidity. Birth and profession become hereditary. And ethics becomes an 'ornamental fiction'. The economic basis begins to break down, and a 'decrepitude' takes over. 'That in visible fact is the last and present state of the caste system in India.'[2] The conventional period fixes and formalizes a system. It does have a golden age where its spiritual inspiration, though confined, still exists, and people look back on it as if it is something splendid, but it is not a *Satya yuga*. To them, this was the period when people lived according to the *shastras*, but even that was nothing but a Copper Age.

The conventional age becomes static, fixed and unchanging, as well as corrupt and is followed by the age of individualism which is an attempt to get back to Truth. The individual now finds the true law within himself. In Europe the age of individualism began with the exercise of reason. It was the questioning of authoritative religion, the pope and the Church. The individualistic age of Europe led to the concept of the democratic rights of all, followed by progressive nations 'and is the basis of the present socialistic tendency of the world.'[3]

The individualistic age develops in search of the lost truths overlaid by convention, but something new is required, as one cannot return to the past. Truths are eternal, but its forms need to change with time. This leads to a stage of critical reason, which though 'largely destructive in its action is an imperative need for human progress.'[4] Sri Aurobindo comments that there have been repeated attempts to remove 'stifling conventions' and restore truth from the time of Buddhism in India, but these have not gone far enough. It is only with European influence that 'the beginnings of a new age of radical and effective revaluation of ideas and things have come into existence'. [5] In this new age, the individual tries to use reason to reconstruct religion, science, art and philosophy and to analyse the world through scientific and socioeconomic laws. But these too have limits and do not explain the self and soul. The individual is a part of society, but at the same time, the soul needs freedom to grow and develop.

Then, living according to laws of physical nature 'is replaced by the effort towards living according to the veiled Law, Will and Power'.[6] Then, the rational and utilitarian that has created the subjective age of society begins to change. There is a vital movement of force and action in life, rather than a focus on the soul, art, literature and music are correspondingly transformed. Literature begins to focus on psychology and often on the dark side, and this type of writing reaches its height in Russia. Then another change begins, where the vital aspect is replaced by the psychic and an attempt is made through intuition to penetrate into the hidden side of things. Sri Aurobindo finalized this book after the Second World War and explained that the changes which preceded and succeeded the war were 'the result of a confused half struggle half effort at accommodation between the old intellectual and materialistic and the new still superficial subjective and vitalistic impulses in the west.'[7] Progressive tendencies took the place of subjectivism as seen for instance in new educational concepts focusing on the child. This was on the right path to lead to the psychic and soul.

Self-development is the main aim of human life, the primal law. A person is not just a body and mind, but 'a living power of the eternal truth, a self-manifesting spirit'.[8] A nation, too, seeks its self-development and has a group soul, its land is only the shell, and is nothing without the people. To be oneself is good, but to solely live for oneself, as Germany did, is a disastrous error. Germany's subjectivism was not based on its soldiers and statesman, but on its great philosophers, thinkers and musicians. There were Kant, Hegel, Fichte, Nietzsche, Goethe, Beethoven, Wagner, representing Germany's soul. There were also diligent and industrious scholars, scientists, educators and organizers. But 'if it neglects to cultivate this lower side of our complex nature, it will fail to build that bridge between the idea and imagination and the world of facts, between the vision and the force, which makes realization possible; its higher powers may become a joy and inspiration to the world, but it will never take possession of its own world until it has learnt its humbler lesson.'[9] In Germany there was 'no pure transmission from the subjective mind of the thinkers and singers to the objective mind of the scholars and organisers.'[10] There was 'obscure transmission' when Treitschke misapplied Nietzsche to national and international uses. Germany had created something immense, but it was 'misshapen and disconcerting' in a few directions.[11] Why did Germany fail and collapse? Why was there a worldwide reaction to the Nazi state? According to Aurobindo, Germany followed a false light, leading to spiritual ruin. She mistook her vital ego for herself and was attached to her body, life and mind, forgetting her soul. 'We have all to do the same thing which Germany has attempted, but to take care not to do it likewise.'[12]

As seen earlier, after symbols, types and conventions, comes the subjective stage, which is a step towards self-knowledge, but the dangers of error are great here. The earlier stages, through a wall of self-limitation, avoid these dangers, though self-limitation is also self-ignorance. Sri Aurobindo explains that within our being, there are many selves, and only one is secret and real. Mistaking the apparent for the real is the cause of suffering. The subjective aspect is evident in new trends in child-centric education, efforts to reform and understand crime and prisoners instead of simply punishing them, and similar attempts at transformation driven by compassion and intelligence. The community or nation can be seen as a living, growing organism with its own subjective existence; however, errors can occur, as exemplified by Germany. Individual egotism in this stage can give rise to a more significant error of great communal egotism.

To seek the Divine, individuals must recognize that the Ego is not the true self and that there is one Self in all, with the soul being a part of universal divinity. The fulfilment of individuals lies in the blossoming of wisdom, power, love and universality. The will to power, the will to be, and the will to know are legitimate, and they should not be discouraged or repressed. However, their satisfaction must not be driven by egoism, as this only leads to conflicts with other egoisms and mutual destruction. We cannot act differently until we possess self-knowledge, and subjectivism is an attempt to attain self-knowledge.

Society has no right to crush the individual, and the individual cannot ignore their fellow beings. Nevertheless, the true 'I' is a Supreme Being. Analysing German subjectivism, Aurobindo said its main characteristic was seeing the individual as a 'cell of the collective ego'.[13] It perceived itself as the superior entity, and thus believed that its growth and dominance were its rightful prerogative. As the individual was considered a mere cell of the collective ego, the German state, supported by many of its people, propagated the notion that individuals must be subservient to the nation. They were to be educated and trained solely to function as machines. 'Let the state be perfect, dominant, all pervading, all-seeing, all effecting; so only could the collective ego be concentrated, and its life be brought to the highest pitch of strength, organization and efficiency. Thus Germany founded and established the growing modern error of the cult of the State.' It gained efficiency, strength and power, but it began to lose 'all that deeper life, vision, intuitive power, force of personality, psychical sweetness and largeness which the free individual brings as his gift to the race.' The individual ego had to be subsumed within that of the state, but clashes arose when the state ego encountered others. For the state, 'inefficiency, incompetence, failure are the only immorality'. Every aspect of the state then became preparation for war, and even 'peace between nations is only a covert state of war.'[14] Even commerce, he explained, is 'another kind of war, another department of the struggle to live, one physical, the other vital.'[15] Survival of the fittest was deemed the ultimate good, leading to the elimination of the unfit, assimilation of the less fit and the imposition of German culture through conquest. It is not that everyone in Germany held these beliefs, but an 'energetic minority' with strong personalities imposed these ideas, which consciously, semi-consciously, or subconsciously permeated the German mindset. Germany merely systematized preexisting notions of racial superiority. Instances of massacres, cruelty during war, commercial exploitation and repression of revolts can be found elsewhere, but Germany's mistake lay in equating the body with the Self.

Individualism allows for individual freedom to develop while obligating individuals to grant others the same freedom, creating a balance between the individual and society, rights and duties, permissions and restraints. International law developed along similar lines, and wars were fought to preserve the liberty of nations. When science views life as a struggle for self-preservation and self-fulfilment, it can lead to the belief that using and exploiting others is justified. Nietzsche's philosophy, certain forms of anarchism and imperialism reflect this perspective. However, science also recognizes that individual life is best secured through the development of the community, whereas nature seeks to preserve the type rather than the individual. Amidst the conflict between individualism and national and imperial egoism, a new concept of universalism is emerging. Objectivism perceives the world as an object, whereas subjectivism sees everything as containing consciousness in some form. Each life evolves from the subconscious and half-conscious to full consciousness. 'The ideal of human existence, personal and social would be its progressive transformation into a conscious outflowering of the joy, power, love, light, beauty of the transcendental and universal Spirit.'[16]

Sri Aurobindo explained that we can discover the ideal law of social development only when we understand our future mental and spiritual destiny and place in nature. Existence is infinite and it has an essential law. 'That law is all things are one in their being and origin, one in their general law of existence, one in their interdependence and the universal pattern of their relations; but each realizes this unity of purpose and being on its own lines and has its own law of variation by which it enriches the universal existence.'[17] There are limited variations in species and sub-species, but innumerable variations in humans. Man is an individual soul, so 'that the One may find and manifest himself in each human being,'[18] Every human being no matter from which culture is an expression of the universal being and therefore, society should provide the conditions for personal growth, so that each, following one's own nature, can reach the highest perfection possible. No church, guru or shastra can limit the ways in which he does this and though the individual can temporarily be helped by teachers, finally one proceeds only through one's divine freedom. A person can help the world only by being his own real self, drawing inspiration from others in the past and present, but assimilating it according to his own nature. 'Individual man belongs not only to humanity in general ... but to his race type, his class-type, his mental, vital, physical, spiritual type in which he resembles some, differs from others.' According to Sri Aurobindo, people form groups, but cannot be limited by a social or national group. The individual has to perfect his free development from within, and help others to do so, and the law for nations is the same. Of course, the ideal law has not yet been attained.[19]

Perfect individualization and reciprocity form the ideal law for individuals, community and nation, and perfect union and 'oneness in a free diversity is the goal'.[20] The Self is hidden; it is distinct from the mind. As a whole, humanity remains unaware of the truth about itself. Only a few individuals possess the vision and self-experience, while others may venerate but cannot emulate these avatars, saints and prophets. The Oversoul, the guiding force behind our evolution, operates according to its own timeframe. While the semi-divine individual can transcend this framework, the half-animal race cannot. Evolution progresses from the vegetable and animal realms to the sub-human and human stages. Humans must assimilate and transcend the mineral, vegetable and animal instincts within themselves. Inertia, attachment, rage and many other physical and vital tendencies stem from these instincts.

Everyone seeks the deepest reality, God or the Divine. This is also a seeking for one's best or highest self. Religion and art provide glimpses of the truth as temporarily through these we can enter God's kingdom of beauty and delight. Though in practical life, too, the Divine is the true goal, we don't acknowledge this. 'All life is only a lavish and manifold opportunity given us to discover, realize, express, the divine.'[21] The truth of practical life is in our ethical being, the ethics we follow that are actually beyond any practical use. Sri Aurobindo explains, this is not the utilitarian ethics of the nineteenth century, or anything else formulated by reason, but that which comes from within. The ethical being grows from within, but behind it are the inalienable eternal laws. The pursuit of the Divine is inherent in the concepts of goodness, beauty and spirituality, even in their nascence.

In all higher powers of his life, man is seeking the Divine and eternal, even if blindly. He seeks it in himself and in the world and attempts to harmonize them to arrive at his most perfect self.

The Ideal of Human Unity

In two parts and thirty-five chapters, *The Human Cycle* tries to understand how nations and humans in all parts of the world will unite. It was first published in *Arya* between September 1915 and July 1918, and as a book in 1919. It was revised in the 1930s and in 1949, and a final chapter was published as a postscript.

Among its themes is the concept of internationalism. Sri Aurobindo explains that as an idea the concept of all humans everywhere being the same was growing, but still it had not taken root. It remained an intellectual idea, its political expression developing into the different concepts of socialism and anarchy. Scientific and other knowledge provided scope for the concept of internationalism, but only a few could really embrace it. Socialism, for the time being, retained a nationalist identity, leading to more uniformity within Russia and until there was a psychological transformation, it could only be introduced by force. The world war had revealed the evils of nationalism, but were the worst aspects of it burnt away and purified, or would they revive? 'Until man in his heart is ready, a profound change of the world conditions cannot come; or it can only be brought about by force, physical force or else force of circumstances, and that leaves all the real work to be done.'[22]

The idea of humanity already exists, but Sri Aurobindo asked the question: how will it proceed? The family, he says, grew out of a vital need. The clan and tribe had a similar origin, though not so compelling. 'These were natural aggregations, evolutionary forms, already prepared at the animal level.'[23] The nation was not like this. It arose 'not from a vital, but from a geographical and historical necessity'.[24] It was either created by force, by a conquering king or tribe or a revolt against such force. 'A revolt against conquest and domination that brought a slow or sudden compactness to peoples who, though geographically or even historically and culturally one, had lacked power of cohesion and remained too conscious of an original heterogeneity or of local and regional or other divisions.'[25] After failures and partial successes, a nation is formed with a psychological core of patriotism. Without this, the nation cannot exist. That is why there were few nations in the ancient world, and artificial empires declined. People function fine without international unity, which is desired only by a few. But the individual has to be transformed, and the world has to move towards unity, as that is the only way forward.

War and Self-determination

This concise book comprises six essays that hold significant importance. Originally published in *Arya* between 1916 and 1920, with the addition of an essay on the League of Nations in 1920, these writings were composed during and immediately after the First World War. Despite their age, these essays remain relevant today as they delve into the nature of war and emphasize that true elimination of conflict requires a transformation within the individual.

In the foreword to the first edition, Aurobindo acknowledges the critical nature of the time, where hopes of freedom, equality and unity faced 'powerful obstacles'.[26] These obstacles, he emphasizes, originated from within society itself. Various groups held differing stances on war, ranging from those advocating peace and unity to those seeking to protect their labour and productivity. Even governments did not want to disturb the peace. Great industrial nations sought to maintain a peaceful status quo, without revolts and revolutions, to continue to exploit and dominate the world. It was hoped that war would become impossible, which has not happened. War could only be eliminated when the inner causes were removed, and 'the constantly accumulating karma of successful injustice, of which violent revolutions are the natural reactions'.[27] There are not only intelligent minds and intellectual reason, along with science, but also a universal will, force or law. Outer results come from the spirit of our being. The realization of ideals such as truth, justice and love can bring about a better world, even if they are currently mere concepts. The timing of this transformation depends on the level of knowledge individuals possess and their willingness to align their actions with that knowledge.

'The Passing of War?'

In this essay, Aurobindo sees the idea of the passing of war as an illusion. The first aspect was that commerce would do away with war, but indeed, the desire for 'unnecessary necessities' has caused many wars, and commerce and militarism go together. Another illusion that prevailed was that the growth of democracy would lead to pacifism and end wars. Similarly, could international organizations end war? These expectations have proven unfounded. There are other illusions and false ideas too, but the only way to end war is when it becomes psychologically impossible. Even so, to struggle through illusions towards the right end is something pushing onwards to make it a reality.[28]

'The Unseen Power'

In this essay published in *Arya* in December 1918,[29] Aurobindo explains the necessity for sincerity, truth and higher ideals. He wrote that the physical war had ended, but the mental war of propaganda, conflicting parties, etc., continued. What was the unseen force or will behind the war? Despite the suffering and ruin, a powerful force stood behind the war, aiming to bring about a wider and increased spirituality, leading towards a greater purpose. This is not the power of nature but of something much vaster: 'an ineffable perfection, an infinite Light, an infinite Power, an infinite Love, a universal Good and Beauty'.[30] It is the invisible spirit of the universe and of each person. If one builds one's outer world according to one's ego, passion, interest and vital needs, then the karma of that is ours. Sacrifice and effort will bring rewards, but if one goes against the law, karma strikes without mercy. If we live according to an ideal, we must follow our inner truth or disaster will strike again. Using the imagery of Vedic deities, Sri Aurobindo explains that the first brings the wrath of Rudra and the second the noose of Varuna. It is the anger of Rudra that has brought about the war. 'The one safety for man lies in learning to live from within outward, not depending on institutions and machinery to perfect him.'[31]

'Self-determination'

In another essay, Sri Aurobindo looks at concepts of freedom and their practical application.[32] Self-determination, he says, is a condition for a better world, but it can't stand by itself, as freedom must move within a framework of unity, of freely coming together. Commenting on the League of Nations, he remarks that it is only a partial step forward, as it still follows the old ways. True freedom is only possible when one lives in the infinite, but one can experiment with its outer form. Apparently, there was democracy and liberty in ancient Greece, but as he explains, this was just the rule of a minority over slaves. In recent times it is the rule of the bourgeoisie, or then of the emancipated proletariat which is equally tyrannical. 'And just as the glorious possession of liberty by the community has been held to be consistent with the oppression of four-fifths or three-fifths of the population by the remaining fraction, so it has till lately been held to be quite consistent with the complete subjection of one half of mankind, the woman half, to the physically stronger male.'[33] He adds that they no doubt intend to extend freedom to the exploited at some later date, but meanwhile only they benefit. Despite these problems, or anomalies, as he said, there was at least some progress, and more liberty of thought. The true turning point would be when thought reflects the soul, the inner being. Within every human being, or every collective, there is a self that 'has the right to grow in its own way'.[34] Despite this, self-determination can be egoistic and though ethics is a corrective, this only checks it. It is when one recognizes the Divine in oneself and in others, that one would arrive at 'a harmoniously self-determining united existence'.[35]

'The League of Nations'

People look back to a golden age, but in this essay Sri Aurobindo questions: did a perfect age ever exist? Or was it just a reflection of a dream, a hidden ideal within the heart? People also look to a future golden age, and to some sort of redeemer, saviour, *mahdi*, messiah, avatar, and then there is a secular dream of at least a half golden age, which is more peaceful, rational and cooperative. The League of Nations[36] was the first step to this, replacing the earlier 'balance of power'. As Aurobindo says, war was its father, and an armed and enforced peace its mother. To be effective, it had to include all existing nations, but in practice, it was oligarchical. It may serve an imperfect and temporary purpose, he said, but a golden age can only come when the 'soul and body of the divine, becomes the ideal of our perfection'.[37]

1919

The year 1919 marked the conclusion of the First World War, and with it came the establishment of the League of Nations, carrying the hope for a better future. Sri Aurobindo analyses the events of the preceding five years, highlighting the Janus-faced nature of the era, with one side turned towards the past and the other towards the future.[38] German militarism and imperialism stood in opposition to the partial democracy of Western Europe, and even the League of Nations was regarded as a temporary and makeshift solution. Sri Aurobindo believed that the destruction caused by the war paved the way for the forces of the future. He also delves into the reasons behind conflicts within nations, stating that law is consistently imposed by the stronger upon the weaker. 'The history of mankind has largely been a protracted struggle to replace unjust laws with justice.' He further emphasizes that much has been lost in this process, but the human spirit still needs to discover its essence, its idea, and its greater orientation.[39]

After the War

The Great War had ended some time ago, yet the future appeared uncertain and ambiguous. Disappointment and disillusionment prevailed, accompanied by the failure of great hopes and ideals.[40] The war fought to end wars had only given rise to new conflicts. Sri Aurobindo commented on the state of the world, remarking that the League of Nations had become a mockery. Africa was partitioned as if it were the private property of a few European powers, and West Asia was placed under mandates. However, he affirmed that this was not the final outcome, as the mistakes of the past could not vanish in an instant. Two aspects that were unlikely to change immediately were the division between labour and capital and the resurgence of Asian nations.[41]

Sri Aurobindo analysed the global changes and pondered on the causes of war and the necessity of unity for development. Until his passing, he continued to provide commentary and analysis on the issues plaguing the world.

Examining India

In some of his early works, Aurobindo wrote about India's past and present.[42] These writings included essays on the Indian Renaissance, Indian culture, external influences, as well as pieces titled 'Is India civilised?' and 'A defence of Indian culture'. They were initially published in *Arya* between 1918 and 1921, carrying significant historical significance. Minor revisions were made and Aurobindo intended to make more before publication, but he was unable to find the time. These works encompass several noteworthy ideas.

One collection features four essays on the Indian Renaissance.[43] Aurobindo questions the meaning of an Indian Renaissance, emphasizing that spirituality is the essence of Indian life. In the past, there existed a vibrant vitality that permeated all aspects of Indian society, including philosophy, art, architecture and even the economy. This was followed by a period of stagnation. What could the future hold? Aurobindo asserts that it should not be a blind adherence to any particular religious form, dogma or tenets. As he states, 'Spirituality is much broader than any specific religion.' True spirituality involves seeking the Divine and eternal, incorporating these values into everyday life. No aspect of life should be excluded from this pursuit.[44] He further adds that 'The highest spirituality should be followed, not the tenets of any religion'.

In 'Indian culture and external influence',[45] he wrote about how India had to meet the challenge of Western civilization in her own way, and not to blindly follow their path.

His essay 'Is India civilised?'[46] is based on the title of a book by John Woodroffe, responding to a very critical work written by Scottish writer William Archer. Sri Aurobindo appreciated Woodroffe's work, but also commented that the past was not always entirely admirable.[47]

'A Defence of Indian Culture'[48] consisted of another series of essays partly based on Archer's criticisms while extending far beyond them. In them, Sri Aurobindo wrote about history, spirituality, art, literature and politics, reflecting a vast knowledge and deep understanding of all these spheres.

He explains that foreign critics are useful in our own evaluations of India; however, not people like Archer, rather those who have some knowledge and substance, particularly those with some spiritual propensity. He was referring to Schopenhauer, Nietzsche, Cousin, Shlegel and Tolstoy.[49]

Expounding his perspective on Indian history, he points out that the Mughal conquests of South India were possible because of the help of the Rajput princes, and this happened because the Mughals ceased to be foreign very soon. 'The vast mass of the Mussulmans in the country were and are Indians by race, only a very small admixture of Pathan, Turkish and Mogul blood took place, and even the foreign kings and nobles became almost immediately wholly Indian in mind, life and interest.'

Analysing the Maratha revival under Shivaji, with the impetus of Ramdas's spiritual inputs, he remarks that 'it failed as all attempts to revive the past must fail'. With his knowledge, perceptiveness and analytical mind, Sri Aurobindo also examines

Akbar's attempt to bridge the gap between the two religions and that of Guru Nanak and the Sikhs. In Akbar's case, 'the living assent of the people' was lacking, while Nanak had tried to create a universal religion, which according to Sri Aurobindo, had dwindled into a sect after him. As he said, conditions were not at that time right for it to succeed.[50]

Sri Aurobindo, writing a hundred years ago, was knowledgeable, perceptive and analytical in his assessment of the problems facing India and the world. Remarkably, many of these issues persist to this day, making his incisive analysis still relevant and pertinent.

But all these works pale in significance to his later spiritual analyses and great works, namely, *The Life Divine*, *The Synthesis of Yoga* and *Savitri*.

5

Philosophical Backgrounds

The East and the West

In developing his philosophy, Sri Aurobindo delved into some of India's ancient texts, providing new interpretations of them. At the same time, we should not forget that he was proficient in Greek and Latin and had read classics in the original languages. He was fluent in French and could read German and Italian. He commented on some of the works of the Western world, but his appreciation and connection with ancient Sanskrit texts were more significant. We have already looked at his commentary on the Vedas, the Upanishads and the Bhagavad Gita, and in that context have briefly touched on these early texts. In addition, in his great philosophical works, he often referred to and explained aspects of the six classical systems of philosophy, particularly Vedanta, Samkhya and Yoga; the other three being Mimamsa, Vaisheshika and Nyaya. He also mentioned Tantra and the Puranas and certain aspects of ancient texts, such as the *koshas* and *chakras*. He explained some of these, both in his major works and in his many letters, in detail.

Vedanta

The term Vedanta comes from 'Veda' plus '*anta*', indicating that the Upanishads form both the last part of the Vedas and its ultimate or highest part. The main features of Vedanta were summarized by Badarayana in the fifth to third centuries BCE in the *Brahma Sutra*, alternatively known as the *Vedanta Sutra*. The *Brahma Sutra*, the Upanishads and the Bhagavad Gita are the main texts of Vedanta and are known as the *prasthana-traya.* Vedanta developed further through commentaries and interpretations of these and other texts. Some early Vedantic teachers, such as Yajnavalkya, are referred to in the Upanishads and in the *Brahma Sutra.*

Over time, different schools of philosophy developed within the broad framework of Vedanta. These include *Advaita, Vishishtadvaita, Dvaita, Dvaitadvaita, Shuddhadvaita* and *Shivadvaita.* Vedanta focuses on Brahman, the eternal, unborn substance underlying the world and all creation. Brahman, the One Reality, has always existed and will always exist. Beyond time and space, it never changes, grows or diminishes. It is complete and perfect and is not similar to anything else. But what is the relationship of Brahman with *Ishvara*, or God, the atman, or soul, which has an essential identity with Brahman, the *jiva*, or individual incarnating soul, and the world? Each Vedantic philosophy interprets this differently. A main aspect of Vedanta are the *mahavakya*s, the great sacred statements in the Upanishads, such as '*Aham Brahmasmi*' or 'I am Brahma', indicating the essential unity and oneness of all.

Advaita

In Vedanta, Advaita, meaning monism, is the most widespread and influential school of thought. Though there must have been ancient teachers, the earliest available texts are those of Gaudapada, a philosopher who lived in the seventh or eighth century, followed by those of Shankara in the ninth century. Gaudapada revealed his ideas in an analysis of the Mandukya Upanishad. His *Karika* is a lengthy commentary on this short Upanishad of only twelve verses. Shankara further commented on Gaudapada's Karika and also elaborated on the principles of Advaita in several other commentaries and texts. Shankara had a logical and analytical approach, questioning prevailing assumptions. We think we know what reality is, but experiences, senses and memory may deceive us. However, we are aware that we have consciousness and knowledge of ourselves and others. This confirms that there must be an atman, an inner self, through which we are aware of this. The nature of the atman can be nothing other than pure consciousness, *chaitanyam,* and eternal knowledge, but we do not perceive it correctly. And if there is the atman, Brahman must exist, as the substratum of all atmans. In its essence, each atman is identical with Brahman, and both have the characteristics of *sat-chit-ananda.* Brahman is the only reality; therefore, the world, with its multiplicity of forms and various components, is unreal, an illusion. This unreality is known as *Maya* and is a product of *ajnana* or *avidya*, that is, of ignorance. The world is always changing, and whatever changes and is non-eternal cannot be real. Similarly, the Ego, or individual personality, which is subject to birth, growth and death, cannot be real. Realizing the self as Brahman brings bliss, joy and freedom. Jnana, or wisdom, is the direct route to such realization.

Shankara did not deny the existence of Ishvara or a personal god, as the shruti scripture states that it exists. Ishvara is *saguna* Brahman, limited by qualities, and the apparent creator related to the world, to Maya, which is not only a term representing unreality but also refers to an illusory creative power, and to the individual consciousness, or jiva. The jiva incorporates the *antahkarana,* or personal inner self, including the mind, ego and thought, and thus is not the same as the atman. It is subject to rebirth and to its individual karma. Yet, in essence, all is the same, as all is Brahman.

The concepts of Shankara, such as the relationship of Brahman and Ishvara, the atman and the jiva, Maya and the world, as well as jnana and ajnana, were further clarified by commentators on Shankara's work, who explained them in different ways.

Advaita is considered the most influential philosophical system in Indian society even today.[1]

Vishishtadvaita

Vishishtadvaita can be defined as 'qualified monism'. The main proponent of this philosophy was Ramanuja of the eleventh century, though aspects of it can be traced to earlier times. Though Ramanuja accepted Brahman as the only true reality, he believed that the world, matter, and soul were also real as they were part of Brahman. The Brahman has the power to create, and creates all that exists, including the various souls. Once created, souls are eternal. Their actions and karma lead to their taking on various forms, such as gods, people, animals and plants. The souls have to strive for perfection, and when this is attained, they lose their material form and become part of Brahman, but they do not merge with it, retaining their individuality and consciousness. The path to perfection is explained and includes worship and bhakti. Brahman and the gods are compassionate, guiding the souls towards moksha and ultimate bliss.[2]

Dvaita

A form of dualism, though this is not absolute, as in this philosophy, Brahman is supreme, perfect, self-created and independent and has no equal. He is both creator and destroyer, transcendent and immanent, and is the inner ruler and *antaryamin* of all souls. But the dualistic component is that souls and the material world, once created by Brahman, have a separate existence and do not merge with Brahman. Madhva, who lived in the thirteenth century, founded this philosophy, which is explained in his many writings, including commentaries on the *Brahma Sutra*, some Upanishads, the Bhagavad Gita, the Bhagavata Purana, and the first forty hymns of the Rig Veda.

Madhva explains the famous mahavakya that Brahman is One without a second, '*ekam evadvitiyam brahma*', as merely a statement on the supremacy of Brahman. Madhva goes on to equate Brahman with the god Vishnu. The god manifests himself in forms called *vyuhas,* or incarnations, called *avataras.* Lakshmi is the personification of his creative energy and is *nityamukta*, eternally liberated. The jivas, or individual souls, are innumerable, and though dependent on Brahman, they act on their own. Liberation could be attained by worshipping gods such as Vishnu, Shiva, the avataras, the Panchayatanas or the five deities, along with knowledge and study of sacred texts, bhakti and leading an ethical life. However, even those who had attained liberation remained separate individuals, in close contact with the deity but without merging with it.[3]

Dvaitadvaita

Another variation of the philosophy of Vedanta is Dvaitadvaita, in which both duality and non-duality exist. It was founded by

Nimbarka, probably in the twelfth century. The soul and the world emerge from Brahman and are not illusions, but Brahman is supreme, and realizing one's identity with Brahman leads to divine bliss. Nimbarka equates Brahman with the god Krishna. Bhakti, surrender to the will of God, and leading an ethical life are essential to realizing Brahman.[4]

Dvaitadvaita, Dvaita and Vishishtadvaita have very subtle differences. All believe that Brahman is supreme and that souls and the world emanate from Brahman but are not identical with it.

Shivadvaita

It was founded by Shrikanthacharya, who lived in the twelfth century. He identified Brahman with the god Shiva. Brahman is sat-chit-ananda, but at the same time it contains the world of matter. The world is created through shakti or energy, also known as Maya or Prakriti. At the same time, Brahman remains transcendent. Thus, the material world is neither identical with nor entirely different from Brahman.[5]

Shivadvaita agrees with other Vedanta schools, that Brahman, the Absolute, transcending time and space, is the ultimate cause of all creation and that its true nature is concealed because of ignorance.

Bhedabhedavada

Bhaskara explained this philosophy around 900 CE through his commentary on the *Brahma Sutra* called *Bhaskarabhashya.* According to him, Brahman is One, but evolves into multiplicity. These two aspects coexist and are equally real. The world is real and essentially the same as Brahman. The jiva, or individual soul, has the same essence as Brahman but is limited because it is contained in matter. Moksha is attained through karma, or right action, which leads to knowledge (jnana), which leads to moksha liberation.

Thus, the unity of Brahman and the multiplicity of forms are both real. An active life should be lived, withdrawing from the world only after fulfilling one's dharma.[6]

Shuddhadvaita

It was founded by the Vaishnava philosopher Vallabhacharya in the fifteenth century. Shuddhadvaita is considered *Shuddha* or 'pure' non-dualism. The individual is part of God, who is whole and complete, but both have the same essence and hence are essentially the same. Differing from other forms of Vedanta, the goal here is not union with God or liberation, but the service of the god Krishna. Vallabha had seen Krishna in a vision, and then this philosophy was revealed to him.[7]

Sri Aurobindo differs from Advaita, but his philosophy can be considered closer to the other forms of Vedanta, such as Vishishtadvaita and Shivadvaita.

Samkhya

Sri Aurobindo constantly refers to Samkhya theories; hence, these are given here in some detail. Samkhya provides a whole theory of evolution through two main principles: a passive but eternal Purusha and an active Prakriti. Traditionally, the founder is the rishi Kapila of the seventh to sixth century BCE, but available texts said to have been composed by him are much later. The earliest text is the *Samkhya Karika* of the second to third century CE, written by Ishvarakrishna.

The universe arises through the action of Prakriti. Literally meaning 'nature', here Prakriti means something different. In Samkhya, Prakriti contains the three gunas, or qualities, of sattva, rajas and tamas. Sattva is everything that is good, leading to a state of consciousness that is perfect and full of happiness. Rajas is the element leading to activity, through which both enjoyment and pain arise. Tamas is the quality of inertia, leading to indifference and slothfulness. These three are contained together in Prakriti. When all three are in equal quantities, there is a state of equilibrium, and Prakriti rests. This state exists after *pralaya*, or the dissolution of the universe, but then creation begins again through the movement of the gunas. And the aim of creation is actually to realize Purusha. Though Purusha can be compared with Brahman, it is somewhat different.

Mahat

In the first stage, Prakriti becomes Buddhi, the higher mind or intelligence, in which sattva predominates. In this stage, the minds of all the Purushas that were in a dormant state after the pralaya again become aware. This stage is called *Mahat* or the Great One, holding within it the Buddhitattva and all the Buddhis. It is also known as the *linga* sign, as it is a sign of what is to come.

Ahamkara

From Mahat, *ahamkara*, or the Ego, develops, which is of three kinds, the first being the sattvika or *vaikarika* ahamkara. From this, through the action of rajas, the various senses develop, including those of sight, hearing, touch, smell, taste and movement, as well as *manas* (mind). From the *tamasika* ahamkara, also known as *bhutadi*, again with the help of rajas, the *tanmatras*, which are the preceding cause of gross elements, come into being. These contain the potential elements from which the five classes of atoms, *paramanus*, develop.

Twenty-five Principles

Most Samkhya texts list twenty-five tattvas, or aspects or principles, that emerge during evolution. These are Prakriti, Purusha and twenty-three manifestations of Prakriti.

Purusha is similar to the concept of a soul. In each living being, there is a Purusha, yet in essence, all Purushas are the same. According to S. Radhakrishnan, it is 'not the mind, life or body, but the informing and sustaining soul, silent, peaceful, eternal'. It illuminates all the activities that take place but does not participate in them. It is pure, inactive intelligence. Yet, the concept of Purusha in Samkhya philosophy indicates that it is different from Brahman as it does not participate in creation. Creation arises from Prakriti, though it comes into being for Purusha. It 'excites prakriti to activity and development', for Prakriti exists only to serve Purusha. The empirical self is the union of the free spirit, Purusha, and Prakriti. Purusha is the knower, and the known is Prakriti. The purpose of Samkhya is to free the knower from the known.

Samkhya sees the world as full of sorrow and all experiences as sorrowful. Purusha is eternally free, but to realize this freedom, the individual self must establish virtue in itself, along with unselfish activity, *vairagya* or detachment, and higher knowledge. The Buddhi reflects the Purusha, but when the Buddhi realizes its difference, the Purusha is finally freed and can never again be bound. Thus, with the right knowledge and discrimination, freedom from bondage is achieved.

To Samkhya, Vedic sacrifices have no value, and the path to liberation is only through knowledge and understanding. There is no Ishvara, but only a natural process of causation. Though the first cause is Purusha, it is only a mechanical cause.

Samkhya is concerned with both *avirbhava* (evolution) and *tirobhava* (involution). The world evolves from Prakriti, but through correct knowledge, Purusha is freed from Prakriti.

There are cycles of creation. After dissolution, or pralaya, components of the world continue to exist in Prakriti, in which the three gunas lie dormant in a state of equilibrium. When equilibrium is disturbed, creation begins anew. We find a similarity here to Sri Aurobindo's theories of how creation begins and also to his theories of involution and evolution.

There is no concept of God in early Samkhya, but Vijnanabhikshu, a later writer, put forward the theory of a universal Purusha, which would be similar to Brahman.[8]

The basics of Samkhya philosophy were accepted by the system of yoga, with the addition of the concept of Ishvara, or God. The Samkhya theory of evolution is also described in the Upanishads and in the later Puranas, though with some modifications.

The Philosophy of Yoga

The earliest available text for the philosophical system of yoga is Patanjali's *Yoga Sutra.* Yoga literally means union, implying the union of the individual self with the Divine. This is attained when the individual self, the atman or jiva, also known as the Purusha, realizes its true being by stilling the mind and body. In its philosophical base, yoga is similar to Samkhya. Yoga accepts the Samkhya theories of Purusha and Prakriti but adds to these the concept of Ishvara. It differs from Samkhya in its method of reaching the goal. In yoga, a systematic effort is required to detach Purusha from Prakriti, and Patanjali describes this unified system. Patanjali's yoga was later called raja yoga to distinguish it from other forms of yoga. This form is also known as ashtanga yoga or the yoga with eight limbs, or eight parts, sometimes translated as eight steps. Both *abhyasa* (practice) and *vairagya* (dispassion) are required to follow this path that consists of eight steps or stages. These are: *Yama*, or five ethical restraints; *Niyama*, or five positive observances; *Asana*, or postures to stabilize and improve the body; *Pranayama*, or breathing practices; *Pratyahara*, or withdrawal of the senses from the outer world; *Dharana*, or concentration; *Dhyana*, or meditation; and Samadhi, or union. These are explained in the *Yoga Sutra* and in numerous commentaries and form the basis for all later systems of yoga.[9]

The Mahabharata describes Samkhya and yoga as two aspects of one whole, the former being the theory and the latter the practical aspects. The Bhagavad Gita also relates Samkhya and yoga. The Gita uses the term yoga in many different ways but basically in the sense of 'joining' or 'union'. Yoga can be attained when all desires have ceased and the mind has been controlled, becoming single-pointed in its focus on God.

Vyasa's *Bhashya* or commentary on the *Yoga Sutra*, from about the fourth century CE, explains the basic principles of the system. Additional texts on yoga do not exactly follow Patanjali and some list ten yamas and niyamas. Later texts explain various forms of yoga in detail, such as hatha yoga, mantra yoga, bhakti yoga, jnana yoga, kundalini yoga, likhita yoga, laya yoga, siddha yoga along with Integral Yoga and Tantra Yoga, as well as several modern hybrid forms, such as power yoga. Texts on yoga include the *Gheranda Samhita*, the *Goraksha Samhita* of Gorakhanatha and the *Hatha Yoga Pradipika* among others. All traditional forms of yoga are not mutually exclusive, each employing some of the techniques used by other forms, though the emphasis is different. The prerequisites of each form are basic ethics, morality dharma and discipline or regular practice sadhana.

Yoga is also described in Vaishnava, Shaiva and Tantric texts, in the Puranas, and in the works of several other writers. Sri Aurobindo did not focus much on the other three classical systems, and they are therefore only briefly mentioned here.

Mimamsa, Vaisheshika, Nayaya

Mimamsa

Jaimini from between the fourth and the second century BCE is said to have founded this school, and his work *Mimamsa Sutra* explains its philosophy. This early form of Mimamsa, known as Purva Mimamsa or Karma Mimamsa (analysis of action), focused on the Vedas as the ultimate source of divine knowledge and the correct performance of rituals and sacrifices.

Purva Mimamsa examines the nature of dharma and tries to show that every part of the Vedic texts can be related to dharma. It accepts a plurality of selves, and the early writers do not concern themselves with moksha or ultimate liberation; they accept a number of deities, the worship of whom leads to heaven. Later commentators began to deal with higher philosophical concepts and this philosophy became almost identical with Vedanta, known as Uttara Mimamsa or later Mimamsa. Badarayana's Brahma Sutra is also known as Uttara Mimamsa. According to some commentators, Jaimini's Purva Mimamsa and Badarayana's Uttara Mimamsa formed one whole, the former emphasizing dharma, ethics and ritual, and the latter philosophical aspects.[10]

Vaisheshika

The traditional founder of Vaisheshika, was Rishi Kanada, also known as Uluka Kanada, who probably lived between 250 BCE and 100 CE. It has similarities with the Nyaya system of philosophy, and by the medieval period the two schools had almost merged.

Vaisheshika deals with physics, metaphysics, logic and methods of knowledge, and its central feature is considered its theory on the atomic structure of the universe. Kanada's Sutras do not directly refer to god, but later writers accepted a divine principle because of existing contradictions in the philosophy.

Nyaya

Nyaya means that by which the mind reaches a conclusion, based on logic and analysis. According to tradition, it was founded by Akshapada Gautama, though some hold that Akshapada and Gautama were two different people who both contributed to its philosophy. The basic text is Gautama's *Nyaya Sutra*. This Sanskrit text contains five books, each with two sections, and also looks at how to arrive at right knowledge. It provides arguments to prove the existence of a permanent soul. Salvation *apavarga* is attained when the manas (mind) separates from the soul (atman) after all karma has been destroyed. Both Nyaya and Vaisheshika analysed the world through logic and experience. Ishvara, or God, is mentioned, though not prominent in the *Nyaya Sutra*, but later Nyaya was clearly theistic, with Shiva as the chief deity and cause or origin of the universe. [11]

Other Philosophies

Between the sixth and fourth centuries BCE, other types of philosophies coexisted. Buddhism and Jainism developed, and they are also commented upon by Upanishadic philosophers. The Ajivikas, Keshakambalins and Lokayats or Charvakas were other streams of thought. The Shaivite Pashupata sect developed slightly later. In later centuries, there were further developments in Shaivism, Vaishnavism, Shaktism and Tantrism.

Shaivism had many different schools, and here we look at just one aspect, that put forward by Abhinavagupta, with whom Sri Aurobindo has been compared. Abhinavagupta lived between c. 975 and 1025 and followed Trika Shastra, one of the main branches of Shaivism in Kashmir.

His vast knowledge included Buddhism, Jainism and Shaivism as well as Kaula Tantrism. Apart from describing Trika Shastra, he explained the related *Pratyabhijna* philosophy, which involves a recognition of the world as a manifestation of the god Shiva. He wrote a number of texts on Trika and Pratyabhijna, aesthetics and aspects of Tantrism, as well as commentaries on earlier works. In his books, he also explains how dance, drama and poetry, can lead to inner Bliss, and to an experience of the Divine.[12] This was a theme in fact that was explored by the Mother.

In his philosophy, Shiva can be considered equal to Brahman. His encyclopaedic knowledge and the fact that he also wrote on poetry, dance and drama, have led to him being compared with Sri Aurobindo.

Shaktism

Shaktism can be linked with Sri Aurobindo's focus on the divine mother. It is based on the concept and worship of Shakti or divine feminine energy. This energy, represented by Devi or Mahadevi is said to pervade the universe. Both outer and inner forms of the deity are worshipped and advanced practices involve raising the kundalini, the hidden power within the body. Both the Mother and Sri Aurobindo were said to have done this. Shaktas have ascetic, philosophic and tantric practices.[13]

Tantrism

Tantrism is a form of religion or spiritualism which originated in ancient days but gained popularity by around the eighth century CE. As a method of religious practice, its exact origin is not known, but certain concepts and practices are traced back to the Atharva Veda.

Tantrism aims to gain control over all the forces of nature and to obtain the power to accomplish any task. At its highest level it seeks union with the Divine, while at its lowest its powers can be used to harm others.

There are numerous Tantric texts, which are both philosophical and provide various practices. These form part of both Hinduism and Buddhism. The texts are composed in Sanskrit and in regional languages. Tantric practices include the cultivation of jnana or knowledge, both outer and mystical; *kriya* or action and *charya* or right conduct. Specific methods of practice are prescribed, including techniques for *shuddhi* or purification, *uddhara* or elevation and *chaitanya*, the reaffirmation of identity in consciousness. Several tantras focus on the chakras, raising the kundalini and the practice of *nyasa*.[14]

The Body and its Sheaths

Although Sri Aurobindo does not employ precisely the same Sanskrit terminology, he alludes to these concepts. The body, known in Sanskrit as *sharira*, has been extensively analysed in ancient texts, extending beyond its physical manifestation. The *sthula* sharira, or gross body, contains the atman or soul. Within it are also chakras and *nadi*s – subtle centres and channels, which, if purified, can lead to Bliss and perfection. Surrounding the gross body are other subtle bodies, such as the *linga* sharira or *sukshma* sharira, the subtle body, which persists beyond the physical body and retains the impressions and experiences of past lives, transferring them to another body during reincarnation. The *karana* sharira or *para* sharira, known as the causal body, preserves the record of successive births and guides the selection of a particular body, time or place for the next birth.

Apart from these bodies, there are koshas or sheaths. The *annamaya* kosha or 'food sheath' corresponds to the *sthula* sharira. The *pranamaya* kosha, *manomaya* kosha and *vijnanamaya* kosha are contained in the linga sharira, while the *anandamaya* kosha is part of the para sharira. The pranamaya kosha is the body created by *prana*, the breath, and the manomaya kosha by mana, the mind. The vijnanamaya kosha represents the wisdom sheath, and the anandamaya kosha represents the sheath of bliss.[15]

Yugas

The yugas represent cyclical, long periods of time and are mentioned here to highlight the correspondence between the future Supramental age of Sri Aurobindo and, to some extent, the *Krita* or Satya Yuga.

The four yugas, namely Krita, *Treta*, *Dvapara* and *Kali*, constitute one *mahayuga*. The cycle commences with the golden age of Krita or Satya Yuga, followed by progressively declining yugas, until the Satya Yuga begins again. *Manvantaras* and *kalpas* are larger cyclical periods of time, resulting in creation, re-creation and intermittent periods of rest.

The Krita Yuga is the golden age characterized by truth and righteousness. Negative emotions such as envy, malice, hatred and deceit do not exist. All individuals are equal and worship the same deity, and there is only one Veda, known as the Brahma Veda. Humans live for 4,000 years, possess gigantic stature, and have significantly enhanced mental abilities. Procreation occurs through the power of the mind rather than through sexual means. The duration of this yuga is 4,800 divine years, equivalent to 1,728,000 human years and is symbolized by the colour white.

Subsequently, the Treta Yuga ensues, in which righteousness decreases by one-fourth compared to the previous yuga. Knowledge becomes the primary virtue. Four Vedas emerge, sacrificial rituals commence, and people begin seeking rewards for their actions. Humans now live for 3,000 years, still retaining superior powers. Procreation occurs through a simple touch between two individuals instead of through sexual means. The duration of this yuga is 3,600 divine years, equivalent to 1,296,000 human years and is symbolized by the colour red.

Following the Treta Yuga, the Dvapara Yuga unfolds. Righteousness decreases by half compared to the initial yuga. The primary virtue of this age is sacrifice, and the sacred texts of this era are the Puranas. Only a few individuals adhere to truth and duty without seeking rewards. Suffering, diseases, disasters and the caste system emerge during this period. Human lifespan decreases to 2,000 years, and procreation occurs through sexual means, which was not the case earlier. Men are permitted to have only one wife, and marriage can only take place at the time of a woman's first menstruation. The duration of this yuga is 2,400 divine years, equivalent to 864,000 human years and is symbolized by the colour yellow.

The Kali Yuga follows, signifying a general decline and possessing only one-quarter of the righteousness of the initial yuga. The primary scriptures of this age are the Tantras, and people prioritize the body over the mind. This period is characterized by anger, hatred, discord and strife. Human lifespans vary, with some reaching one hundred years. The Kali Yuga is believed to have commenced in 3102 BCE and will last for 1,200 years of the gods, equivalent to 432,000 human years. It is symbolized by the colour black. Subsequently, a new cycle of the mahayuga will commence, once again starting with the Krita or Satya Yuga.

Even larger periods of time exist, including manvantaras and kalpas. Seventy-one mahayugas constitute one manvantara, and fourteen manvantaras form one kalpa, representing one day in the life of Brahma, the Creator.

One month of Brahma encompasses thirty kalpas, and twelve months make up one year. A hundred such years constitute the lifetime of Brahma. Jainism and Buddhism also incorporate similar concepts of kalpas or cycles of time.[1]

Lokas

In *Savitri*, Sri Aurobindo describes the different worlds traversed by Aswapati and Savitri. The Puranas and other texts mention 'lokas,' which are worlds of different types. The number of lokas typically varies from three to fourteen. Various worlds associated with different gods, such as Vishnu, Indra, Agni, Varuna and Brahma, are also mentioned. The commonly described fourteen worlds include seven in the upper world and seven in the lower world. The seven upper worlds are as follows: *Bhuloka*, representing the earth; *Bhuvarloka*, situated between the earth and the sun, where *munis*, *siddhas* and perfected beings reside;

Svarloka, the heaven of Indra; Maharloka, inhabited by saints like Bhrigu; Janarloka, where Brahma's mind-born sons, Sanaka, Sananda, and Sanat Kumara, reside; Tapoloka, the abode of Vairajas; and Satyaloka, the heaven of Brahma, reaching which one is liberated from rebirth.

The seven lower worlds are: Atala, ruled by Mahamaya; Vitala, governed by Hatakeshvara, a form of Shiva; Sutala, under the rule of Mahabali; Talatala, under Maya; Mahatala; Rasatala, where the Daityas and Danavas reside; and Patala, ruled by Vasuki and inhabited by the chief Nagas or serpent gods. The seven lower realms are collectively referred to as Patala. It is important to note that these realms are distinct from '*Narakas*' or hells. When the sage Narada visited these worlds, he described them as marvelous and superior to Indra's heaven. Different Puranas present varying lists of these lokas.

Naga Loka, the world of the Nagas, is also mentioned. According to the Mahabharata, it extends thousands of *yojanas* in all directions and features several walls made of pure gold. In a mystical sense, all the lokas are represented within the body, where the seven upper worlds can be associated with the seven main chakras, and the lower worlds correspond to chakras located in the lower part of the body.

The term 'naraka' commonly refers to hells, of which there are many mentioned in various texts. 'Naraka' can also be interpreted as a state of mind that causes pain or sorrow, which should be avoided.

Knowledge and ignorance are frequently addressed by Aurobindo, and these concepts are analysed in various texts. Jnana, meaning knowledge, plays a significant role in the path to Brahman. *Jnana marga* refers to the path of knowledge leading to the realization of God. Jnana yoga is a similar term denoting the union with the Divine through knowledge. To utilize knowledge in attaining divine unity, it is essential to comprehend the nature and structure of knowledge. Ancient schools of philosophy such as Samkhya, Vaisheshika, Vedanta, Yoga and Mimamsa extensively analyse knowledge. Although these analyses differ in details, they generally differentiate between valid and invalid knowledge and attempt to classify the means of knowledge, or *pramanas. Vidya* is another term used for knowledge, while vijnana is often translated as wisdom. Jnana is contrasted with ajnana, specifically referring to spiritual ignorance.

In Samkhya philosophy, ajnana is identified with Prakriti. Prakriti, consisting of the three gunas (sattva, rajas and tamas), obscures the truth of Purusha. In Samkhya, the identification of Purusha with Buddhi represents another form of avidya. In Yoga philosophy, avidya occurs when Purusha cannot distinguish between Buddhi and itself and attributes the transformations and impermanence of Buddhi to itself.

Other philosophers like Madhva and Nimbarka provide various definitions of ajnana or avidya. Sri Aurobindo extensively describes karma and rebirth, which are also elaborated in ancient texts, but he highlights the differences between traditional views and his own in his writings.

Chakras and Kundalini

Chakras

Derived from the Sanskrit word meaning 'wheel', this is a term used to describe the mystical energy centres within the human body. There are seven main chakras through which the Kundalini or divine energy is raised along the Sushumna Nadi located in the spinal cord. These are the Muladhara Chakra at the base of the spine, the Svadhishthana Chakra just below the navel, the

Manipura Chakra at the solar plexus, the Anahata Chakra in the center of the chest, the Vishuddha Chakra in the throat, the Ajna Chakra in the center of the forehead, and the Sahasrara Chakra located on the crown of the head. These seven main chakras are believed to play a significant role in spiritual and energetic practices. It is worth noting that there are also many other chakras dispersed throughout various parts of the body, each with its own unique functions and significance.

Kundalini

Referred to as a coiled serpent residing at the base of the spine, Kundalini represents a latent source of powerful energy within the human body. When awakened, it is believed to bestow extraordinary abilities upon the individual. Various spiritual, breathing, and physical practices are employed to activate the dormant Kundalini energy and guide it through the chakras or energy centres along the spinal column, eventually reaching the crown of the head.[20] This process is said to facilitate spiritual awakening and transformation. In the Mother's vision of the future, she envisioned a different kind of body that operates without internal physical organs. This concept may be related to the understanding of chakras and the existence of a subtle or ethereal body beyond the physical realm.

Gunas and Tattvas

Sri Aurobindo uses the term guna quite often, and at times, tattva. Guna, which means quality, refers to the basic qualities or characteristics according to which people can be classified. Most often, three gunas are mentioned. These three are sattva or serenity and purity, rajas or energetic activity and tamas or dullness. Though not exactly the same, these have a relationship with the mental, vital and physical bodies described by Aurobindo.

Tattva is a term for the principles of Prakriti or matter. The term also refers to categories of various phenomena. It is an element or elementary property, the essence or substance of anything. Tattva-jnana indicates the knowledge of truth or the true principles of something.[21]

While his theories are interrelated with his philosophy and described in his major works, he also provides straightforward explanations of some of these philosophies and philosophical terms in his letters to his disciples, and in his essays.[22]

In addition, Sri Aurobindo comments on other mystics, saints and gurus of India, including Sri Ramakrishna, Swami Vivekananda, Ramana Maharshi, J. Krishnamurti and many more of the past and present. It was Swami Vivekananda's voice he heard internally in prison, which set him firmly on the spiritual path. Among his numerous musings are those on the Vaishnava Bhakti saints and the Tamil Alwars, including Andal, the woman saint-poet.[23] Additionally, Sri Aurobindo frequently discusses aspects of the gods, not limited to Vedic deities but also including Shiva, Narayana and Sri Krishna, with whom he identified.

Western Philosophy

With his vast reading, Sri Aurobindo was not only familiar with Greek and Latin classics but with some later European philosophers too. As S. K. Maitra says, Sri Aurobindo's knowledge of Western philosophy was immense.[24]

Among the early Greek philosophers, Sri Aurobindo particularly appreciated Heraclitus (c. 535–475 BCE), whom he commented on in 1916–17. Heraclitus brought out the idea of involution and evolution from a single element, that of fire. Heraclitus had some mystical concepts that were difficult to understand, but Sri Aurobindo found similarities with Vedic symbolism. For instance, Heraclitus saw the thunderbolt as the eternal fire, which would find correspondence in Indra's *vajra* in the Rig Veda. The eternal fire was One, which multiplied and became many, and can be compared to the concept of Brahman. Heraclitus also wrote about right consciousness, wisdom and truth, which resonate with Sri Aurobindo's developed philosophy.[25]

Sri Aurobindo had also read Plato; in fact, he had read some of his works in the original Greek in his younger days in England. In Greek, Plato is Platon. In his philosophy, Sri Aurobindo brought in the concept of 'real ideas', which are similar to Plato's 'fixed ideas', which exist at an eternal level as ideals. Plato's 'ideas' are perfect and represent the truth that exists behind all creation. They are interconnected and exist at a higher level than the gods, who attain their divinity by accessing them. K. D. Sethna is among those who have compared Plato and Sri Aurobindo.[26] However, there are differences in the concepts, as pointed out by S. K. Maitra.[27] Both Plato and Pythagoras also believed in rebirth, and Sri Aurobindo commented that 'The ideas of the Upanishads can be rediscovered in much of the thought of Pythagoras and Plato and form the profoundest part of Neo-Platonism and Gnosticism with all their considerable consequences to the philosophical thinking of the West.' He added that 'Sufism only repeats them in another religious language'.[28]

Plotinus (204–70 CE), the Greek philosopher who founded Neo-Platonism, was deeply appreciated by Sri Aurobindo, and he stated that his philosophy 'was founded on Yogic experience and realization'.[29] Plotinus put forward the concept of Nous, or the Supreme Intelligence, which emerged from a divine being infinite and beyond time and space, similar to the concept of Brahman. Nous, as a term, was already known in earlier Greek philosophy.

In his early writings, Sri Aurobindo commented that the intuitive vision of Schopenhauer, Nietzsche and Wagner led to a change in the thinking of Europe.[30] The German philosophers Fichte, Kant, Hegel and Nietzsche are mentioned by Aurobindo in *The Human Cycle*,[31] but Sri Aurobindo particularly appreciated Nietzsche and said that neither Hegel nor Kant meant anything to him,[32] though he occasionally referred to them.[33] He has, in fact, been frequently compared with Hegel.[34] Seeing a similarity with Hegel, Sri Aurobindo is even said to have 'appropriated' aspects of Hegel's philosophy.[35] However, Odin also praises Sri Aurobindo's approach as having overcome the shortcomings of traditional Hindu thought and also going beyond that of Bergson and Whitehead. Aurobindo found such comparisons difficult to understand.

In *Essays in Philosophy and Yoga*, Sri Aurobindo writes on the concept of Nietzsche's Superman.[36] At the same time, Aurobindo believed that Nietzsche's concept of the *Übermensch* (or Superman) was confused, as it was not a sufficiently moral concept, even though at times he reached close to the truth. Nietzsche's Superman was often egoistic rather than spiritual and had no clear concept of the nature of the higher self he sought to reach.[37] Sri Aurobindo's comments on Nietzsche have been summarised by Huchzermeyer.[38] In his own philosophy, Aurobindo uses the term Superman in different ways, sometimes as the perfected individual but at other times to refer to lesser beings such as Napoleon, Ravana and others. He explained that there were some men who embodied a supreme force; they were not human, and were above all morality. He refers to them as '*vibhutis*' and discusses others who had this force to a greater or lesser degree.[39]

The French philosopher Henri Bergson (1859–1941) provided a different concept of time along with his theory of 'elan vital'. Sri Aurobindo, commenting on him, says he has a perception of 'dynamic creative intuition.'[40] S. K. Maitra discusses Bergson, Sri Aurobindo and Bergson's great work, *Creative Evolution*.[41]

Aurobindo also comments on H. G. Wells, *God the Invisible King*, in which Wells writes about how the kingdom of God that is within, can also appear on earth.[42]

Comparisons between different aspects of Sri Aurobindo's philosophy and other theories are numerous. He has often been compared with Jung, for instance by David T. Johnston, who delves into several aspects of Sri Aurobindo's philosophy and compares Jung's Rotundum and Archetypal Psyche with Aurobindo's Unconscious and Circumconscient, his Anthropos with the Matri Mandir, and the Supermind and Overmind with Jung's *Unus Mundus*.[43]

Though Sri Aurobindo does not mention him, the German philosopher Schelling is thought to come close to his philosophy.[44] Sri Aurobindo was not aware of Teilhard de Chardin (1881–1955), but the latter saw similarities in his theory of evolution with that of Sri Aurobindo.[45] Teilhard's main books are *The Divine Milieu* and *The Phenomenon of Man,* and he himself was influenced by Bergson's work, *Creative Evolution*. Many books compare the philosophy of both.[46]

Jean Gebser (1905–73) was another philosopher influenced by Sri Aurobindo who had some similar ideas even before he came across him.[47] Gebser put forward the idea that evolution was already contained in the Invisible and then revealed in the Visible, but Ego distorted how it should be expressed.

Alfred North Whitehead (1861–1947), a mathematician and philosopher known for 'process philosophy, has most frequently been compared with Sri Aurobindo, and this is examined by Maitra.[48] Their ideas were parallel to some extent, but Aurobindo probably did not know of him. Others have also compared him with Whitehead.[49] Of particular works, several people have compared Sri Aurobindo's epic *Savitri* with Dante's *Divine Comedy*.[50] *Savitri* has also been compared with the *Odyssey* of Nikolas Kazantzakis.[51]

Some find Christian elements in his work, and though at times Sri Aurobindo refers to elements of the Bible and uses Christian imagery, these often mean something different to him. A line in *Savitri* reads: 'Through a false poignant figure of grief and pain / Still dolorously nailed upon a cross', but Sri Aurobindo explains that 'this is not about Christ and Christianity, the symbol of the cross represents the world soul.'[52]

Many people in the past and present have put forth theories of evolutionary spirituality. Another example is Madame Blavatsky's theory of 'root races', further expanded upon by other Theosophists. According to this, human evolution could be traced through a series of such 'races'. There were seven races, each subdivided into seven sub-races. Five root races had already appeared, and the sixth sub-race of the fifth root race, which they named the Aryan root race, was imminent. Each root race proceeds from the previous one and this sixth sub-race would consist of highly evolved humans.[53] Sri Aurobindo, though critical of some aspects of Theosophy, also believed the organization could make Indian concepts acceptable in the West. He wrote, 'Theosophy with its comprehensive combinations of old and new beliefs and its appeal to ancient spiritual and psychic systems, has everywhere exercised an influence far beyond the circle of its professed adherents. Opposed for a long time with obloquy and ridicule, it has done much to spread the belief in Karma, reincarnation, other planes of existence, the evolution of the embodied soul through intellect and psyche to spirit, ideas which once accepted must change the whole attitude towards life.' This could bring the understanding of East and West closer, he added.[54]

Though these largely form part of his early writings, they show how Sri Aurobindo had read and thought about the major events in history and the ideas that prevailed, and how these are part of the background to his philosophy. However, in his interpretations, he differed from the traditional philosophers, whether of the East or the West. He was not influenced by them, but he sought passages, particularly in early Indian texts, to support his philosophy. Speaking to Nirodbaran, Sri Aurobindo said he had read Plato and Nietzsche but could not read more than one page of Kant. He had never read Hegel. He read some commentaries on Shankara but did not find much in them. He explained, 'I have written everything from experience and spiritual perception.'[55]

6

A Life Divine

The main theories of Sri Aurobindo on spiritual evolution are in *The Life Divine*.[1] He explains in the book that all humans are evolving to a higher consciousness, and with this evolution a new type of individual will emerge, which will bring a new dawn to life on earth, where all will live in peace and harmony. He goes into great depth to explain how this will take place, analysing different philosophies and texts, and even the origin of the universe and its development through different stages.

Book 1

Book 1 begins by stating that every person's ultimate preoccupation is attaining perfection, searching for pure truth and bliss.[2] Even Vedanta says that 'Matter is a veiled form of life' and 'Life a form of veiled consciousness'.[3] Therefore mind, that is, one's mental consciousness, has within it higher states that are at present concealed, as if behind a veil. However, each person is evolving towards a manifestation of God, no matter how limited they may seem at present.

Both materialists and ascetics deny and negate this future.[4] For the materialist, only matter exists, but the Upanishads state that as Brahman contains all, even matter is part of Brahman. If we separate spirit and nature, we deny one or the other, but not if we see the links between the two. Sri Aurobindo now introduces the concept of the Supermind, towards which all are evolving. The Supermind is a superior state existing beyond the mind and between the mind and Supermind there are other intermediate levels. This is explained further throughout the book, but here he emphasizes that either by objective or subjective methods, one has to reach an ultimate unity, without denying the energy of multiplicity.

Unlike the materialist, the ascetic takes an opposite stand and says that only the eternal spirit is real while matter is unreal. The ascetic therefore seeks to transcend the world and enter into eternal divine consciousness or unity with god or Brahman. If, as some Vedantists do, we see the world as Maya or illusion, the individual, ego and personality become insignificant and can be discarded in the quest for divine unity. Or, if we believe that the material universe has an eternal self-existence, beyond life and mind, this too makes the life of an individual insignificant.

He affirms that there is more to life than this. Perhaps only matter can be seen through the physical senses, but there are higher physical realities and senses, through which we can contact other realms. There are worlds beyond ours, and if we extend our individual consciousness into cosmic consciousness, we become aware of universal existence, and even our sensory experiences change. Then we increasingly get a sense of unity with others.

Explaining Brahman

Sri Aurobindo explains Brahman in his own way. The world is part of a conscious energy. Ancient texts describe two aspects of

Brahman, passive and active, with the passive or inactive being behind and beyond all creation. When the mind through the practice of asceticism reaches this luminous state, it experiences a vast, transcendental silence, and in this state sees the world as unreal and only the Silence as real. This leads to a spiritual negation of life. The ascetic seeks liberation from birth and death, and to live in this supreme silence or in some other divine realm. But Sri Aurobindo says this cannot be the aim of life. The Upanishads contain some key statements, known as mahavakyas, and Sri Aurobindo links two of these. One of the key statements is that Brahman is 'One without a second', that is, that only Brahman exists, there is nothing else. Therefore, ascetics seek to merge with Brahman and deny the existence of the world. But this mahavakya has to be linked to another that states, 'All this is Brahman', indicating that the whole world is Brahman. The ascetic has understood that one must aspire to the Divine but has not realized that if 'all this is Brahman' the Divine has to permeate the world.[5]

He states that spirit and matter meet in cosmic consciousness, where mind and life are 'intermediaries', and not what they seem to the egoistic mentality. Those who have experienced the calm of the passive Brahman, 'can perceive always welling out from its silence the perennial supply of the energies that work in the universe.[6] 'But if we say Being or sat, appeared out of *asat*, or non-Being, does it return to non-Being? Sri Aurobindo affirms that there is no point in time when this happens as both are eternal. Even the Buddha, when he spoke about nirvana, may have meant not annihilation but action out of silence.

Brahman contains everything, and does not distinguish between truth and falsehood, or state that there is anything that is not Brahman. Within us is an inner sense that there will be 'an ultimate victory and fulfillment, not the disappointed recoil of the soul from its great adventure.' It is when our relative consciousness sees evil and pain, that we think there is something like evil, or the devil, or even Maya or illusion, but 'There is one Lord and Self and the many are only His representations and becomings'.[7] Diving deeper, he says there is an omnipresent reality which includes everything but cannot be defined. As such, we arrive at the concept of '*neti neti*', meaning not this, not that. The same is seen in Buddhism and in the Upanishads, where sat–asat or being and non-being are not opposites. Avidya or ignorance is the field, and vidya is the knowledge, but both are required and part of the whole. To know God, one must know him everywhere without distinctions. So, the One and the many, sat and asat, are all real. Brahman expresses itself in successive forms of consciousness but unifies many at one time. We cannot reject the lower or physical but have to transform it with the light of consciousness.[8]

Attaining the Highest Consciousness

Sri Aurobindo identifies three forms of consciousness: the individual, the universal and the transcendent. Rejecting the first two to reach the third is not the way, the three are to be integrated. According to Advaita, the individual soul escapes, the world remains in bondage, and both the individual and the world are illusory. A person who seeks moksha is actually very egoistic. 'The individual soul can only cut the knot of ego through a supreme act of egoism, an exclusive attachment to its own individual salvation which amounts to an absolute assertion of its separate existence in Maya.'[9] The transcendent is free but manifests here for a purpose and the Ego, without escaping, can transcend its personal consciousness and become aware of cosmic unity. This is true liberation, and, 'The liberated soul extends its perception of unity, horizontally as well as vertically'.[10] As he remarks, we don't have to be blotted out, but become luminous centres of conscious divinity.

How does one become this luminous and conscious divinity? This happens in progressive stages, and Sri Aurobindo is convinced that this is the purpose of the universe – to reach 'a transcendent luminous reality'. This aim is concealed in ancient texts, for instance in the story of the three steps of Vishnu and is represented by the third and 'highest step of the world-pervading Vishnu.' The story is first recounted in the Rig Veda, and later modified and expanded in the story of Vamana. Human life, Aurobindo insists, has just one purpose, and that is to ascend to divine life. When sat-chit-ananda – Being, Consciousness and Bliss – is established in the mind, life and body, that is what is known as transfiguration. The first step is for the mind to awake to itself and to the world, and finally, to reach beyond mind to the Supermind. Matter contains life and energy but does not possess that which it contains. Its peace is that of inertia; however, there is a tranquillity which is not inertia, that exists beyond the normal life and mind. The universe is the field for self-realization. 'The animal is satisfied with a modicum of necessity, the gods are content with their splendours. But man cannot rest permanently until he reaches some highest good,' says Sri Aurobindo.[11]

Manu, known from ancient texts, is the son of man, the thinker, the Manomaya Purusha. 'When he has turned Death into a more perfect life, lifted the small things of the human limitation into the great things of the divine vastness, transformed suffering into beatitude, converted evil into its proper good, translated error and falsehood into this secret truth that the sacrifice will be accomplished, the journey done, and Heaven and Earth equalized', then there is supreme bliss.[12]

The peace of the Buddhist nirvana is also sat-chit-ananda where the Ego has vanished, all terms and 'cognitive experience' don't exist. But to realize it in life, one must go below, explore 'the depths of consciousness and identify ourselves with states of being that are not our own'.[13]

Why do dualities exist? There are hidden truths in every text, and Sri Aurobindo was familiar with the Bible and understood its symbolism. Even what seemed to be death, suffering and limitation, or a fall, as described in Genesis, is actually part of sat-chit-ananda. It is nothing but a deviation from the full acceptance of God, into 'a dividing consciousness.' Adam and Eve, Purusha and Prakriti, the soul tempted by nature, have, he says, eaten this fruit of division, leading to life and death, good and evil, and other apparent opposites. With the recovery of the universal in the individual, and the spiritual in the physical consciousness one can eat instead the fruit of the tree of life. A higher knowledge transforms these opposites, 'into something surpassing them that effaces their opposition'.[14] There are states of consciousness in which these opposites are seen differently, but unless we have that higher knowledge, we cannot and should not go beyond the dualistic sense-mind. If we can do so, the dualities can cease here, death and other worlds are not required. Humans are evolving further and can conceive of a supreme state as divine consciousness already permeates everything. The egoistic construction dissolves by opening itself to the universe and God.

How does sat-chit-ananda work in the world? It is important to know this. Reason, Sri Aurobindo explains, is of two types: first when it tries to make sense of experiences, and second, pure reason that looks at wider issues. Through pure reason, we move from physical to metaphysical knowledge, beyond that which is known by the senses. Manas or the mind, too, has a double action, one dependent on the senses, the other that comes in contact with higher things, which could be called the sovereign sense-mind. Through this mind, other senses can be developed, but the Truth is beyond them, though in theory, mental self-awareness can be extended 'to awareness of the Self beyond and outside us, Atman or Brahman of the Upanishads'.[15] But these would still only be a reflection. Beyond our mind and reason, evolution is upwards, to the superconscient, and the waking consciousness is a mediator between this and the subconscient. Vedanta is built on these truths, and this is the best foundation on which the new ideas can be built. At times, efforts have been made to combine Vedanta with different philosophies and arrive at a unified whole, but using intuition and reason, one has to move even beyond this.

When we search for truth, setting aside our egoistic preoccupations, we first become aware of 'a boundless energy of infinite existence'.[16] It does not revolve around us, but nor are we insignificant. This great energy is Brahman, it is neither whole, nor does it have parts, and is impartial and equal to all. In Vedanta we are told that there is a stable base, out of which movement appears, and we, as movement are subordinate to it. But the idea of eternal stability is a fiction, as energy is movement. Is there some existence beyond this energy? Sri Aurobindo says there is infinite existence, beyond time and space, beyond all we see and know. It is existence without, or beyond, quality, quantity and form. It cannot be defined and is the source of all. From Brahman which is this pure existence, comes sat or truth; chit, which is a force of consciousness; and ananda, the joy inherent in existence. He questions whether the force is Prakriti, which indicates a movement of nature, an unintelligent energy, or a power of chit, which is a conscious force. In any case we can't know the Absolute, which is beyond both stability and movement.

Expanding on this theme, Sri Aurobindo says that a force or movement of energy is part of all existence. It emanates from pure Existence, sat, and is part of the absolute reality that one may call Brahman. The conscious force or chit is involved in creation, but its conscious component is then lost in matter, even though as we know from science that matter too is energy. As pure being, or sat, descends to life and matter, its consciousness is hidden. He analyses five aspects of material force: sound, contact, light, diffusion and cohesion, and also looks at Mahat and ahamkara of the Samkhya theory as preceding these. But the key element in his analysis is that consciousness in material forms is concealed. There is force, but not conscious force. But then, through an evolutionary process, the force becomes conscious again.[17]

Finding Delight: The Reason for Creation

Even if we accept the reality of Brahman, he says, we must ask why it creates. Brahman of course has the potential to do so, but in no way is it compelled to create. From Brahman comes sat, then chit, and then ananda. The last is the delight of Creation, the reason for which creation began. It is ignorance and division that leads to the experience of pain and sorrow, instead of joy. We will realize this ananda when our consciousness reaches a higher level. For our original being has all the characteristics of sat-chit-ananda. Then why is there pain and suffering? This, says Aurobindo, 'is often further confused by a false issue starting from the idea of a personal extra cosmic God, and a partial issue, the ethical difficulty.'[18] There is no easy solution to the problem of pain and suffering. If it is a test or trial, then the one who invents it is either deliberately cruel or morally insensitive. If we look at it in the context of the usual theories of karma and rebirth, the dilemma remains. Who created this moral evil which is punished by pain and suffering? If moral evil is only a form of mental disease or ignorance, then why torture anyone for it? 'The inexorable law of karma is irreconcilable with a supreme moral and personal deity', which is why the Buddha said there was no god. The problem arises if there is an extra cosmic personal god who creates the opposites of good and evil etc., but remains above it. In Brahman and sat-chit-ananda there is no such god, but the problem remains.

Sri Aurobindo explains that this confusion is because of forcing our concepts on nature. 'We do not live in an ethical world. The attempt of human thought to force an ethical meaning into the whole of Nature is one of those acts of willful and obstinate self-confusion'.[19] Material nature is not ethical, it is governed by habits and ruled by a force that disturbs or destroys according to its secret will. Animal or vital nature is also non-ethical, i.e., the tiger killing a deer. We do not blame it, nor the storm that destroys. Disapproval of what threatens us, approval of what pleases us, and along with us the larger community, lead to the concepts of good and evil. The beginning of true ethics is the concept of self-blame and self-condemnation. Man wants self-expression and self-development; what hinders this is seen as evil, what helps it is good. Ethics is only a stage in evolution. Below, is infra-ethical, above, it may be supra-ethical. What is common to these three stages is the conscious force, seeking to reach delight through its own development. Delight is not pleasure or joy, it is beyond cause, 'universal, illimitable and self-existent.'[20] Spiritual development can lead to this state.

Thus, the solution to our problems is in the delight of existence. Ananda or delight is concealed but gradually reveals itself in creation, and is even greater when it appears in creation, than in its origin in the unmanifest state. As life evolves, it emerges in different ways, but we can bring ananda into our lives in its full form by raising our state of consciousness. It is through attaining a calm and detached state and opening to the Divine that ananda can manifest in us. Sat, or pure existence, allows ananda to manifest in various ways before it reaches its full expression. We find it in the depths of our being, and in the heights. As we focus on the higher aspects of mind, we open ourselves to this delight.

It is through the psychic being that we reach and discover the divine ananda. The two souls in a person are desire soul and psychic soul. The psychic soul is a subtle centre of love, light, power and joy. Seeking delight, the soul ascends through stages of desire. First, it is an inconscient desire, then a more conscious desire to possess and give; this leads to the desire to love and be loved, and then higher desires. The psychic being is the flame of the godhead, the silent witness, and the inner guide. It is the imperishable evolving soul. Through it, we develop a psychic personality, which changes and grows as we move through different bodies. The desire soul seeks power, knowledge and happiness, but everything it gains is temporary, whereas if we connect with our psychic being, our nature is illumined. Through it, we can touch the Supermind.

The True Creator: The Supermind

The divine maya is the creative force. The infinite behind all creation, creates through divine maya. But Maya is not illusion, as is commonly supposed, instead it is the creative capacity of the infinite. Reaching the Supramental level we can see not only how Maya creates, but how every aspect of creation is linked. Sri Aurobindo strongly contradicts the Advaita theory that the world is unreal, an illusion or Maya. The philosopher Shankara in his logic says: that which appears and disappears, i.e., life forms and matter, cannot be real. But Sri Aurobindo says that it is only the lower consciousness that sees forms as separate from their source, while the higher consciousness knows that everything is an integral part of the Divine. It is the Supermind, using the creative power of Maya, that creates this world of form and shape. We have to raise our consciousness to Supramental perception, to understand this higher Maya. In this state of consciousness, we have transcended our egoistical limited viewpoint.

The Supermind is the true Creator. Earlier, Sri Aurobindo had indicated that from Brahman came sat-chit-ananda. From these comes the Supermind. The fundamental truths, or real ideas emanate from the Supermind through Supramental action. The Supermind has supreme knowledge, and also the power to create. If we raise our consciousness, we can also reach that Supramental state and the power to create. Mind is a lower level of the Supermind, but it can first become spiritualized and then rise higher to the Supramental level. Supermind creates the many from the one and thus various truths are manifested in the world. Sri Aurobindo uses the term 'real ideas' for the truths that the Supermind wishes to manifest. Real ideas are the spiritual attributes that come from sat-chit-ananda. These include Silent Witness, Harmony, Oneness, Wisdom, Truth, Beauty, Love and other divine attributes. They manifest in actual forms, and in basic principles and idealistic movements. All life is the manifestation of the Divine. The Supermind is the power, knowledge and will of the Divine, that exists beyond ordinary life, mind and matter.

The Supermind is the 'nature of the divine being',[21] not in its 'absolute self-existence', but as the creator. This being can be called God, but is not the personal, limited deity, conceived in our own image, though this too is part of the all-existent. Truth-consciousness permeates the universe, where it is reflected as 'an ordering self-knowledge'. If there was no order based on truth and harmonious self-knowledge, creation would be random and chaotic. It creates through the seeds of real ideas, contained in itself and knows the truth of everything. At one level it is the cosmic vision, holding within itself the seeds of creation, and at another also the Creator, through which space, time, and various forms emerge. Even though we may not be aware of it, the Supermind is hidden in every form, and is revealed as 'the indwelling light'. In the Supermind, the knower, the known and knowledge are one.

The Supermind has a triple status of sat-chit-ananda. All existence is 'one being whose essential nature is consciousness'.[22] The active aspect of Consciousness is force or will, and every aspect of it is Delight. Consciousness is Bliss, whether at rest or active, and this is God as well as ourselves in our essential being. It is already in us, so the divine life can only be attained be realizing this veiled self. Sat-chit-ananda is a unity yet a divided mentality seems to exist. If we abandon life here in order to reach the One, then a divine life here is impossible. There must therefore be an intermediate link between our normal lives and the Transcendent. This link is the Supermind or Truth-consciousness. The Supermind is above and superior to the ordinary mind. It is sat-chit-ananda in principle but proceeds out of its infinite consciousness as a form of energy. Consciousness and Force are the twin aspects 'of the pure Power of existence'.[23] Knowledge and Will are the form the Power takes in creating within time and space. Though we humans are limited, the divine consciousness is not. We are subject to time and space and know one thing at a time, but the divine consciousness can be many things. The Supermind has three main aspects: First, it contains the unity of everything; second, it modifies this unity to support the creation of many in one, and one in many; third, it further modifies it to support the evolution of individuals. It is through ignorance, that the individual at the lower level suffers the ignorance of a separate ego. The Supermind is not the same as sat-chit-ananda, which has a pure unitarian consciousness beyond time and space, but is an extension of it, and in its primary state retains its universality. In the second stage, it realizes itself as the stable, conscious self in each. It is the same in essence but varies in form. It can be equated with the individual divine self or *jivatman*,[24] different from the universal divine self. In the third, the individual divine while remaining separate, would be aware both of the joy of differentiation and of unity. The Upanishads, he says, imply the validity of all these truths. The error arises when there is an insistence that the only eternal truth is the one Consciousness encompassing all.

By understanding the Supermind, we get an intellectual understanding of the Divine, and the realization that whatever emanates from the Divine must return to it. The gods have never known the fall, and are in a different category, but the human can move beyond them. When a person accepts the descent into matter, and then moves upwards again, even the lost godhead can be conquered. The divine soul, if it had not descended into matter, would be self-contained in sat-chit-ananda, immortal, without death, birth, or change of body. It would have an eternal and luminous tranquility, but it would also explore knowledge and forms of conscious power.

It would live in natural harmony, with 'an inalienable delight in its eternal self-experience', without any dislike, hatred or suffering. It would know the absolute truth and live in eternal freedom in the presence of the Absolute. Aware of variations, yet in its essence it would be concentrated in the One. We would experience the Transcendent and universal divine, even while retaining our individuality. While living in time, we would know timelessness. We would know the aspects of the Supermind and of Supramental existence. This realization of the Divine that is already within us will take place when the separative ego is removed.[25]

The Supermind creates the universe, through divine maya, but our own minds are limited as they are rooted in the physical consciousness of the body. The human mind too, has different aspects, and Sri Aurobindo analyses it. There is the physical mind, aware of its location in the body; the subconscious dynamic mind; and a reflective mind behind the dynamic, which is the source of the pure thinker. This Higher Mind is beyond the physical and vital, it can conceive of unity, but still remains separate. It strives to arrive at its own higher self. When the divided mind is silent, there is a luminous mentality, an instrument of the divine realities.[26]

Life and Death

What is life and what is death? Sri Aurobindo provides an explanation of how life energy descends into matter from sat-chit-ananda, and then emerges in creation. Death is only a process of life, as the life energy also destroys and renews. He had already brought this out clearly in his commentary on the Bhagavad Gita, but here he expands on his views. While descending into matter, he says, the conscious energy creates the

Supermind and next the Cosmic Mind, and then becomes latent in matter. With evolution it gradually reemerges, but even in humans it does not at first reveal itself. One has to understand that the energy in different life forms is related. Sat, or True Being, as seen earlier, is the first manifestation of Brahman. Its conscious form exists in varying degrees in all life, plant, animal and human. The energy does not die when a material form dies, hence it is clear that death is just a process of life.[27]

All life is a product of the intention of the Divine, and life forms have an interchange of energy. Yet the Divine is not fully realized in our lives, and death takes place because the souls are striving for sustenance and immortality, seeking this through different forms. Each form they take brings a different experience, and this is essential for the soul's evolution. All desire is actually a seeking of Bliss, which is the ananda or Delight of being, it begins with small and mundane things, then proceeds to greater forms. Though the individual is subject to disease, incapacity and death, humans can move beyond this when the self awakens and the Supramental Truth and Power come to the forefront. It is an imbalance of forces and energies that leads to disease and disintegration, and when we can contact the Supermind, the balance is restored. Through the Supermind we access perfect knowledge, and create a perfect vital and physical being, which could even lead to physical immortality.[28]

Life, therefore, is a process of the ascension of energy through different forms. It begins with an unconscious movement, the will to survive. Next the individual ego comes into being and interacts with other egos. The movement is from the physical to the vital being, while at the same time, the Conscious Mind emerges. Third, there is harmony when the individual, though still separate, reaches a higher level, and interacts in a mutually beneficial way. The conscious mind predominates, and there is the quality of love. Finally, there is the level of spiritual unity. As our Psychic Being develops, we can see the process of this evolution.[29]

Sat-chit-ananda are one but become divided as consciousness and force when they descend into matter or the subconscient. As life develops, they begin to unite again, and with the higher mind, Supermind and Supramental, Life and Consciousness are reunited. As Force and Consciousness begin to unite, four aspects have to be resolved. We have to understand the subconscious or the subliminal mind, and not just the surface mind. We have to bridge the differences with others by contact with the universal. The physical, mental and vital within us are limited and separate, but each also has a higher consciousness, and as one becomes aware of these, they can be harmonized. These are some of the ways in which the Supermind can be reached, uniting Consciousness and Force, so that the principle of harmony and joy in the universe can be rediscovered and realized.[30]

Understanding Life in Matter

We need to understand matter, as it developed from energy in the process of Creation. The vital and then the mental planes emerge out of matter. But why was this limiting matter created? Sri Aurobindo explains that it is so that the highest consciousness can inhabit every possible form. The Universal Mind created matter by separating energy into its different components. It seems inert and inconscient, but Consciousness, Delight and Force are its essence. In fact, matter is no different from sat-chit-ananda. It is just another aspect of Brahman, but it has a specific role in developing different and diverse forms in which divine consciousness will grow. Matter has 'infinite potential', just as consciousness does.[31]

As matter is an aspect of sat, the Divine is always in it. Yet matter limits higher life and mind, through ignorance, inertia and divisiveness. This can be called the knot of matter. It is the unconsciousness of matter that causes ignorance; as it operates through mechanical laws, it leads to inertia. It is a result of a division of energy, which therefore leads to struggle and contradictions. Pain and suffering arise through this knot of matter. But the true aspects of matter can be realized, leading to transformation of the body. When a higher power descends into the body, it is transformed and is then beyond death and suffering.

How can consciousness ascend to higher planes? As consciousness ascends from matter, it is less associated with the body and physical form. We are not just the physical body, though that is the basis for our existence. If we can open to the Supermind, its power affects even the body, ultimately leading to a bodily state beyond death.[32]

Seven Levels of Life

Sri Aurobindo ends Book 1 by explaining and summarizing the seven expressions of the one reality, which exist both in involution and evolution. Sat descends to chit, then to ananda, then to Supermind, to Mind, to life energy, to matter, and then ascends again in reverse order. The higher planes are reflected in the lower, thus sat=matter; chit=energy life; ananda=the psychic self; supermind=mind. They are also reflected in the human being. Matter is the body; life energy is the life force and vital being; and mind, the power to think and reason. These are our powers which help us to evolve further upwards, towards the higher states. Above everything is Brahman. In this whole process, the Supermind is the intermediary between sat-chit-ananda and the mind-energy-matter and has an important role. It is the force which brings sat-chit-ananda into the lower planes and enables humans to access the upper planes.

The Superconscient and the Subconscient are generally beyond the reach of our mind. Beyond the mind is the Higher Mind, Illumined Mind and Intuitive Mind, and as we get in touch with these spiritual levels, we access the sources of original thinking and genius. Beyond these is the Overmind and Supermind. The Supermind is the intermediary for even higher stages, but Overmind exists between the mind and Supermind. Overmind perceives unity and oneness, but also brings in division, through which Ego arises. It sees the whole, but from a single point of view. The Supermind perceives from the consciousness of unity. A million godheads can emerge as invisible sources of power from the Overmind, but each remains separate. The cosmic Maya comes from the Overmind, creating differences and separation from truth. Maya is the creator. To summarize, therefore, there is Brahman, then sat-chit-ananda, Supermind as intermediary, followed by the Overmind, Intuitive Mind, Illumined Mind and Higher Mind, above the ordinary mind.[33]

Through involution sat-chit-ananda descended and created their opposites. Sat becomes asat or non-being, leading to the opposites of life and death; chit or conscious force becomes unconsciousness, or the inconscient. Ananda becomes insensibility, leading to pain and sorrow.

The Overmind can be seen as a delegate of the Supermind, which provides flashes of light to ignorance, which would not be able to bear the full light of the Supermind. The Supermind holds the essential truth, and transmits it to the Overmind, but the Overmind's dynamic capacity gives each aspect or power an independent and separate action. We have Purusha and

Prakriti, the One and the Many, the divine personality and divine impersonality. Each is part of the One Reality but gains the power to act independently to fulfil its potential.[34] The Overmind creates infinite possibilities out of the One.

The global consciousness of the Overmind is different from our separative consciousness. To the Overmind, all religions would be the true expressions of one eternal religion, all philosophies valid in its own views of the universe, all political systems the legitimate working out of an Idea-Force, but to us they seem opposed. The Overmind contains the original cosmic maya, the maya of knowledge, which has yet made ignorance possible. It is all these powers that make a divine life on earth not only possible, but inevitable.

Book 2

Divided into two parts, the second book[35] further explores how human beings can transform themselves and develop their higher aspects, thus transforming life on earth.

Knowledge and Ignorance

In Part One, the infinite consciousness and ignorance, Sri Aurobindo discusses knowledge and ignorance. A conscious force creates the worlds, but in our material world and in ourselves, it has two aspects, knowledge and ignorance. As he says, 'In the Infinite consciousness of a self-aware Infinite Existence' knowledge is its essence.[36] But the material world begins with inconscience. As life evolves, knowledge too begins, but at first knowledge consists only of all that can be seen or accessed through the senses, and not of the reality behind these. Within the infinite, the universe appears paradoxically like a 'boundless finite', remaining a mystery. In science, the infinite reveals itself as energy, in various atoms and their components. We know of genes, chromosomes, psychological variants, cells, glands, but what produces a Plato or a Shakespeare? Science explains evolution, but can it explain the reason behind it? Does evolution take place through chance? Is it a mechanical activity of nature? Or is it the work of an extra-cosmic divinity with 'an omnipotent and omniscient Mind and Will?'[37] If so, couldn't the so-called God have created a better world? Once again, Sri Aurobindo traces creation from sat-chit-ananda, through 'real ideas' or truths. He describes Purusha and Prakriti, seeing Purusha as the mental being influenced by consciousness, and further explains the nature of the Overmind, a state beyond individual mind, which carries within it the knowledge of cosmic truth. But what the Overmind can be, depends on what the individual can receive. Within the Overmind is both the pure silent, self-sufficient self and the dynamic creative power.[38] These are apparently in opposition, but we find the truth in the Supramental beyond the Overmind and further beyond the complete experience of sat-chit-ananda.[39] Sri Aurobindo examines in detail the methods by which sat-chit-ananda appear in creation, the nature of the atman, Brahman, Purusha and Ishwara, the divine force or Shakti, the concept of Maya as creative power, infinity, space and time. Our own mind as well as our ego are limited, and they view everything personally, unless we move on to a greater self. This becomes possible when we come in contact with our true self or soul that provides connections with other souls and higher aspects. He again explains how the 'Undivine' is allowed to exist and what its uses are. Ignorance and imperfection, which can be termed the 'undivine', actually provide the widest possibility of experiences and because of them, divine delight enters every sphere. As one proceeds from ignorance to knowledge and imperfection to perfection, divine joy increases. Every possibility must exist, or the movement towards the Divine would be pre-ordained and have little meaning. In essence, it is preordained as only that can give one joy. And so, evil, ignorance, grief and sorrow, are actually part of the divine plan, as realizing the problems these create, one moves beyond them. When one reaches a higher consciousness, these do not exist.

Life and the world are not Maya or an illusion, it is the ignorance of the mind that prevents one from seeing the Truth, and we don't see things as they really are. Sri Aurobindo clearly explains the three aspects of Mind: physical, vital and mental.[40] The physical mind sees things through the prism of matter, the vital mind through emotions; the vital also has a life will, while the mental or thinking mind, reasons and inquires. Inquiring into the world, it feels there is something beyond it, and thus perceives it as an illusion. When we dream, the Subconscient and the Inconscient behind or below it are expressed. In dreamless sleep we are in contact with the subliminal, and if one goes deeper, with the universal unconsciousness. Dreams, he says, are not an illusion, but an attempt of the limited mind to discover something beyond itself and imagination too is a method of touching the Unknown. But though dreams and imagination are not illusions, they are a product of ignorance. The true nature of reality can only be perceived through a higher consciousness and when this consciousness prevails, even Brahman and the unmanifest can appear in the world.

The average mind sees things as separate, prioritizes one over the other, and divides people and ideas into categories, and all this is the action of ignorance. At the same time, both knowledge and ignorance are equal powers of divine consciousness. By observing the limits of our consciousness and moving to a deeper and higher level, ignorance is removed, and one will be able to recognize that there is only One reality, expressed in different ways. The Inconscient, the Superconscient, and every level between these, are all part of the whole.

How do we gain right knowledge and remove ignorance? Ignorance leads us to live in the present, with a limited knowledge of the past, and only inference for the future. Memory, imagination, thoughts and ideas, developed because of this and memory succeeds to a limited degree, to connect with the past. But memory is selective, it does not know the whole past. It is when we reach beyond the limited mind that we can see this, and understand the eternal, which is beyond time. Ignorance is a mediator between knowledge and the inconscient.[41]

We are caught in time, but we can move into timelessness through realization of the true self. We reach the psyche or the psychic self in a state of detachment. When we stand back from what is happening around us, we can analyse it and get the right perspective. We find the eternal self through silence and stillness.

Discovering Integral Knowledge is essential. We get superficial knowledge in many ways, but true knowledge is found when we can move beyond our surface egos. Then we see the source of our thoughts, feelings and actions and through this we reach higher levels of existence. In our inner consciousness, the psychic being enables us to overcome subconscient aspects of fear, memories of failure and other aspects.

Sri Aurobindo further explains the different aspects of our being, i.e., the Subliminal, the Subconscient, the Waking Consciousness and the Superconscient. We are ignorant of most of these selves, of different planes and levels, and of the nature of time and space. But when we are conscious of ourselves and our limits, we start moving to a higher level. The ego serves a purpose, as it unifies our different aspects, and provides the base for further growth. How does this self-limiting ignorance arise? It is not directly from Brahman, nor in creation, but from a separative movement in chit, the consciousness force, when it is involved in involution. First knowledge emerges out of consciousness or the conscious force, and ignorance comes later when the cosmic mind separates from the Supramental.

Sri Aurobindo continues to explain the source and nature of ignorance but repeats that it has a purpose. Through it, a person can live as an individual in the confines of time and space. The individual then would be able to get the joy and delight of Integral Knowledge and Truth. Ignorance begins in the Overmind, but not in the Supermind. Unlike Vedanta and most other philosophies, Sri Aurobindo affirms that ignorance is a power of knowledge, which enables self-limitation and the ability to concentrate on a single thing. We need it to function in life as ignorance is required to develop individuality. But we also become ignorant of our true self and nature and of awareness beyond time, and this can be remedied when one goes deeper into oneself. Just as ignorance and knowledge are both required, the opposites of good and evil, too, serve an evolutionary purpose, as one can lead to the other. In addition, our ideas of these differ according to societal norms. Evil does not exist either in Brahman or in sat-chit-ananda but is below the Supermind, in the occult planes, where there are many demonic and titanic forces, powers and personalities, their aim being to prevent the person rising out of ignorance. Man is an instrument of both good and evil energies and forces. The Ego is necessary, but within it evil, falsehood and ignorance can establish themselves as the material realm is not advanced enough to expel evil. Evil and falsehood can also establish themselves in the vital mind of desire and sensation.

To understand the existence of ignorance and evil, we need to analyze how the mind works. Our consciousness includes the physical and vital aspects through which the thinking mind emerges, with its various powers of intelligence, observation and purpose, and behind it the vital mind of feelings, personal values and beliefs. The subliminal acts on the person, providing a different dimension of intuition and instinct. As mind emerges, a greater capacity for error and falsehood too are born, and in the human ego, ignorance takes place when there is a focus on one's own needs. This is an error in thinking, and attachment to this leads to falsehood. Unrestricted action emerging from falsehood, is the power of evil. Ego divides us from other beings, and therefore is a distortion of truth, leading to ignorance. When ego clings to these distortions, there is falsehood. When ego, in its limited, narrow knowledge, starts believing in the greatness of its own ideas, and these lead to hatred, dislike, violence, cruelty, opposition, then evil is present. Yet ego is necessary to distinguish ourselves from others, for the emergence of the many from the one. Through Ego, we go within and find our true soul or psychic self. Then we lose the separateness of ego and discover unity and harmony. To completely overcome ignorance-falsehood-evil, we have to connect with the Divine, experience the eternal self, and become its instruments of light and power. Even beyond that, we open to the Supramental, which is connected to sat-chit-ananda. We move from ego to the psychic self, then to the eternal self and the awareness of the Divine and finally the Supramental.[42]

The second part of Book 2 begins with an attempt to look at reality and Integral Knowledge. How does one overcome ignorance and attain Integral Knowledge? We will get this knowledge when we are in touch with the Supreme or Omnipresent Reality. To start with we have to understand the dualities that exist, life and non-life, the one and the many; knowledge and ignorance, time and timelessness. These dualities are aspects of the One Reality and are not opposites but complement one another. We have to also explore and understand all levels of consciousness, the mind, vital, physical, and lower and higher states, all the basic aspects of the world such as matter and evolving life. And we will be able to understand all this through an analysis of our various experiences, after we get in touch with our psychic self. Integral Knowledge thus is a knowledge of the One Reality in all its aspects.[43]

Sri Aurobindo explains that in the upper hemisphere there is sat-chit-ananda, in the lower is mind, the vital and matter, and between the two is the Supermind. Most theories of life can be summarized into four, the first being that only the Supreme is real, and the second that only matter is real. The third is more complex as it transcends the earth and sees that both the spirit and the different planes of life are real, but it is not able to explain the connections between these. Fourth, we have Sri Aurobindo's integral view that the individual, the universal and the transcendent are all real, and their connections and integration too are explained.[44]

Both involution and then evolution are part of life, as sat-chit-ananda is concealed in the universe and in the individual and can reveal itself, and the aim of life is to embody it in our daily life.

The evolutionary process of ascent and integration, begins with the conscious force, chit, that leads the upward awakening. As it evolves in matter moving upwards, it receives help from higher planes. This chit-force exists in every plane of life. Chit moves through the physical, vital and mental selves; limitations remain, but they can be removed by connecting to the psychic being within, and to the Supramental above. Science sees the outer forces in evolution, whereas Sri Aurobindo sees evolution occurring through this inner force.[45]

Thus, evolution occurs through simultaneous ascent and descent. It occurs because of the heightening of the cosmic force, i.e., chit. We are at present a half-animal humanity, and we will evolve towards a very different way of life, a spiritual consciousness. Sri Aurobindo presents seven types of ignorance that have to be transformed. First, there is Practical Ignorance: we don't know how to act or think rightly and use our mind and will as expressions of the Divine. We don't understand situations and reach wrong conclusions, leading to error, falsehood and various problems. Self-knowledge is the remedy for this and leads to our nature becoming luminous and divine. The second is Constitutional Ignorance, which is part of our own nature, our physical, vital and mental selves. We are concerned with daily life, our material existence, and what we understand through our senses. We have to grow towards other principles within us, of light, intuition and spirituality, and get an understanding of our true nature. We have to gradually overcome the vital and material aspects. The third is Psychological Ignorance, by which we are limited in our views and thoughts, not realizing that there are also occult and divine energies to access. We have to enter these higher aspects of ourselves, and also to understand our different levels of being, including the Subconscient, Intraconscient, Sircumconscient subliminal and Superconscient. The Subconscient has a hidden occult consciousness, with automatic responses, reflecting the lowest levels of the occult sense mind, which are more active in plants and animals. It also has within it, past impressions rejected by the conscious mind, which can reappear in sleep and dreams, or moments when one is unaware. These repressions can also occur as vital impulses, nervousness, imbalance or disease. It is expressed through thoughts, feelings and habits that refuse to change. When we view it from the Subliminal or Superconscient, we become aware of its different aspects and are able to change it. We can flood it with light and then gain control over its actions, which is an essential part of change and progress. The Subliminal is different. It is another aspect unknown to our surface consciousness, consisting of an inner and subtle intelligence of the mind, vital and physical. Its inner action creates our surface self. It has an 'enveloping consciousness' and receives energy from the universal mind. The Superconscient is beyond our present awareness. It includes higher mental levels, the Supramental and pure spiritual being.

The fourth ignorance is Temporal, the belief that we exist within time, and within the limitations of the body. We don't know the full nature of our past, our previous births or our future, and living within the limited present, we don't realize the eternal existence of our true self. To move beyond, we have to open to the subliminal and superconscient. The fifth ignorance is Egoistic: the Ego creates a limited self with a superficial identification with the body and mind. It separates itself from others, from the Divine, and from the highest self which has an essential unity with all. As we move upwards, the Ego becomes universal, with a cosmic consciousness. The sixth is Cosmic Ignorance, that is, ignorance of the true self and the eternal divine. Our true being is immortal and beyond the cosmos and as our knowledge grows, ignorance is replaced with the cosmic truth of sat or true being, by first reaching the psychic within. Original Ignorance, that is ignorance of the Absolute and of the origin of the universe, is the seventh, and has to be replaced with Truth and Integral Knowledge. When these seven ignorances are converted to a seven-fold knowledge, it leads to the establishment of divine life on earth.[46]

Rebirth and Karma

Sri Aurobindo goes on to comment on the three mysteries of the universe, birth, death and life. If we enter life with certain attributes, a certain nature, it is clear that we must have had a past life. In the Upanishads we come across the jiva and the atman, the individual and the universal soul, and Sri Aurobindo comments that Advaita too has the concept of rebirth, and of the individual self, the jivatman. He also identifies two souls, the incarnating soul and the eternal soul. The personal soul has to be reborn, as it begins in matter and ignorance, and then moves towards the light through successive births. It moves through physical, vital, mental and then higher levels. Rebirth is thus a spiritual journey, leading to spiritual evolution. Does the human soul evolve after inhabiting animal forms? And is the power to survive death only for humans? Sri Aurobindo states that the animal 'has some kind of soul formation which after death occupies other animal forms on earth and finally a human body'.[47] However, the animal soul may not be able to move to other planes of existence, as 'the animal's conscious invidualisation does not seem sufficient to bear such a transfer or to adapt itself to an other-worldly existence'.[48] The individual soul, he says, passes 'from form to form until it reaches the human level of manifested consciousness'.[49] Once it is firmly in a human body, can it regress? This would be unlikely but not impossible in certain cases. As he says, 'The movement of Nature is always sufficiently complex for us not to deny dogmatically such a possibility',[50] but usually the soul proceeds upwards.[51]

Our world is not the only one that exists. The Upanishads and even the Rig Veda refer to several worlds or planes of existence, and Sri Aurobindo begins with quotes from these texts. He explains that there are many different worlds and beings. He looks at other possibilities but concludes that as both involution and then evolution take place, and that there are different levels such as the Inconscient and Superconscient, there must also be higher planes of existence. In these, beings may exist in forms different from us, more subtle and less material. Beings of other worlds can influence us and can be positive or Asuric. At times humans can project themselves into these planes or can temporarily reside in them after the dissolution of the human body. As we reach or ascend to our highest selves, powers from these planes help us to ascend.[52]

What is the process of rebirth? Is there an interval between birth? How does the soul mutate in its passage from birth to birth? And how does this help in spiritual evolution? We can connect with these other spheres through our subliminal, and they must exist or the process from one body to the other would be continuous and would be confined to earth. After death the soul probably has to go to other spheres. It may be that all souls have this interregnum, or that there are two types, and that some immediately transmigrate.

Three aspects of life are the individual, the universal, and the transcendent. The universal precedes the individual. The nature of the individual and his progress would lead to different states after death or to rebirth. Sri Aurobindo also looks at contradictions in various beliefs, such as beliefs in heaven and hell.

The concept of karma is also linked with that of rebirth, and Sri Aurobindo provides a very important interpretation of it. As he explains, the theory of reincarnation usually has two aspects, metaphysical and moral. In the moral sphere, the nature of the soul and its incarnation is believed to be the result of good or bad actions in a previous life. Alternatively, a strong personal will or desire in the past life may lead to a new incarnation of a particular type. As he says, 'The inexorable rule of a tooth for a tooth is a frequent principle of the Karmic Law: for this Law is an arithmetician with his abacus as well as a judge with his code of penalties for long-past crimes and misdemeanours.'[53] He also points out that in this system, there are double punishments and rewards, first in hell or heaven, and then on earth. He adds, 'These are very summary popular notions and offer no foothold to the philosophical reason and no answer to a search for the true significance of life. A vast world-system which exists only as a convenience for turning endlessly on a wheel of Ignorance with no issue except a final chance of stepping out of it, is not a world with any real reason for existence. A world which serves only as a school of sin and virtue and consists of a system of rewards and whippings, does not make any better appeal to our intelligence. The soul or spirit within us, if it is divine, immortal or celestial, cannot be sent here solely to be put to school for this kind of crude and primitive moral education.'[54] There has to be a larger principle, a growth out of Ignorance towards Immortal consciousness. 'For such a spiritual growth, this law of Karma is all too puerile.' It is constructed by the 'smaller part of the human vital mind concerned with its petty rules of life and its desires and joys and sorrows and erecting their puny standards into the law and aim of the cosmos',[55] and has no relevance to the thinking mind.

At a higher level, though, aspects of the law of karma can be accepted, as all actions in nature yield results. It cannot, however, be the determinant of how the cosmos works, as it is not a mechanical system. There is not just nature and law, but a conscious spirit. Law and process affect the outer mind, life and body, and 'their mechanical power is absolute only over body and matter'.[56] Laws lose their rigidity in life, and more so in mind. The spirit within is not a slave of its past actions. If there are effects of past actions or lives, the psychic being must have approved of it, and it would be an expression of a 'secret Will and Guidance'.[57] Fate and destiny are complex. That which binds even our physical being, can do so as long as a greater law does not intervene. The law of karma is an over-simplification of the many aspects of life, involving not just actions but feelings, desires, love of beauty, pursuit of knowledge, etc. It can't be limited to a duality of good and evil. What about good and bad luck? Sri Aurobindo says, if we see a good person suffering here, 'it is difficult to believe that this paragon of virtue was in his last life a scoundrel' and is paying for some unknown sins. 'To saddle the new opposite personality with the rewards or punishments of the old looks like a purposeless and purely mechanical procedure'.[58] An ethical being, he says, does not require reward or punishment as such a system debases the ethical values of a good person, 'and turns virtue into selfishness'.[59] There may be a partial truth in the law of karma, but it is not meant as reward and punishment. 'Cosmic existence is not a vast administrative system of universal justice with a cosmic Law of recompense and retribution.'[60] The psychic being is moving towards divine wisdom, thus all experiences are a preparation for this.

Another common and erroneous concept is that the personality of today is the same as it was in the previous birth. This is not correct, as no spiritual growth can be attained by repeating the same character. Personality is only temporary, and in each life there is a new formation to provide for its growth. It may even be opposite to the previous one. Thus, a false importance is given to the memory of previous lives. If karma represented retribution, 'then there is evidently a great stupidity and injustice in denying to the mind in its new incarnation all memory of its past births and actions.'[61] As a new birth brings in a new personality for further growth, past memory is an obstacle.

Fragmentary recollections, and sometimes clear recollections, do remain. The psychic entity within represents the divine self, but the person we are is temporary. 'It is one step of the many steps of our evolutionary change, and it serves its true purpose only when we pass beyond it to a farther step leading nearer to a higher degree of consciousness and being.'[62] The outer personality could survive if it was close in nature to the inner mental and vital Purusha and also open to the infinite. These would remain in the subtle body after death, and then return in a new body. The physical body could survive if it kept pace with this, but 'true immortality would still be the eternity of the Spirit; the physical survival could only be relative, terminable at will, a temporal sign of the Spirit's victory here over Death and Matter.'[63]

Evolution

The spiritual evolution of consciousness in matter continues until the 'form can reveal the indwelling Spirit'.[64] Only a human can ascend to a higher spiritual level and reach the Supermind. Becoming aware of the limitations, a person can consciously move to a higher level. When he is in touch with the psychic being, he can reach spiritual and Supramental heights.

Evolution begins with an empty material existence, and then consciousness of mind slowly emerges and moves through various planes. Evolution occurs because of a previous involution, for if the principle of life was not already in matter, it could not have become animate. Life in matter could not begin to think, reason and feel, if the principle of mind was not already there.[65] And spirituality emerging in mind, is the sign of a power that already existed. Gradually it begins to see the soul as distinct from mind, life and body. The first step in the discovery of the spiritual self is to perceive an inner silence separate from the life movements. The next step is to be aware of this self and extend it into universality. The third step is to realize the Supramental.

In the past, Sri Aurobindo explains, four methods have been used to develop the spirit. The first is religion, which provides faith in a supreme being and in hidden aspects of life, but in actuality, its rules and laws are against the spirit, though in India, on the whole, many different paths are acceptable. Another method is occultism, the discovery of invisible powers and secret knowledge, which lead one on a spiritual path. A third method is that of spiritual philosophy, which provides an intellectual understanding of the divine spirit, through the power of the mind. A fourth way, which may be the most direct, is to aim to get spiritual experiences through meditation, prayer and other practices. This is the best way, even though the spirit is beyond experience. These methods help in spiritual realization, but actual realization can only take place when one is totally dedicated to attaining this realization.

Whether or not a person can reach any spiritual realization also depends on the nature of the aspirant, as those who aspire may be at different stages of development. For instance, the sage or seer lives in harmony, and has cultivated an inner stillness; this, along with flashes of intuition can lead to Supramental realization. The devotee aspires with self-surrender and love, while the saint is already in touch with the psychic being. Finally, the liberated person has realized the Self and the spirit within and acts according to it. In each of these broad categories there are many different stages and types.[66]

A conscious evolutionary change can be made through first getting in touch with the psychic self, and obtaining a different dimension to life, of harmony, universality and joy. Next there is a total spiritual transformation, with light descending on all aspects of the individual. Finally, there is a Supramental transformation of the entire being. With the Supramental transformation of even one person, the possibilities of a divine life on earth increase.

Sri Aurobindo elaborates on this triple transformation. As we contact the psychic, we begin to change. Contact is made with the levels of the spiritual mind, i.e., the higher mind, illumined mind and intuitive mind. The Overmind is next and has a universal sense of things, and finally there is the Supermind. We simultaneously have to move inwards, and open upwards towards higher spiritual planes. The Supramental can't be understood by the average person, one has to start from a different level and proceed step by step, till one reaches the Supermind at the highest level. Each spiritual level has a higher Knowledge, Energy and Consciousness, with the Supermind being supreme. The Supramental is a gnostic being who has integral truth knowledge, oneness, delight and freedom, and is in communication with the Divine. When many gnostic beings emerge, there would be a movement towards a collective gnostic life. In such a life there would be no suffering and no problems, and though differences would exist, there would not be divisions. Non-gnostics too could live together with gnostics, and all would be living a divine life. In the gnostic vision the inner, the outer, and the world, are all part of a whole and a world consciousness is attained, in which the individual and the world are interrelated. The gnostic individual knows the higher divine self, and lives and works for the divine purpose. The supreme spirit is reflected in all the actions of the gnostic, who is a Supramental being, a manifestation of the divine Shakti or world mother, and someone who can access all the planes of life, with power and influence over the physical, mental and vital planes of life. The universe exists in oneself, and when one is in touch with the Divine, the joy and delight of the fulfillment of purpose is within. The impersonal and the personal are the two selves of the individual, but in the Supramental, both coexist. The gnostic has a life of total freedom as ethics, dharma or religious rules and regulations cannot apply to him, but these are not necessary as he is guided by a true spirituality which permeates every aspect of the Self, and in every cell of the body. For the gnostic being, freedom and order are the same and there are no actions according to one's own desires.

It is the vital aspect of the person that connects with others and the Supramental person connects with love and joy. This experience of love and joy is a dynamic one, experienced through diversity and multiple connections. The gnostic or Supramental person would also become aware of the subconscient and its dual nature and light and consciousness would even flood the subconscient and transform the inconscient, despite its lifeless and ignorant nature.

Sri Aurobindo next categorizes people into five types: manners, a person who follows others and can't think for themselves; behaviour, someone acts on his own, but not in the right way; character, someone who has certain fixed qualities, and a greater sense of self; personality, who expresses his individuality, a pioneer and who meets challenges; and person, the true spiritual individual, the gnostic being.

Sri Aurobindo says that physical consciousness would change when the real or true ideas of the spirit, such as peace, harmony, truth and love reach it through the Superconscient. Acting on the body, the Supramental force would increase strength, health, delight and goodness. Guidance from the Subliminal would be more easily available, intuition would grow. The body would derive new and higher energy from the cosmic force, and soon the person would cease to identify with the body, even though the body is not to be discarded, but perfected.[67]

As people partially or wholly move into the gnostic consciousness, there will be a new way of living, a collective divine life. This will be a life of peace and harmony, free of sorrow and conflicts. The gnostic person would listen to truths revealed by other people, and not insist on his own view, the gnostic can lead and yet subordinate himself to the whole. It will be a life of diversity, and yet of Truth, Delight and Joy, and cannot be compared with our present existence. But this new world will be possible only when a substantial number of people reach the gnostic, Supramental level. In the course of evolution, Sri Aurobindo envisages such a future, but if enough individuals aspire to this divine life, the future could become the present.

7

The Synthesis of Yoga

The Life Divine provides a complete overview of what a life raised to the level of divinity would look like on earth and offers insights and guidance on attaining the Supramental self. It traces the journey of divine consciousness from its descent into matter to its ascent through humans, leading to the emergence of Supramental or gnostic beings who will dwell in this earthly paradise.

In comparison, *The Synthesis of Yoga* is a more complete account of possible methods to reach the Supramental through Integral Yoga, which synthesizes and moves beyond traditional practices. It also goes deep into ancient texts to understand the methods presented by them and to indicate where and how Aurobindo differs.

It was first serialized in *Arya* between 1914 and 1921. Some sections, i.e., Part 1 and some chapters of Part 2 were revised in the 1940s. Although the first section was published as a separate book in 1948, the entire work was only combined and published after his death in 1955.

The integrated book, along with his revisions, starts with an introduction that provides the conditions for the synthesis, followed by four sections: 'The Yoga of Divine Works'; 'The

Yoga of Integral Knowledge'; 'The Yoga of Divine Love'; and 'The Yoga of Self-perfection'.

Introduction

Sri Aurobindo asserts that all life, whether consciously, or subconsciously, is yoga.[1] Yoga signifies a union, specifically with the Divine, and all life inherently moves towards this union, irrespective of its awareness. When we examine systems of yoga, however, the concepts and methods we encounter are often compressed and narrow, highlighting the need for a wider synthesis that reunites god and nature in a perfected human being.

Using ancient texts, Sri Aurobindo refers to the body, which has emerged through evolution in nature, as 'the food sheath' – also known in the Sanskrit of the Upanishads and other texts as annamaya kosha. There are four more koshas, or sheaths, of the individual according to these texts: pranamaya, manomaya, vijnanamaya and anandamaya, meaning the breath or life, mind, wisdom and bliss sheaths or bodies. While Sri Aurobindo does not follow this classification precisely, he looks at three manifestations of nature that can be seen as progressive steps: the body, mind and spirit. Progressing through these steps can be called the 'triple birth'.[2] The body is linked with matter, but the mind has different aspects. Mind energy can change, rise to a higher level and reorganize itself. The spirit, the highest aspect, has 'self-existent perfection and immutable infinity'.[3] Nature exists in all these aspects, and the whole aim of the human being is to live in the best way possible. The mind, which seeks a poetical imagination of perfection, is restricted by the material world. Spiritual force, however, has no limits. The schools of Indian yoga seek individual liberation and, traditionally, the teacher passed on his knowledge to very few, but *The Synthesis of Yoga* has a more complete aim.

God, nature and the human soul, or in other words the transcendental, universal and individual have to unite to attain perfection in the world. This can be seen in the traditional yoga systems of devotion or bhakti, knowledge and works. He looks at the merits of some of the existing systems in ascending order. Hatha yoga, using asana and pranayama, seeks perfection of the body and vital. And raja yoga leads to overall development, with Samadhi as the goal. But the integrated triple yoga of works, knowledge and devotion, he says, is the best path.

Commenting on Ramakrishna Paramahamsa, who was in touch with the Divine and realized God through different religions, Sri Aurobindo affirms that such a person is unique, and the majority cannot do this. He points out that the integrated yoga he suggests is partially described in the system of Tantra, but not as it is popularly interpreted. In Tantra, Prakriti acts in the universe, whereas in all Vedantic systems it is the Purusha or conscious soul that acts and governs, with energy or Shakti as an illusory power. In the integral system, Purusha is the conscious soul with the nature of sat; Shakti or Prakriti has the nature of chit; and ananda as creator uses Tapas or the force of Purusha's consciousness to bring Truth and real ideas into the world. We can use the terms will and faith to explain these – a will that is based on knowledge, and a faith reflecting unrealized truths. There is nothing that is not divine, but there is a distinction in practice, as we have to move from the lower to the higher levels. We start from wherever we are, rejecting nothing in our being. Through the integral method, we can identify with the One being in all. The material life, too, is being divinized, and this method and goal transcends all religions.[4]

Part 1

The consecration and offering of all work to the divine is part of the Bhagavad Gita, as are the other two paths. But Aurobindo explains these more completely, linking them to form a whole. There are four aids, he says, on the path: a knowledge of the eternal truths that he refers to as shastra; patiently acting according to these truths through personal effort; raising knowledge and effort leading to spiritual experiences in which a guru can provide help; and *kala* or time, recognizing the cycles of action and divine movement.[5] Everything is already known – it only has to be revealed. Shastra usually refers to texts, but in Integral Yoga there is no fixed text. There can be general guidelines for the *sadhak*, but these are only signposts, a partial guide, not something to be rigidly followed. The ideal sadhak has a yearning for the Divine, but in addition, three successive stages can be discerned in Integral Yoga: there must be an effort to transcend oneself and contact the Divine, to receive the inputs from the divine source for our self-transformation and then to become a centre of the Divine on earth. As he puts in effort, the sadhak will find the divine force also working within him and, as he merges with it, his transformation takes place. Then the purified, illumined, liberated person becomes the means through which the supreme power descends.

Integral Yoga does not just seek the infinite, 'but we call upon the infinite to unfold himself in human life'.[6] The aspirant seeks through the inner guide. 'He has no method and every method', that is, anything the aspirant is capable of, through his own nature, can be used, as long as it is part of the aspiration for the highest goal. Finding the inner teacher is best, but there can be outer teachers and guides, as long as they do not pretend to be gurus. If the sadhak aims for this highest goal, time, life and death, have no meaning. Patience through lifetimes will ensure success.

All yoga is a new birth, as the person sets aside mundane concerns and moves towards the highest. There has to be a total self-consecration to achieve the desired end, the entire being has to be concentrated on the 'One who is the All'.[7] Time may be taken to arrive at this total concentration, either through the higher mind, or the inner heart, but it will be realized. At first, it will be through the lower element of desire, though this desire has to be transformed into desire for the highest. The yoga starts with an effort to see the Divine, not only in ourselves, rather in all things, beings, and events. The first step is to accept the One divine working in all. Gradually, the higher nature acts and then Shakti, or divine power, transforms the limited individual. To prepare for this, one must reject all that is not true, not part of the Divine. This is the process of consecration to the Divine, leading to the second stage of self-surrender to the highest. Sri Aurobindo refers to this as 'all comprehending absolute surrender'.[8] The two processes can overlap, though.

Integral Yoga has to be worked out in life. We have to dedicate our entire being to the Divine, which is greater than us, and work through the Divine, not through the Ego. This will speed up the process of the descent of the Divine on earth. Our capacities have to be surrendered 'into the hands of a greater power', so that the egoistic sense of being the doer disappears. Consecrating one's works and actions is a part of reaching the Divine, and the way for this has been described in the Gita. However, while karma yoga is perfectly described in the Gita, some of its aspects remain hidden, as they cannot be revealed to all. The Gita explains that performing actions without any desire for a reward is essential, but it does not mean we go on performing the usual actions; rather, as far as possible we contact the Divine within, focus on that with our mind and heart and then act according to the divine will. This is true freedom, as otherwise, actions are pushed by natural forces through a confused mind. Nature is both mechanical and free and, in ignorance, we are aware of the mechanical aspect. If the soul is embodied in Prakriti, it has the limitations and consciousness of the Ego. When it sees its oneness with all, in every situation equanimity arises. We have to act without ego or desire; however, the Gita does not aim only at 'a stoical fortitude or a religious resignation'.[9] Instead, it seeks something that will transform the individual, asserting that 'All action must be done in a more and more Godward and finally a god-possessed consciousness'.[10] But these are described in the Gita as equanimity, renunciation of desire for the fruits of one's work and action consecrated to the Lord.

More aspects of this path are explained in this section, along with how to guard against believing that a lower or intermediate consciousness, represents the highest. This yoga is undertaken only to unite with the Divine, and not to attain the Supermind or any type of power. The Supramental and Supermind is a far distant goal, though it is the ultimate one.[11]

Part 2

In the second section, Sri Aurobindo explains the path of Integral Knowledge. The path of knowledge is described in the Bhagavad Gita, and is the focus of the Upanishads, of the philosophical systems of Vedanta based on these, and particularly of Advaita. In the traditional systems, higher knowledge, jnana or vijnana, is arrived at through a process of discrimination, leading to the realization of an ultimate truth. Along with this is the concept that the ternal or bsolute is beyond the world, and the world has no relevance. The goal is moksha or nirvana. Sri Aurobindo points out that in the traditional view, jnana yoga, the union through jnana or knowledge, is attained by the intellect, but even the intellect is then transcended. 'The thinker in us separates himself from all the rest of what we phenomenally are, rejects the heart, draws back from the life and senses, separates from his body that he may arrive at his own exclusive fulfilment in that which is beyond even himself and his function.'[12] It thus rejects life in order to arrive at the peace and joy of the eternal.

The path of Integral Knowledge and its goal is different from the traditional path of knowledge. Only unconsciousness and ignorance are to be eliminated in this integral path. Ignorance includes the mechanical way of living and the false desires of the Ego. The right path of Integral Knowledge will reveal the joy of the infinite in the conscious self. Spiritual knowledge leads to the Divine. The universe and the individual are not what they seem to be to our ordinary vision. But the knowledge of truth consciousness reveals the light of reality of the true self. The Supreme, known as Brahman, is the one reality from which everything comes – Purusha and Prakriti, name and form, force and matter. Our own Supreme Self, and the Supreme existence that has become the universe are the same. The traditional path does not consider either the individual or the universe, and focuses on the transcendent, which is infinite and eternal. But in the integral way the consciousness of Brahman is within us, on earth, and the liberated soul, the *jivan mukta*, does not reject life.

Yogic knowledge takes us to a secret consciousness that normally remains concealed. We cannot know this through the senses or the body, or through the intellect. The intellect can reveal certain truths, but not the highest knowledge. Neither will it bring about a transformation of our selves. Right thought is an essential preliminary, but it has to be followed by vision, experience and realization.

Right thought and meditation will lead to the purification of the Self and then to a tranquil mind. It is only through self-knowledge, however, that we will understand and realize the true consciousness in ourselves. Self-knowledge is not merely an intellectual concept, though one can get an intellectual understanding. Self-knowledge requires actually seeing the inner self, an inner *drishti* or vision. At first the vision may be temporary or fleeting. Then once it occurs more frequently it can become permanent. The true self can also be experienced through Knowledge, Love, Delight, the body and vital elements. Vision and experience go together and culminate in identity. To realize the Transcendent is the status of knowledge required on this path. The first step towards it is a purification of the understanding, i.e., of the higher Buddhi, the higher intelligence. It is not intellectual thought that is the highest; instead, it is the one which comes from intuition, without interference from the senses. We have to learn to recognize true intuition descending from a higher level.

It is only when purity is established that one can proceed to the next step – of concentration. Raja yoga describes concentration too, though in Integral Yoga, the aim is not Samadhi. The aim is to reach the Transcendent, without excluding what it transcends.[13]

Renunciation is another step on this path, but in Integral Yoga renunciation is not because the world is unreal, or for personal salvation, or through weakness and disappointment or indifference to suffering humanity. Divine strength, courage, divine compassion and helpfulness are essential to Integral Yoga. Within it, renunciation is not of worldly existence or of life. It is an inward renunciation of attachment and desire. One has to end attachment to family, nation, work or whatever one sees as one's mission in life. This is not an ending of love, but of selfish love. Renunciation is only a step, through which we attain all.

In this path of knowledge, the world is real and the individual is real; however, we don't know the truth of either of them. We first must have a realization that the individual self is the same as the Divine, the 'I am That' of Vedanta, then next we will realize that the world too is That. To realize the true self, we must understand that the Self is not the body, life or mind. We have to reach a state of indifference to exhaustion, illness and death. Moderation is good, yet the food eaten is not as important. We have to also detach ourselves from the physical life energy, or prana, and from the activity in the mind, so that the mind, as a representative of Purusha, can affirm, 'I am not the Life; the Life is not the Self of the Purusha, it is only a working and only one working of Prakriti.'[14] Life has action and movement. It reaches out to draw satisfaction from what is around and this characteristic of life, of action, desire, liking and disliking, are part of nature. Our motives are formed by desire, and in the emotional mind we live in the confusion of joy and grief, anger, fear and other emotions. On the divine path we have to step back from this, and discover the real soul, the psychic, which has pure love, joy and luminosity. The thought-mind needs to delight in knowledge and be open to illumination. We have to detach ourselves from our heart and mind, and from the Ego as a whole.

The discriminatory path of knowledge implies withdrawing from everything that is not eternal, removing the false idea of the Self, and seeking the true, eternal self. We use this knowledge to understand the universe and ourself. As Sri Aurobindo says, 'It is the science of Yoga to know, and the art of Yoga to be unified with the highest.'[15] Thus, using knowledge is one aspect of the unification and realization of the higher self. Knowledge is also of the essential principles of being, of sat-chit-ananda, of the truth of our being. If we mentally seek to realize sat-chit-ananda, it seems very far away, very difficult. The mind can be aware of it, but it is beyond us. And even if we have a vision of it, it is beyond our reach. With a supreme effort, as in raja yoga, we can see it in a state of Samadhi, but then the individual consciousness has itself vanished. In Integral Yoga, the mind itself has to be divinized, not abolished. As one ascends to gnosis, the soul is elevated in a glory of light and bliss and power. Sri Aurobindo also explains Samadhi, raja yoga and hatha yoga, and says the methods can be used at times while practising Integral Yoga but are not indispensable.[16]

Part 3

The third aspect of the triple path of Integral Yoga is divine love. Life begins with action and proceeds towards knowledge. When our will and work find their unity and origin in the omnipresent, love is the next step. 'Knowledge is the action of the consciousness, the light by which it knows itself.'[17] The height of knowledge leads to a love of the Divine, and thus the three aspects are united. In the union of these three powers lies the base for self-perfection and true bhakti is when external worship changes into inner love for the Divine. When the Supreme is reached, action proceeds from the power of knowledge and from 'the outpouring of love'.[18] Devotion and worship is common in religion, though it usually arises from the mixed motives of desire and fear. But there is also a bhakti yoga, in which the emotions which have transcended these elemental feelings are used to reach the Divine. Even if one begins with fear and awe, a concept of ethics develops which leads to right and pure action. Then a love emerges, for the one who directs our works. As one moves closer to divine love, the original fear vanishes.

The universal will, the Transcendent, proceeds according to its aim and is not deflected by egoistic prayers. Yet there is no mechanical law, and crude prayers are also part of will, aspiration and faith that help to bring one closer to the Divine. Prayer helps to prepare one for the higher level of devotion, and in adoration of the Divine, even in its beginning stages, there is an aspect of consecration. Works and knowledge too are offered to the Divine, but it is the consecration of love, rather than an understanding of the divine will. Bhakti can result in a focus on the Divine, neglecting all else. An ascetic path, or in its wider aspect of Integral Yoga, is a consecration of all aspects of the Self – all action and all knowledge. With intense devotion, one sees the Divine everywhere, leading to universal love. The most beautiful art and literature result from bhakti. But when it comes to bhakti, it is difficult to love an impersonal divine, so a divine personality is chosen, but both are aspects of the one. The divine can be represented in an idea or a person. He is each deity separately, and all of them together.

Yoga is the union of the soul with the immortal. Through Integral Yoga, we are united with sat-chit-ananda, Being, Consciousness and Delight. And Delight has the power of love, and the joy contained in love presents itself through a vision of beauty. In the bhakti of Integral Yoga, the deity has to be universalized, to be seen everywhere. He is in nature, he is in every being, in every object. This leads, at its highest, to 'a supra-cosmic union'.[19]

Part 4

In the last part, 'The Yoga of Self-perfection', the three paths are integrated, and a synthesis of yoga is provided, in which different aspects are combined. Hatha yoga focuses on the body and breath, raja yoga reaches heights through the mind. The discipline of Tantra itself provides some kind of a synthesis, as it shows there are two poles of existence, Brahman and Shakti, spirit and nature, and in their union, there is a heightened spirituality. The yoga of Tantra is not just of liberation, though that is the final aim. There is also enjoyment and perfection, power, light and joy in human existence. The synthesis 'starts from the method of Vedanta to arrive at the aim of Tantra'.[20] Tantra also focuses on the six lotuses chakras and the perfection of the individual. According to tradition, the chakras are the main invisible energy centres of the body.

The Integral Yoga thus focuses on perfection of all aspects of the individual, with a higher spiritual aim. In the first stage, the movement towards perfection is through effort. In the second stage, one allows the Divine to act through oneself. The individual who has divine self-perfection has a divine nature, though this develops gradually, with just hints of divinity in the beginning. Supermind, mind, life and body are the four instruments leading one towards perfection.[21] Supermind is spiritual consciousness, with self-luminous knowledge, power, energy and joy. Mind is partial and limited, even though the Supermind supports it, while life is an energy of the spirit, subordinate to mind and body, and an intermediary between mind and matter. Purusha or soul is the spirit, aware of the workings of nature, and nature too is a power of the spirit, the same as Prakriti, Maya and Shakti. Purusha is both individual and universal, and the universal Purusha is the Divine and can dwell in any of the higher planes, sat, chit or ananda, or in the Supermind. But the normal individual lives in a lower hemisphere, and there is a veil between the upper and lower planes. To cross this veil, one must become the highest possible, in the mental, vital and physical nature, by totally purifying the lower mentality. The Buddhi, or intelligence, is the highest aspect of the mind and also directs the higher will.[22] Once these are purified, it is easy to proceed. Within the *antahkarana* or the inner self, the psychic prana presents the psycho-physical basis for enjoyment, which has to be raised to the higher level of ananda or Delight, by ending vital desire, the root of sorrow and affliction. Sri Aurobindo explains that one has to distinguish between will and desire. There is a will to delight, which will lead to pure motivation, but desire is the craving of the mind and body, and the prana of desire has to therefore turn into that of will. Prana here can be interpreted as essence. However, desire cannot just be eliminated, leading to indifference or a peaceful impartiality, and Integral perfection neither shuns love, nor the movements of delight.[23] As he says, the purified heart has no anger, fear or hatred; instead it has universal love, and can appreciate the delights of the world without desire.[24]

Within what we refer to as 'mind', is the *manas* or sense mind, and the Buddhi, which has a higher intelligence and will. But to purify the Buddhi, we must first understand it. The Buddhi is the instrument of the soul, the Purusha, but is only partially developed within us. Gradually, the Buddhi has to detach itself from lower suggestions, and move towards truth, light, goodness, strength and purity, reflecting the spirit and self. The beginning is establishing a calm peaceful mind, without the circular and repetitive thought mind. Creation, action and will become its motive, and it accesses changing aspects of truth. It moves further into a higher, self-existent, truth and knowledge. It begins to reflect truth, but to actually access the Truth, one must go beyond it. One cannot rise into divine knowledge immediately. The process has to be gradual, or one would overshoot the mark, 'breaking or slipping through the gates of the Sun, *suryasya dvara*, without near possibility of return.'[25]

The mental being, the psychic prana, the physical prana and body, all have to be purified – that is the basis and ground for liberation. But as one rises from the lower being, the first tendency is towards inaction, as sattva gets rid of rajas, through the aid of an enlightened tamas. These are the three gunas of Samkhya philosophy. Such people have a rich inner life but are either inactive or ineffective outwardly.[26] In the higher being, the three gunas actually represent divine powers. Tamas, instead of being seen as the darkness of inertia, is equanimity in the face of all upheavals; rajas becomes perfect Shakti and will; and sattva, the self-existent light of the Divine. When the Self is purified, divine action begins to operate and a sense of samata or equality, emerges, which sees Brahman as the self of all. Next, all parts of the human nature have to be raised to the highest that they are capable of. In practical terms, these are the understanding, heart, prana and body. In addition is the dynamic force or *virya* of the temperament, and the *svabhava* or characteristics of the soul nature. The perfected person then has to call on divine shakti, to replace human energy with that of the Divine. Further, the ordinary mental being has to rise to the level of the gnostic being. Gnosis or vijnana, itself has several gradations, which proceed towards ananda. Gradually, the light converts even our lowest aspects into the highest. Siddhis' special powers may appear, but they are not indispensable. 'The siddha or perfected soul will live in union with the Purushottama'[27] and will be conscious of Brahman, who is in all, and will see the universe as the manifestation of Brahman. The perfected soul dwells in the light of the Divine.

To get the essential state of samata or equality, the emotional and vital being has to be conquered. The thinking mind and the entire ignorant nature has to be regulated. There are two actions of equality. One is a passive acceptance, the other a higher understanding of the divine element in what is taking place. Withdrawal, and even understanding, are not enough, but rather the attitude should be to accept and perform the smallest work allotted by the Divine, without any egoistic desire. The higher person can also act through his own creative force, 'because by its detached and yet intimate acceptance it carries into both an infinite calm, knowledge, will and power'.[28] The sadhak must have self-surrender, which is not the same as indifference or quiescence. The Buddhi can learn to deal with disturbances, though once the higher self takes over, there is none. Calm must be pervasive in all states, in pleasure and pain, health and disease, failure and success, praise and blame. As the calm persists, the vital and mental lose the force of desire.[29] Purified of defects, the mind, life and body is capable of greater action.

After establishing the principle of equality or equanimity, one has to move on to right Shakti, or the right use of the powers of the intelligence, vital mind, heart and body. The first step is controlling the body and life by mind and its power of thought, and in succeeding steps, mind is replaced by spirit, the Supermind and the Supramental force. The body too has to be prepared for this, so that it can suddenly take in a great force without breaking. Pranic Shakti has to be developed, not just by systems such as hatha yoga, but also by invoking a higher force. Desires should not be sought after; yet they will be fulfilled in the right way, and there will be an enjoyment, which has spiritual bliss as its essence. Next *chitta*, or conscious force, needs to be perfected, through which a calm and non-egoistic power develops. The third step is faith in the heart, belief in a universal good, and openness to ananda. Finally, the perfection of Buddhi, the intelligent thinking mind, is required.

With these efforts the psycho-physical self is perfected, ready for the divine force or Shakti. The soul and nature, also referred to as Purusha and Prakriti, work together in humans. But the Shakti of Ishvara is the force behind this, supporting the reason, mind, life and body. Depending on the nature of the person, and the predominance of one of the three gunas, the divine power will manifest differently.

The divine shakti is a power beyond time. It is the power that acts within us, initially through the Ego. Whether predominantly sattvic, rajasic or tamasic, Ego is essential in the lower levels of our development, but as we ascend higher, it has to be eliminated. A sense of oneness develops, and the Ego diminishes as the divine shakti acts, gradually bringing perfection. The individual doer disappears, even though thoughts and actions continue through the Shakti. The jiva or individual can even become one with the Shakti. In the third stage, the Ishvara, the power of God, manifests in the jiva, and the distinction between the Ishvara and Shakti disappears. The divine acts within us, and the joy of the spirit is realized. It is only faith or *shraddha*, that is accompanied by self-surrender, that can bring about this transformation.

Integral Yoga intends to raise the human to the Supramental and perfecting the various aspects of oneself is a preliminary step. Does the divine act through the purified mind? The perfected human in fact, has to rise beyond the mind, reaching some level of Supermind. In the Supermind, all knowledge is through identity and oneness. Such knowledge, being real, is total and universal and has a transcendental vision, and the Supermind has a direct consciousness of the truth of the universe. All realities are revealed through a luminous consciousness. The Supramental nature is harmonious, with the divine spirit infusing Will, Knowledge and Power. The Supermind sees the past, present and future as an indivisible movement, and is aware of all three. But there is a difference between the Supermind that can be attained by Ishvara, and that which the jiva can reach. There are grades of ascension, and the jiva starts with lower grades.

Can one silence the mind and allow the Divine to work? It is good to know how to silence the mind, but the Supramental will not immediately replace the lower mind and reason. The inferior mentality still has to be transformed. There are different ways to move closer to the Divine, through bhakti in the heart centre, to the centre above the *sahasrara* chakra, and through raising one's intellect to a higher level.

Sri Aurobindo explains and analyses the stages of growth on the path to the Supermind. The intuitive mind is higher than the mind, revealing some Supramental truths. Intuitive discrimination has to function along with a suggestive intuition, to avoid errors. Inspiration and revelation are also part of intuition and are the two higher aspects of intuition. The intuitive mind receives the knowledge of the Supermind through these four powers and transmits it and though a universal mentality and luminosity develop, the development through intuition is usually in a confused way.

The intuitive mind then proceeds a step higher to that of Supramental reason. Thought is now formed above the mind, and there is a different quality of will and knowledge, but this higher reason, is still operating through the mind. The mental, vital and physical, after purification have to be Supramentalized, only then can Supramental reason start the process of this transformation.

The mind then actually begins to act from a secret Supermind, but it must be prepared, calm and open to receive the suggestions of the Supermind, otherwise causing disturbance and collapse. A genius, saint, mystic or artist reflect a one-sided development through the Supermind, but an integral and harmonious development is necessary. Supramental knowledge is conveyed through an identity with it, rather than via thought and, at the highest level, the knower, the known and the knowledge are the same. It can also be revealed through a vision, or through words, as one gradually proceeds to the Supermind and an identity with the Supramental. The Supramental has supreme knowledge of this and other worlds. The person who has raised themselves to the level of the Supramental can act in the world but is totally transformed, with even every aspect of the senses revealing their deeper and hidden aspects.

Summarizing the whole movement towards perfection, Sri Aurobindo says that one sees the eternal as beyond time, but in the Supramental there are three types of time-vision. There is, of course, an eternity that is not bound by time. There is also a vision of the past, present and future, and of these three aspects of time as a whole. Thus, we move forward, through the preparation of the body, mind and senses, the heart, psychic self, intuition and other aspects, towards a Supramental being in a luminous world.[30]

8

Savitri

> 'Let a great word be spoken from the heights,
> and one great act unlock the doors of fate.'
>
> Book 3, Canto 4

Savitri, based on a story from the Mahabharata, is perhaps Sri Aurobindo's greatest work, and the one closest to his heart. Continuously refining it until his final days, Sri Aurobindo regarded it not only as a story of love triumphing over death but also as a symbolic myth. As per the Mahabharata, Savitri, the daughter of Aswapati, falls deeply in love with Satyavan, the son of Dyumatsena. Despite the prediction that Satyavan will die within a year, she marries him. After his inevitable death, she confronts the god of death, Yama, who ultimately restores Satyavan to life.

In his version of the story, Sri Aurobindo provides the symbolic meaning of each character. Satyavan represents the soul containing the ultimate truth, 'but descended into the grip of death and ignorance'. Savitri is the divine word, goddess of truth, who descends to save the world; Aswapati is the Lord of *tapasya*, the concentrated energy required for spiritual endeavour; Dyumatsena is the divine mind which has 'fallen blind'. The characters represent incarnations or emanations of conscious forces.[1]

When Sri Aurobindo first composed *Savitri*, it was a short text. However, he later expanded it multiple times, describing it as a reflection of his inner consciousness and 'a means of ascension'.[2] While large parts of *The Life Divine* and *The Synthesis of Yoga* were written before 1920, he continued writing and revising *Savitri* in his last years, lending it a special significance. In 1936, when asked for the reason, he replied, 'It is very simple. I used *Savitri* as a means of ascension. I began with it on a certain mental level, each time I could reach a higher level, I rewrote from that level.'[3] The first, a much shorter version, was in fact written even before the Mother had settled in Pondicherry. In addition to what he had written at the beginning of the text, he explained that *Savitri* represents an incarnation of the divine Mother. In its revised form, he said, it is a poetry deeply influenced by the Overmind, which is higher than the normal mind.[4]

Nonetheless, the Book of Death and Epilogue were never revised and, by early November 1950, he considered the work finished. The final version comes to around 24,000 lines in verse. To go through it, even by reading a few lines at a time, is to follow Sri Aurobindo on his spiritual journey, which culminated in a vision of the future. The path is not easy or straightforward, moving through different realms, many levels of existence, joy and sorrow, shadow and light. All kinds of beings appear on the way that may have a certain reality or are entirely symbolic. And despite the summary below, one cannot simply read through *Savitri* and expect to arrive at an understanding of the perilous journey. Each part has to be carefully read and meditated upon, and the summary merely offers cues towards it.

Part 1

Book 1: The Book of Beginnings

The first line of this epic poem is 'It was the hour before the Gods awake'. It describes a state of nothingness, the state that must exist in pralaya. Everything is contained in it, yet it is silent an 'unlit temple of eternity'. Then, a movement begins, something stirs, there is a desire, but the aim is not clear. There is a thought, a memory, a hope, as a spark of eternity stirs the darkness and then withdraws. But, 'A sacred yearning lingered in its trace, The worship of a presence and a power.'

The Divine withdraws; gradually, the world and life, with their grief and ignorance, come into existence. Then Savitri is born, and she is unlike others on this earth, who are caught up in the pursuit of temporary pleasures. Within her is 'The calm delight that weds one soul to all, The key to the flaming doors of ecstasy'. Yet the earth rejects Savitri's gift; the Light and the Truth are too difficult to bear and thus her light too is dimmed and hidden, though never lost.

The second canto takes a leap into the future, when Satyavan dies. Savitri's inner thoughts move through her past lives, and then to this life, her childhood and youth, and finally the joy of love, and how after 'twelve passionate months', the day of fate arrives. This is the destiny of the past, though somehow Savitri has to use her inner force to dislodge it. She has to face the universe, reshape her fate, and affirm that she has the right not only to live, but also to love. She has to gaze into the void where there is the loneliness of 'Immortal Death'. The entirety of life provided a background to her present state, but she is someone with such sincerity, compassion and love, that 'The whole world could take refuge in her single heart.' The godhead could dwell within her, in whom there is light, stillness and peace, strength and the silence of the gods.

She was a joyful person during her youth, until darkness came upon her so that she could fulfil the reason for her existence. To one who tries to move upwards towards the Light, pain may stop them, or joy may lead them on a different path, or even a dark power can prevent them, but there was a force in Savitri that could transcend it all.[5]

The third long canto begins with how and why Savitri was born. The earth requires Savitri, and therefore her 'radiant power' descended on earth. Her descent is because of her father Aswapati, who had ascended to the level where he could see the whole cosmos. The 'flame of god', the divine spirit that dwells in each person, is described, and the journey of the soul is traced from the first life form to the time it is part of a human being, and further to a recognition of the Divine within and without. As the text says, 'And in the worm foresees the coming god'. We also find here a mention of the 'Oversoul'. As the eternal light enters Aswapati's heart, his thoughts expand into infinity, and 'His soul breaks out to join the Oversoul'. Divine creative Power enters him and is reflected through his life. Still, he continues his search, 'for something or someone never found'.

The embodied soul passes through the struggles of life. As it begins to glimpse the Divine there are moments of insight and peace, visions of other realms, but it is a long journey. Slowly, light enters the limited mind, and there is an experience of infinity. As Aswapati grows into this 'larger self', there are many changes, miracles become normal, hidden worlds are seen, divine sounds are heard. He touches the Subconscient too, where 'primal ignorance' can be found. Even visions and dreams are symbols, cues to that path.

Dualism also finds mention here in 'the kings of evil and the kings of good' and also 'the gods of light and titans of the dark'. There is danger, but he passes through it and arrives at 'a silent self' and 'a nameless vast' where there is no duality or differences, love prevails and the conflicting thoughts and struggles of the world have ended. The soul is now free, both witness and king, beyond thought, and has experienced the Superconscient level of peace. These states are initially temporary, but they exist for longer periods, and a sudden ray of joy, light and vision can be experienced. Then his soul is released from ignorance, and through him, a power works in the universe.[6]

Within us, is always 'a magic key' or a 'timeless light' that is aware of life's goals even if we are not conscious of this. But unless we look within, life seems to have no goal, and life on earth appears to be just an accident: 'A net of death in which by chance we live.'

At times, a vision is glimpsed, of power, strength and joy, providing hope. Everything that happens here is part of a plan, taking place through unknown laws. Focused on the external, we do not realize what is within and cannot understand the 'cosmic will'. Only the immortals, beyond time, space and thought know this. Eventually, the truth and light of spirituality shall enter the heart on earth. Then life takes on a different meaning, though initially, the conscious self will not know how to access or use this, and the light may be filtered and distorted. Those who know it live in 'self-knowledge and power'. They are beyond grief, as well as the good and evil of the world, and have nothing to attain. They do not respond to ignorant prayers or cries, yet without them, nothing would exist, and the unseen presence is everywhere. Within the world two aspects are described – male and female, a reference to Purusha and Prakriti, albeit without any mention of the terms, or 'He moves there as the soul, as nature she'. He withdraws his own omnipotence, and focuses on making her great, supporting both the world and her; even so, his actions are shaped by her. She, the world-nature, seems capricious and he is dependent on her. Nevertheless, the Divine is within nature. The Absolute and perfect One has created millions and dwells in all, so that each one may reach his stature and divinity. He is Truth, yet he seeks Truth. 'He is the Thinker who has become the Thought', and the many who is One. It is the spirit, seeking to realize itself through matter. Just like a boat clings to the shores at first, then journeys further, finding unfamiliar coasts and lands and then crosses the last lands and ultimate seas, the same way the soul finally turns to the eternal. Even with his mortal eyes, he looks into eyes that see eternity. There is a new vision, as he moves through a world of thought that exists in matter, to a spiritual sun. Sailing through life and death, and life beyond, through waking and sleep, he has left infinity behind to bring the truth-light to earth.[7]

Canto 5, ending the first Book of the text, begins with the line: 'This knowledge first he had of time-born men', indicating that the knowledge was first introduced to him by a person. He then describes the 'occult cave' within, with all the mysteries it encloses, a place of magic containing everything known by the gods, including the secrets of numbers and symbols, of metres, along with the 'Vedic truth' and 'the secret code of the history of the world'. It was through this he could understand the nature of the universe, and of life's place in it. And it would enable one to understand life, death, the spirituality contained in matter and the ultimate infinity. He gets imperfect glimpses through the chaos that exists but finds no perfect answers. Nevertheless, he can change and even recreate himself, moving towards the Truth of the eternal spirit. Retiring from all he had done or 'Silence was his sole companion left'. Then, a universal life and force enter him, along with a 'nameless joy'. Only one among many thousands can move upward like this, and as a power moves down through him, and through an 'omniscient knowing, without sight or thought', a new self emerges. He is no longer bound by laws or protected against the forces of the universe. Everything is uncovered and known. The outer world seems solid, but there is something else behind it, and the hidden power, harnessed by the mind, could change earth's laws. In those secret regions, 'She meditates upon mighty words and looks / On the unseen links that join the parted spheres. / Thence to the initiate who observes her laws / She brings the light of her mysterious realms.' The Superconscient is also mentioned as something miraculous, beyond normal laws.

Therefore 'he', the male principle, reflects the concrete world and 'she' the creative power. This creative power can also be evil and dangerous, but she now surrenders to the Supreme. The invisible begins to be visible, the 'Oversoul' can be seen, with forms 'projected from the Unknowable.' The universe that we see hides many secrets and an eternal mystery and there is a descent from the eternal into Time, and then a return journey, 'Up a golden ladder carrying the soul.' Then a world is seen, where all worlds meet, and there is neither night nor slee A glimmer of eternity was then restored to earth, where there is 'A deep spiritual cry in all that is'. Thus, through unknown paths, 'He broke into another space and Time.'[8]

Book 2: The Book of the Traveller of the Worlds

The second book starts with the following lines: 'Alone he moved watched by the infinity / Around him and the Unknowable above.' Things that cannot be seen by mortal eyes became visible, the continuous self-creation, immortal thoughts and words that were silent again emerge, and the eternal stillness rejoiced in the workings of the universal power. Whether there is pleasure or pain, it is all according to a plan. A thousand realms and a thousand expressions of the One were known, as well as many strange occult and rare elements. The way to the infinite appeared like a temple tower that led to heaven, and eternal silences revealed worlds and heavens, as his soul was drawn by an invisible magnet to ascend.[9]

In his secret self he finds a light through which immaterial things could be seen, as he entered the kingdom of subtle matter. Here all things were true and beautiful; here was the shining origin of the earth nature. Perfect plans and distant outcomes were seen in advance; also, there was much there that we can never dream of, which have 'no earthly counterpart'. Matter and soul are joined together, and even the higher and lower worlds. The spirit outlasts death and birth and is beyond change and time. It is 'more real than this grosser frame' and takes the soul to higher worlds. Before the earth began, the secret spirit already existed, it pervades everything, and even 'invests with grace the demon and the snake.' It is in everything, even in our 'fallen strengths', thoughts, and body's reflexes. The Divine is concealed in the world, but then, in the apparently meaningless void, a Being awoke. In earth, there was 'a subconscient yearning memory', which forced creation. Thus, man was given this stupendous task of living a difficult life in the field of death, and yet fixing the eternal here, recovering lost words, and bringing through glimpses of beauty and thoughts from the eternal. The divine idea is immortal and immaculate, and only when we have gone beyond ourselves does 'a line of the transcendent' meet us, connecting with the Divine. The imperfect earth is our sphere, but 'the mortal body becomes godhead's robe'. We can look beyond the mind and communicate with greater things, with 'brighter earths and wider heavens'. Some aspect, some vision, rapture, beauty and light come down to us. There are worlds nearer to those absolute realms, where 'love and sweetness are the law of life'. We draw closer to this, following the signs and guides of beauty, love and happiness. We evolve through many stumbles, with brief visions of light, yet the full vision remains behind a veil. A perfect realm beyond our own is described next, where there is a perfection of beauty and form, no fear, grief, fault or error, no 'futile effort's broken heart'. It was a divine yet kindred world, deathless, but still limited. The vast desires, heights, and shadows were forgotten, there were no perils. At the same time there were no vistas or mighty dreams. He spent a short hour of bliss, which it could not satisfy him and, thus, he moved onwards.[10]

Aswapati continued to ascend, crossing 'the limits of embodied mind', and next he entered a world of doubt and struggle. At every step, he wrongly assumed he was nearer to the goal. In this region, life, referred to as she, is 'the manifest incalculable'. She accepts disaster, suffering, sin and fall, danger and discovery. She represents 'The hazard of a seeking ignorant Force / That tries all truths and, finding none supreme, / Moves on unsatisfied, unsure of its end.' Life proceeded in an inconsequential way, based on inner thoughts, sometimes uplifted, sometimes fallen, at times a powerful ruler, at other times drowning in sorrow and grief. 'Or she lingered tied to an inadequate joy / Missing the turns of fate, missing life's goal.' A scene was planned for every mood, and everything that happened, even grief, was of her own choice. 'Yet pure and bright from the Timeless was her birth', and suddenly, 'the antique face of joy' was revealed. Now he once again has hope of a different life beyond grief, and saw a world of beauty, beyond death and time. Glimpses of blissful eternal worlds could be recalled. A divide was crossed, and dreams took the shape of reality. The world force had come down to earth, but she, the force, acts capriciously, while his wisdom steadies her. 'His timeless still immutability / Must standardize her creation's immutability.' this is again a reference to Purusha and Prakriti She sees the Light by flashes, and it is her will that brings down the Supermind, her force feels, but does not know, and the power of the Supermind guides her. Yet it is a hazardous movement upward. A movement or passion of inviolate purity, broke through, bringing a ray of bliss. Sri Aurobindo adds, that if the earth was pure, these joys would be here, but the earth's dreams were still contained in matter. There were other beings, including 'Immortal figures of embodied joy'. Love's sweetness was appealed to, and it descended to include everyone in its embrace. There were worlds of great happiness. No one aged, and there was universal love and peace. Her luminous heart was her only guide, and she could build any number of Edens. Each act was perfect and joyful, but though he saw this world of Bliss, he could not enter it, as 'A darker air still encircled his soul', and he lived too close to suffering worlds. The transformation of the world could not take place yet.[11]

The next canto describes how Life, the feminine energy, meets and enters matter, and how Aswapati follows the course of this journey. An uncertain world was born. Memories and hope arose, to fill that 'aching gap' between earth's pain and the remembrance of the Bliss of life's origin. A power had touched the world, and now he could no longer move on the earth like the happy and unmoved flowers and trees, or the animals who soon forget pain. 'The animal's thoughtless joy is left behind. / Care and reflection burden his daily walk; / He has risen to greatness and to discontent.' The earth and matter can sense the new dimension in him. Now power and energy arose in him, but the aim was not clear. This power and energy is represented as 'she'. In her was instinct, the seeds of hope, and a tireless search. At first, there was the worship of 'dim dwarf gods' with ignorant priests. Moving on, she conquers earth and claims the heavens, but even so there is no transformation. She begins with ignorance, acquires knowledge, but does not find wisdom. She continues 'Fumbling through fog in search of Paradise.' In this slow upward advance, he has to follow her pace, and look at the subconscious beginnings, 'far away from Truth and luminous thought'. There he saw 'the original seat' of the deformed and suffering power. As she first emerged, 'darkness clung to her.' In the dark mists of space, a formless mind sought 'a body to translate its soul'. But, struggling in the void, he could hardly live. Then mind flickered and random energies grew in an anarchic world. Efforts seemed meaningless, there was 'suffering and a grey unease'. Yet his 'spirit's wakened eye' saw a purpose and 'the secret crawl of consciousness to light' began.

There is a veiled reference to sex, when 'the mystic presence' 'Asks from the body the soul's intimacies / And by the swift vibration of a nerve / Links its mechanic throbs to light and love.' The flame of truth is behind everything but is disguised as feelings and desires. Beings are born in time, from eternal Bliss. The ecstasy of the infinite is behind all actions, but momentary delight ends in failure, and 'a dark and evil start' is like a ghost, pursuing all we do. But Life had plunged into the dark void, 'Carrying with it its triple mystic cross'. Only gradually a struggling energy could emerge, first through insects, reptiles and animals, while so many lives perished without trace. There was a half-conscious force, a dark, crude rapture, without spiritual form. Then there was 'a third creation', a mind with a glimmer of light, an evolution from below with 'a masked intervention from above'. The power moved, building a wall against death and a bride to eternity. 'A thinking entity appeared in space' and a small, ordered world emerged, where there was scope to act, but as if in a prison. It could have a little joy and knowledge but could not reach the unseen. It could think and plan 'But for small aims within a narrow scope.' Its power was limited, and there was no glimpse of the vast spirit, but through a confused self-search, the mind gained clarity, and a small light was born within a great darkness.[12]

This small life had a rigid form, protected by ignorance. Aswapati saw it but tried to look beyond at the source. Here 'little deities' 'work remote from Heaven's controlling eye'. These elementals, imps, sprites, genii etc. are ignorant and dangerous, yet they have power. They curse joy with sorrow, turn truth to 'falsehoods ends', corrupt everything and make knowledge a poison, and virtue a dull pattern. They extend their reign to all half-conscious worlds and people. The Life Supreme is far away, but though it can't be seen, God's action and will are everywhere, and even the Inconscient works according to 'God's intelligence'. But Consciousness and Bliss remained hidden. Scattered worlds and stars were created. Next Sri Aurobindo speaks of wave-particles, atoms and photons, for instance, 'Light flung the photon's swift revealing spark', indicating his awareness of scientific developments. Looking at the world through ignorance, Aswapati sees it as Maya. Returning again to the growth of life, Sri Aurobindo explains that gradually, matter became conscious. 'A serpent Power twinned the insensible Force', and gradually there was the beginnings of life, which 'followed Matter's law', but became aware of something more. Very gradually, Spirit grew in matter, and sense, thought, brain and nerve, emerged. A heart's love and the soul's witness entered the body. The animal self was happy to live for a while, even if death followed. Then came the human with a 'thinking mind', but still half developed. There was a temporary beauty, human love that could not last, and hopes that faded. Inner meanings and the greater light, remain unknown. This stage is compared to that of a 'thinking puppet' or a 'conscious doll', pushed this way and that. 'Unwillingly they serve a mightier Power / Ananke's engines recognized Chance.'[13] This continues 'as long as the human animal is lord', with earthly desires, cares, griefs and pleasures. He dreams, but 'sees the Dionysian gesture pass'. There are small pleasures and friendships, love and hate. The conflict and pettiness of daily life are described, as very few can 'climb to a greater life'. But there is 'a bliss that sleeps in all things', and at times this breaks through 'in a small joy of life', which reconciles him with his small life and small world. He plays a trivial part in life, walking through 'an ignorant dream'. There are speculations in science, maths, reason and thought, while religion 'presents its dubious riches to our hearts'. But this is a provisional scheme, a first experiment. A witness soul awakes then and gazes into the unseen. It searches for the unknown guide and self. A deeper mystery, a secret sweetness, an unknown bliss is behind these apparently small lives. When the greater self comes down, all is transformed, and there is a realization of what lives within. Then 'Adventuring once more in the natal mist' he descended to be born again, and 'His only sunlight was his spirit's flame'. Here he describes an ordinary human life, with a glimpse of something wonderful.[14]

Next, he recounts the world after reaching death: 'Where being from non-being fled and dared / To live but had no strength long to abide.' It was a strange, uncertain tract with an eager power that could not quite find its way. There were dim tokens of splendour, not real. Beings were drawn to that region of promise, but they were too divine to 'share the fate of perishable things'. There were entrapped spirits, and souls there who were trying to be born, the truth eluding them. Then there was a greater seeking. The kingdom of the morning star, and a 'great and doubting sun' arose. There was a desire for beauty, joy and truth. It was an intermediate realm, which provided the signs to move forward. Whatever we seek and have not known is already there. Life continues to try is to bring the spirit into a physical form. The eternal and timeless enters material bodies that exist within time, and that which is timeless becomes contained within time. This greatness had to be created on every plane. She – Life – is the same everywhere, on earth, heaven or hell. Even when dumb, she is the word, and when inert, she is still the Power. Even when unseen, she works; she is in every atom; she is there with death and in all calamities. She remembers lost eternity and tries to recreate it. The mind provides a glimpse, but not the whole. Each creature lives to get her power within and grow towards heights. Some are guided by the inner light, while others choose different gods, and there is a battle between the true and the false. There are warriors of both good and evil, and sin too is a divinity. Some revere falsehood and worship false gods, and the dual energy that exists can lead to heaven or hell. The outer is based on inner values. Words were not required as thoughts and emotions could be understood without them. A being could feel another even when far away, but still there was a separateness. The Superconscient remained unknown. There the beginning and end were occult, but reality was hidden. They knew only what mind could create and build from the huge store of the Supermind.

Aswapati follows her – Life – through death and birth, at first without a clear aim. She revealed secrets that he cannot understand. He loses himself in her without being able to reach her. 'Yet it is joy to live and to create / And joy to love and labour though all fails, / And joy to seek though all we find deceives /

And all on which we lean betrays our trust; / Yet something in its depths was worth the pain.' The aim is to bring eternity into time. But the journey continues, from birth to birth and world to world and no end can be seen. Though defeated, Life struggles on, dies and lives again. There is no escape.[15]

During the journey some terrible and horrific worlds are also reached, where Aswapati calmed his mind and tried to look into the 'formidable unknown infinity' in order to discover why the world had failed. He looked into the abyss and sees how death, error, grief and pain overlay the light and joy of life. It corrupted the truth, removed the 'signposts of Life's pilgrimage', deformed the divine creations and laid the foundations of misrule. It sowed a dark seed in ignorant hearts, and the black fruit of it was death and suffering. There were invisible evil messengers of great power. The evil powers came to him 'armed with beauty' and to understand their nature, he entered 'the night from which they came', an intermediate level 'between the world and hell' – a space where nothing was true. Here, 'Love ended early in hate, delight killed with pain, / Truth into falsity grew and death ruled life.' This evil even provided him an untrue scripture and law, spoke as if it was the voice of God and deceived with wisdom, making the false seem true. They all warred against one another, combining to hate those who 'sought some higher good'.

Then the scene changed, and he saw 'a city of ancient ignorance', where everyone walked in darkness, but took different evil paths. 'There Ego was lord upon his peacock seat / And Falsehood sat by him, his mate and queen: / The world turned to them as Heaven to Truth and God. / Injustice justified by firm decrees.'

There was no liberty, freedom, harmony or tolerance. There were groups that pretended to be good and condemned others with 'virtuous wrath'; yet they believed only in 'power and utility' themselves, with the fervour of a zealot. The lies were truth here, and the truth lies, but he survived by uttering a prayer and the Great Name. This was a hell, where he could be pierced by evil, fall, and even the gods would not know, and he would just disappear, but those who kept god in their hearts were safe. Now he entered a greater darkness, where God, Truth and Light had never been, or perhaps had lost their power. Amid squalid huts is a dark, fallen goddess with 'a perilous beauty and charm', but who drew people into the depths. Everything evil was desired and even led to a perverse bliss. As he entered there to search for Truth, the filth of the abyss rose upwards. He met people in houses, streets, councils and courts, 'who looked like living men', but in them was everything vile and subhuman, even though their forms could be fair and virile. Within them was 'Hell's trademark'. There was no sweetness, love or pity anywhere, and no help for those who were suffering. None could resist this tyrannical power and maintained a servile silence. The people here did not even yearn for divine release. Then he reached a dim wall-less space where there were no people, with only a sense of death and of a hostile force. Despite the horror, he tried to shield his soul from despair. The soul was vanquished, the godhead lost, eternal darkness loomed, leaving him to endure it and stilling the terror. Finally, peace returned, the Godhead in him awakened, 'and faced the pain and danger of the world'.[16]

'Then could be seen the hidden heart of Night' the next canto begins. There was 'a black infinity', a denial of spirit and truth in the 'stark unconsciousness', seeking to create a world without God. There were Titan beings, world egos, vast minds and lives with no spirit within. A universe was produced from its lethal sleep, and bliss had fallen into 'a black coma'. There was only matter without soul until life awoke in the abyss and the unspoken word tried to bring forth the spirit before being overshadowed by doom. A non-being took shape and 'covered eternity with nothingness. / A seeking mind replaced the seeing soul'. Truth and Light in the cave of the heart were obscured and an antagonist energy was born, who diverts the pilgrim on the eternal road. In the absence of the Divine, a new order emerges. However, when the Divine aspect is forsaken, it leads to an inner death, a desolated soul. In this state, malevolent forces, who harbour hatred towards Light and oppose peace, gain influence. They assume divine names, guide and rule, but are opponents of the highest truth. There are priests reciting prayers, chanting sacred texts and using incense, yet it is all deceptive. Those who aspire to uplift the fallen world find themselves under their power, for 'None can reach heaven who has not passed through hell'. Sri Aurobindo continues to offer insights into the arduousness of the path and the elements that must be transcended in order to attain the ultimate goal. These stages and states of mind can be understood as inner manifestations and can also be observed in different types of people encountered in the world. Subsequently, the described world that Aswapati enters seems to reflect the actual condition of those involved in war.

Into the dark and despairing night, Aswapati ventured forth with his luminous soul. A realm where people embraced evil and misery as their natural state, where laughter and pleasure were forbidden, and they were 'Glad of one's own and others' calamity'. Because tranquillity presented a state of tedium and ennui, suffering and pain made life colourful. Intense emotions – the fury of jealousy, murderous spite, hate, lust, treachery – provided zest to life. Drama, horror and fear prevailed. 'Uprooted cities, blasted human homes, / Burned writhen bodies, the bombshell's massacre'. And they sang of their fallen enemies, and thought, 'How great we are, how merciful art Thou'. They thought of reaching God in this way. 'It was a world of sorrow and of hate, / Sorrow with hatred for its lonely joy.' Hate glowed like a black jewel in the heart and spilled over into inanimate things. He went through this infernal realm 'to know her dreadful heart'. While in Hell, he looked for its cause, and went alone into this 'mindless Void', where thought and sense failed, but his soul still saw and knew. Then he reached the Subconscient and 'saw the secret key of Nature's change.' A light was in him, primal night was shattered, and a spiritual breath brought a new dawn. The light of the soul permeated the body, and matter and spirit became one.[17]

The ninth canto is a short one, on the paradise of the life-gods. It was a beautiful place, 'Immersed in light, perpetually divine'. Bliss was assured, and there was no fear or grief. One was free of the body's frailties. There was rapture, ecstasy and 'scenes of an immortal joy'. Conscious suns illuminated the landscape, revealing serene plains, majestic mountains and violet valleys. Below, the cities of the gandharvas, divine musicians, emanated ethereal melodies across space. Beauty, joy, stillness and hidden mysteries thrived, granting the fulfilment of miraculous dreams. After the anguish of the soul's long struggle was a perfect calm, accompanied by divine sights and music that makes the mind immortal, leaving the 'heart wide as infinity'. Profound thoughts reshaped the universe. The canto ends with 'Immortality captured Time and carried Life'.[18] Following so much hatred and despair, this canto offers a respite – a brief interlude of calm, joy and light.

But this was not the highest pinnacle and so it, too, had to be left behind. Though this limited existence had tasted a 'touch of the Supreme', there was more. Some were satisfied with this halfway point, where there was safety, and the spirit was tied to 'golden posts of bliss', but the wider soul asked for infinity and on the long path to timelessness, this beautiful memory was left behind. As Aswapati moved onwards, he saw a silver-grey expanse where day and night were one. In this realm, Knowledge mixed with Ignorance, where what lay below and beyond was sensed but not fully known. The forms of an ignorant life are devised here. There are some who believe they have already attained great heights, though they are nowhere. But within the human was the future god. Tree, plant, animal and man – all linked through a divine light. Though there were hints, clear knowledge remained elusive. Truth was fragmented 'into manageable bits'. Initially, the soul seemed dead until a wave descended from secret heights and mysteries were revealed through myths, the young formations beginning to feel beauty and know the self. In the first steps forward of the mind, there is ignorance, with a desire to know. Truth and Knowledge remained concealed and had to be sought after. Mind looked inwards, but God could not be seen. Progress was slow, as the earth could not bear more than that, though the strength of mind is more than that of the earth, as she searched for Omniscience.

'A dwarf three-bodied trinity was her serf'. The reference here is to three aspects of mind. The smallest among the three is the physical or mechanical mind, strong, low-browed and heavy-jawed. It resists change or discovery, perceiving the habits of the mind as truth and of the world as laws. It clings to what it knows, the dead past and the ancient ways, like a watchdog that barks at unfamiliar light, yet behind it stands a cosmic might.

The next was the desire-mind, a fiery spirit, descending from the great mystic flame that surrounds the worlds. It had a thousand shapes and innumerable names, bringing 'the burning vision of Desire'. It loved adventure and tried to leap to heaven without being guided by reason or the seeing soul. The greatest of the three was the last mind-power, Reason. She is described as 'the squat godhead artisan'. She tried to see what to make of the earth and stars. Though unconscious of 'the unspoken thought, the voiceless heart', she creates 'mechanic models of all things that are.' She explains through abstract thoughts and myths, and forces 'wide Truth into a narrow scheme'. Her sciences are precise and absolute, and she uses mathematical signs and formulas to create and prove her summary of things. Hers are 'high works of pure intelligence', withdrawn from the senses, though they don't break through the walls of the mind or reach any heavenly light. The path of reason is logical. She looked at a mechanical world, where matter is the reality, and there is no soul or spirit. But then doubts arise, as there may be a different power. Creation did not come from reason, and truth cannot be seen through reason. Thought and ignorance move together towards the sun. Despite this, 'Even now great thoughts are here that walk alone / Armed they have come with the infallible word'. These come from God and eternity and will bring a timeless knowledge.

In the stratosphere, there existed aspirants to a limitless world, beyond 'the dwarfish trinity'. They sought eternity, viewed the world from solitary heights and remained impervious to the cries of life.[19] There is a 'greater mind', and much can be attained through higher thought. Through this mind, a divine ray enters and influences the person, but its divinity is limited and confined. The godhead can't be contained within the mind, and escapes into vast spaces. It is not created by thought and cannot be known through it; yet higher thought has a role and can also conceive of a reality beyond itself. It can visualize the ideal mind that the individual can strive towards in the future – embodying both beauty and power.

The truths of the spirit manifest as 'Living Gods', capable of creating their own worlds in realms far from earth. Within us is a secret self, containing a breath of the Divine, allowing a light to come to us, through a thought or image of greatness and wonder. Even on earth, there lingers a memory of an exalted sphere. The ideal remains in our depths, and the awakened soul can reach it. The thinker can find the pure source and see the worlds where even matter takes on the substance of thought. A golden sun pours down its light from here, conveying 'the mystery of the eternal Ray'. At first, there was 'A triple realm of ordered thought'. Though immortal and divine, these realms were close to the human mind, and they could be reached by the ascending mind and conveyed through knowledge. Here the 'Prophet hierophants of the occult law' were intermediaries between man and God. And gods and living presences were also on earth, symbols of perfection, and for the infant spirit, the infinite was contained in finite forms. Mind and sense could be used to understand these. Indivisible time was cut into small minutes, and infinite thoughts were contained within world laws. The unseen was made visible to the student, but 'the infinite was reduced to square and cube'; the magic and mystery of life were structured and 'the psychoanalysis of cosmic self was traced'. The mighty mother's mystic whims and freedom were replaced by 'an idol of bronze'. The birth and death of the world was dated, unseen heights and depths measured and plumbed, 'Till all seemed known that in all time could be.' Every aspect was assigned number, name and form, yet the ultimate Truth remained elusive. An all-pervading consciousness governs both earth and heaven, with the mind unknowingly serving a higher power. Everything within the cosmos possesses meaning if only we could comprehend that which is concealed. A conscious power is in us but remains hidden. When ego and mind cease their dominance, it can hear the voice and moves towards a greater light, utilizing thought to grasp the absolute truth.

Thoughts discovered the 'seed-sound of the eternal Word' and heard the rhythm and music of the worlds. They created an abstract of the living divinity, and believed the mind's wisdom was complete. Thus 'the bright gods of Thought', brought the timeless light into time. Then she – Truth – was captive in the human mind, a mute treasure, an unchanging goddess. 'She sanctions and inspires his words and acts', and remains his companion and witness, 'The one joy of his body and soul'. She initiates new beginnings, and the individual becomes absorbed in her. However, even for the seer and sage, Truth is limited within the human experience. The timeless Ray descends into our hearts, but 'Truth is wider, greater than her forms'.[20]

'Always the Ideal beckoned from afar', the next canto begins. 'Tireless Thought' moves towards the unknown peaks, looking for the light. Sri Aurobindo writes of 'blue lucency', and various lights, for instance, 'A glory of sunrise breaking on the soul' and the bliss that beauty gives, as well as 'The lovely kingdoms of the deathless Rose'. Above the spirit in a mortal body are superconscient realms, and below, the inconscient. There is heavenly peace above, while below is 'a sullen, dim abyss'. The deathless Rose exists behind everything, and when awakened, it turns the world into 'a temple-ground.' There is a heavenly joy and bliss, through a secret grace. The names of the high gods and their powers are revealed. 'Our hidden centres of celestial force open' and even this transient body feels that bliss. Freed from time, the immortal is felt, and brilliant-coloured worlds are seen. Once the deathless flame is kindled, it is never extinguished and climbs through the mortal world to the 'invisible Throne'. Only through the strength of the eternal in us can we dare to climb towards the goal. There are worlds, 'Where Will is one with Truth and Good with Power'. Aswapati moved through these ideal kingdoms but did not stay there. They had beauty and greatness, and an intense but partial light. Each of these worlds were 'An absolute ideal's perfect home', where there was one supreme power to which other powers were subjected. Each was deemed to be the Truth, 'Yet were there regions where these absolutes met / And made a circle of bliss with married hands; / Light stood by light, fire wedded fire.' But he moved onwards to higher worlds, where there was 'the immutable and inviolate Truth', where all were one, 'united and inseparable'. The references here are to the worlds of different religions, and to find the truth one has to move beyond them.[21]

Then there was the silence of the vast mind that existed beyond the world. It was indifferent to the world, to good, evil, grief and everything in it. It was a witness, consenting to movements of nature. As the Self and energy met, thought and creation arose from that silence. He watched the world without desire. His soul knew the cosmic whole and had peace. Then doubt and scepticism arose. The certitude and firm theory seemed to be a fraud, and Reason lost confidence; the world seemed a failure. 'Deep peace was there, but not the nameless Force: / Our sweet and mighty Mother was not there.' There was yet a greater spirit, but no clear road, neither above nor below. 'Two firmaments of darkness and of light / Opposed their limits to the spirit's walk.' It moved through momentary events, 'Where all must die to live and live to die / Immortal by renewed mortality'. This is the realm of rebirth, of constant cycles of life and death.[22]

Aswapati saw a well or tunnel 'to the depths of God' and felt a wordless call. There was an intimation of joy, and a mysterious sound led him forwards. It was a whisper, like 'the yearning of a lonely flute', or of silver anklet bells, or a temple gong, reviving memories, arousing mystic happiness. 'The silent soul of all the world was there: / a Being lived, a Presence and a

Power, / A single Person who was himself and all.' This person could love without getting love, heal all cruelties and sorrow. 'It led things evil towards their secret good', turned falsehood into truth, and revealed divinity. It was the seed of the eternal within all. Without it there could be no life or love. There was 'A measureless secure eternity / Of truth and beauty and good and joy made one.' Everything there was soul, there was knowledge, but no thought. The souls were deathless, without bodies. The scenery was beautiful, and he could communicate with other souls without words. The beings who once had forms on earth, were there in a spiritual sleep, waiting for 'the adventure of new life'. A person persisted through many worlds, under different names, learning 'by experience what the spirit knew. / Till I can see its truth alive and God. / Once more they must face the problem-game of birth.' Here the spirit finds the silence of its starting point and remoulds its purpose. Here without thought or word, he saw the truth of himself, under the 'eyes of nameless gods'. He saw the source of all things human and divine. There were two souls united in creative joy, and behind them One. She brings them forth from the unknowable and supports all. 'The sole omnipotent Goddess ever veiled. He prayed to her and 'A light appeared still and imperishable.' He was overwhelmed and, surrendering his heart and mind, he fell at her feet.[23]

From this measureless and timeless state, he had to return again. This was the region of thought beyond thought, of the voice we cannot hear of the 'knowledge by which the knower is known, / The love in which beloved and lover are one.' Here a thousand roads led to eternity, and there were multiples of 'one radiant Self'. All creation here was an act of life, it was the birthplace of the infallible word. He reached the unchanging truth and inexpressible light. There were the 'flaming hierarchies' above, their wings enclosing space, 'The sun-eyed Guardians and the golden Sphinx / And the tiered planes and the immutable Lords.' He began to know his self's infinities and hidden universes. In that region there was no Untruth. There was infinite peace, a luminous silence and primal energy. There was overwhelming light in his brain and knowledge in his heart, his actions like those of the gods.[24]

Book 3: The Book of the Divine Mother

In the world, the eternal light is hidden by the cave of darkness. It called him when he was far, but retreated when he came near. It filled the heart when it was there, but when it withdrew, existence lost its aim. In the ascent, 'a height was reached where nothing made could live.' The mind had to surrender to light or die in 'the blaze of truth'. He had to transform himself into a nameless being beyond thought. To become that being, his separate self had to melt or be reborn into truth. With the disappearance of the individual self, there was a blissful nothingness and the godhead of the whole appeared. Everything now born from his knowledge was undone. There was a vastness and peace beyond time, and his soul's passionate search was answered. There was no connection with the universe, no mind, no heart, no person. 'There was no second, it had no partner or peer; / Only itself was real to itself.'[25]

Sri Aurobindo again emphasizes the very important point, that moksha or nirvana is not the aim of life, instead it is to bring light and love, not merely to the individual, but to all sentient beings.

Aswapati reached a realm where there was an absolute stillness, beyond ego, space, time, grief and joy. It would seem that birth, death, work and fate are over, but, 'O soul, it is too early to rejoice!' Where is the Self's mission and power? The divine within has a purpose, and this eternal peace is not it. This is only half, 'the everlasting No', but there is also an 'everlasting Yes'. This is 'the zero sign of the Supreme', but behind is an immortal face. 'A high and blank negation is not all, / A huge extinction is not God's last word'. To free the Self is only one step. Then the divine presence grew close to him, a being of 'power, light and bliss', 'And built a golden passage to his heart / Touching through him all longing sentient things.' A moment's sweetness was felt by the unconscious universe. 'A love that bore the cross of pain with joy / Eudaemonized the sorrow of the world'. A hidden ecstasy was affirmed in life, a truth and power, and wisdom drew near. 'The hidden word was found' and revealed 'the meaning of our spirit's birth'. A burning spiritual love removed all sorrow. 'Wrong could not come where all was light and love. / The Formless and the Formed were joined in her.' She is the golden bridge and the luminous heart of the unknown, the force, the word, the sun, the might of all. Life can be fulfilled only in her. 'Once seen, his heart acknowledged only her.' The seed of an eternal moment, cast into time, takes ages to be expressed. Now, he had to embody her joy in him. 'His single freedom could not satisfy, / Her light, her bliss, he asked for life and men'. Struggle and thought could not attain this light, but only surrender, so that the Power itself could act. All other desires had to be removed, else 'We lose the One for whom our lives were made.' He longed to bring her healing touch of love, truth and joy, into the suffering world.'[26] As Sri Aurobindo reiterates, his work was never for himself, but for the whole world.

But Aswapati recognized that there was more to be done, a descent into the void was necessary, the void from which everything emanates. He needed a strength that 'was not yet on earth'. There were treacherous elements, trying to block truth, and he had to find and transform these elements. The white flame of heaven would seem to have purified everything undivine, but 'The inconscient too is infinite'. He removed all desire so as to bear that immaculate touch. Then, his soul and mind included every other in it, it embraced the universe. He was one with all that lived. 'He felt the joy of others as his joy. He bore the grief of others as his grief.' There was no division between souls or between the world and God. He found that which had no beginning and no end. 'The stable force of all that moves'. He saw the source of all. 'A stillness of cessation reigned, the wide / immortal hush before the gods are born.' Then he saw creation, 'A bliss, a light, a Power, a flame white love', as well as different worlds and regions, but once again his soul descended into earth's obscurity, 'to share the labour of an errant power / which by division hopes to find the one'. He was two beings, one wide and free, and one struggling, bound.[27]

Then a sound came into the void. 'A recognized stream possessed his veins,' his cells awoke to the joy of the spirit. A voice spoke to him from the chambers of his heart.

'I am the mystery beyond reach of mind, / I am the goal of the travail of the suns' / My fire and sweetness are the cause of life. / But too immense my danger and my joy. / Awake not the immeasurable descent. / Speak not my secret name to hostile time; / Man is too weak to bear the infinite's weight.'

He is asked not to merge his heart of flame 'in the wide uncaring bliss', while death and sorrow remain in the world. Next, he is told to 'accept the difficulty and godlike toil'. Man is the only one awake in an unconscious world. He wants to bring about change, but 'His day is a moment in perpetual time'. Tied to matter, he is unable to find the truth. 'An immutable Power has made this mutable world; / A self-fulfilling transcendence treads man's road.'

'There's no rest for the embodied soul', until he has found himself. He has glimpses of love, beauty, joy. The earth mother then speaks to him to move towards the higher self. She offers him her light and strength and grants him a boon. Aswapati replies from his heart, saying he is not satisfied with the slow pace at which infinity is entering the world, and the way life is on earth, with humans somewhere intermediate 'between the beast and God'. Humans still did not reflect God's world, and he asked for a word and act that would lead to transformation. She replied, 'One shall descend and break the iron law. / Change nature's doom by the lone spirit's power.' Aswapati, relieved by this boon, returns to his kingdom.[28]

Part 2

Book 4: The Book of Birth and Quest

The second part of this great epic begins with descriptions of the rhythm of nature. The seasons passed, time and the days moved on, the monsoon came and went, then, then there was a change in the mood of the earth.

'An innermost thought kindled a hidden flame / And an inner sight adored an unseen sun'. Three seasons passed, then came spring. 'Then from a celestial source a human shape descended into earth's imperfect mould'. Savitri was born. At first the child was sheltered in wordless sleep before she remembered her divine home. Her spirit remained near the eternal. She was one with a greater nature.[29]

She grew up in a land of mountains, plains and giant rivers. Her soul soared beyond the known. An adept of truth, initiate of bliss, she moved in higher spheres.[30] She understood the existing knowledge of the universe, of numbers, of stars, but that was not enough. She conceived of an infinite knowledge and happiness, but it still had no form. She was aware of the universal self in all, the great light of the unknowable. This universal self is not the petty reincarnating self. 'She wished to make all one immense embrace / that she might house in it all living things.' Only a few could respond, and even fewer understood her divinity. Some felt there was a power and light in her and worshipped it, some adored and clung to her, but they did not know her mighty spirit. It is in this way men worship a god who is too great, too high and too vast. She guided people on their paths, and faith drew them. But none of these who followed her was her equal. She knew their needs and wants, understood their joy and grief and tried to heal their sorrows. Her greater self lived alone but felt closeness with nature. 'The force in her drew subhuman broods; / And to her spirit's large and free delight / She joined the ardent hued magnificent lives / Of animal and bird and flower and tree / They answered to her with the simple heart.' Her soul lived apart, like a flower blooming 'in an uninvited space'. She was admired by everyone but found no equal heart. 'Whoever is too great must lonely live. Adored he walks in mighty solitude; / Vain is his labour to create his kind, / His only comrade is the strength within. Thus this was it for a while with Savitri.'[31]

Again, a yearning arose, King Aswapati heard the earth's wordless hymn. 'That asks a perfect life on earth for men.' He saw that his cherished daughter was 'a great and unknown spirit'. He appealed to her to find her unknown lover and seek her strength within. Accompanied by the king's courtiers, she crossed many lands searching for him.

The whole world was revealed to Savitri. She saw different countries and places, met those she had once loved, remembered past events. It was summer. She saw the secrets of the world.[32]

Book 5: The Book of Love

Cantos 1–3: Then, in the wilderness, in a forested area, Savitri met the love of her life, Satyavan.

Satyavan and his beauty are described in detail. His face reflected the joy of life: 'His head was a youthful rishi's touched with light, / His body was a lover's and a king's. / A Veda knower of the unwritten book', He was 'One with the single spirit inhabiting all'. The two met, amazed by a joy they had waited for so long. They rejoiced, in a moment's silent gaze, their affinity clear. Then, 'An hour began, the matrix of new Time.'

Satyavan's father was the blind king Dyumatsena, who had been deprived of his kingdom, and now lived with his wife and son in a forest dwelling.

The third canto begins with 'Out of the voiceless mystery of the past …' and goes on to describe how there was an instant recognition as they saw each other, a joy and perfection born of the past. The souls then joined together. They seemed to merge with one another, and Savitri was conscious of nothing but him. 'In a new act of the drama of the world / The united Two began a greater age.' He showed her his hermitage. She would soon join him there permanently, but now she needed to bid farewell to her father.[33]

Book 6: The Book of Fate

Sri Aurobindo now brings Rishi Narad into the story, and he came down to earth from Paradise. Ancient texts narrate how Narad frequently travelled between the two worlds. The rishi was also a singer who could see the labour of the gods and the lives of people and animals, and he sang about the world, about 'the inconscient and its secret self' and reached King

Aswapati's palace in Madra. The wise and thoughtful king, and his beautiful, passionate, wise queen, human mother of Savitri, welcomed him. They listened to his songs, which brought rapture to the earth. By that time, Savitri arrived. 'Changed by the halo of her love she came; / Her eyes rich with a shining mist of joy.' Narad saw and praised her, but he ended with the words: 'If thy heart could live locked in the ideal's gold, / As high, as happy might their waking be! / If for all time doom could be left to sleep!' He did not say what he knew but Aswapati understood there was some shadow behind the words. He asked whether great souls must always be tested. 'Her glad and griefless days bring heaven here,' he said, and wished that they may continue.

At first Narad was silent. Then he asked where she had gone to return with 'glory in her heart / And paradise made visible in her eyes.' Her father explained and asked her whom she had chosen. Then Savitri spoke and said that following her father's instructions, she had found the one she sought. 'Mid Shalwa's giant hills and brooding woods / In his thatched hermitage Dyumatsena dwells, / Blind, exiled, outcast, once a mighty king. / The son of Dyumatsena, Satyavan, I have met on the wild forest's lonely verge. / My father, I have chosen. This is done.' Aswapati looked within, he saw a shadow followed by a light. He approved her choice, but he knew there was more to come. He already knew and before Narad could speak, he asked him, 'Lend not a dangerous vision to the blind.' The queen requested Narad's blessings, 'Pushing the ominous shadow from their days'. But as Narad said, 'A future knowledge is an added pain'. A beautiful picture of a meeting of two hearts, and love at first sight follows. The queen was full of grief as she understood that something was not right. Maybe, she thought, there was an evil being in the shape of the Shalwa boy. This was her well-loved child, and she had to know, and asked Narad, 'Hide not from us our doom, if doom is ours.' Narad assured her that Satyavan was perfect, like 'a golden paradise.' He was a unique treasure loaned by the gods, but the problem was that in one year exactly, he would die. The queen asked Savitri to travel once more and choose again. 'Plead not they choice for death had made it vain', she said and added, 'A choice less rare may call a happier fate.' However, Savitri had chosen. 'I am stronger than death and greater than my fate; / My love shall outlast the world, doom falls from me / Helpless against my immortality.' The queen had no such confidence. She talked of the transientness of love, life and death. How could Savitri break the eternal law? The thinking person had to choose the middle path and follow reason, she said. Savitri should not leave what was good 'to follow a beautiful face'. Only in the eternal calm and vastness, 'Can love be eternal in the eternal Bliss / And love divine replace the human tie.' But Savitri rejected this. Her strength is the strength of God, she said. 'My spirit has glimpsed the glory for which it came.' She added, 'I have seen the eternal in a human face.'[34]

Now Sri Aurobindo, through the words of Narad, discusses the sources of suffering and pain.

After Narad has spoken, the queen continues to question, as she is overcome with grief. She asks why, within time, there is this mystery of grief and pain. 'Is it thy God who made this cruel law? / Or some disastrous power has marred his work / And he stands helpless to defend or save?' In her long speech she adds, 'In the grey sleep of Matters' ignorance / Mind suffers lamed by the world's disharmony / And the unloveliness of human things.' She comments how people have learnt nothing from time and history and kill others' happiness along with their own. They continue to fight wars and to destroy everything.' Battle and rapine, ruin and massacre / Are still the fierce pastimes of man's warring tribes; / An idiot hour destroys what centuries made.'[35]

Book 7: The Book of Yoga

Savitri insists on her choice and returns to Satyavan, to the ashram where there is nature and the only voices heard are of birds and animals. Her parents have stopped questioning and give 'Their pride and loved one to the great blind king', returning with grief in their hearts. Like any daughter in law of those days, Savitri does all the household work. 'She made herself the diligent serf of all. / Nor spared the labour of broom and jar and well.' They are blissfully happy together, yet grief and fear of the fate to come remain with her. Her conjugal love fills her with ecstasy, but her secret sorrow remains and increases as the year draws to an end. She wants Satyavan to give her even more, so that his soul is imprinted in hers. She dreams of joining him in death, but she knows she cannot, because his sad parents would need her here.[36]

One night as Savitri sits in grief, a mighty voice speaks to her. It asks her why she came to this earth if she intends to just helplessly await her doom, and tells her, 'O Spirit, O Immortal energy, / If 'twas to nurse grief in a helpless heart / Or with hard tearless eyes await thy doom? / Arise, O soul, and vanquish Time and Death.' But Savitri has given up. In her heart's reply she says, 'My strength is taken from me and given to death / … Is there a God whom any cry can move? / He sits in peace and leaves the mortal's strength / Impotent against his calm omnipotent law.' She asks why she should strive with earth's unyielding laws. It would be better to cross over to the other world, where they could be together, and forget about life, time, eternity and thought. But the voice replies, encouraging her not to give up. She came to earth for a certain purpose, and the work was still not done. Was she not there to bring a new word and greater light? Savitri felt abashed. She replied that she was ready to do God's work, she waited for the divine command. She is asked to find her hidden soul, and in silence seek God's meaning. She looks into herself, and in a series of visions, sees how creation evolved, the thoughts emerging in matter, the seeds of life, and finally the appearance of the human being. She saw how the world energy was shaping all that exists. The soul within was a part of God, while on the surface, the mind was ever active. Within a human being, all the opposites of nature exist, though they may not be present in the surface mind. In the Subconscient and Inconscient are dark forces that lie in wait, but there are divine forces too. A human being, drawing on these different forces, moves through life, his past leading to his future, his present shaping what is to come. 'All the world's possibilities in man / Are waiting as the tree waits in its seed.' The mind hardly knows the meaning of life, and is surrounded by ignorance, but above is the Superconscient. Each human being too, has heights where there is knowledge and light. It is when this is brought down to earth, that life here will change. In the inner heart and mind is a self that knows the truth. As the person approaches the Divine, he recognized a part of it in his own life. In *Savitri*, a portion of the divine Mother lives and through her, a new world can be created for humanity. Earth would be transformed and become equal to heaven, but for this, the psychic soul must come forward and take control of the mind. Time, life and death, though passing incidents, still occupied too large a space within Savitri, and had to be 'pushed aside to find her soul'.[37] Here, Sri Aurobindo seems to describe his own experiences, and his feelings regarding the momentous task he has set himself.

Savitri has been asked to go beyond thought, beyond the surface of her mind, and sitting silent, she does this. Then a voice again speaks to her, telling her that what she will do is for everyone, not just for herself. Coming out of her material body, Savitri looks into her subtle being and sees her secret soul. She knocks and tries to enter, but a voice tells her to go back, lest she be tortured and die. A hissing serpent arose, 'the hounds of darkness growled', there were scowling gnomes, trolls, goblins and roaring wild beasts, but she continues and enters 'the Subconscient's gate'. There she experiences a blind mass of power, but she forces her way towards the soul. Everything seems chaotic, with half-formed thoughts, then she sees the beginnings of finiteness but still there is a confusion of vision and sound, 'a chaos of disordered impulses / In which no light can come, no joy, no peace'. Moving further, she comes to 'a vast, calm space'. There is light from an invisible sun, a bodyless happiness and a nameless peace. But now there is a bigger danger, 'a giant head of life'. This is the vast and powerful Subconscient that is not governed by mind or soul. This tremendous force wanted the heart's support and the soul's consent. It dreamed of glory, and 'Tempted a deep dissatisfied urge within.' Its force is in the world of opposites, of dreams, darkness and light, sun and clouds, laughter and tears, fear and joy, ecstasy and despair. But all these powers and forms, these joys and sorrows, are not of heaven, even though they seem almost divine. They hold in them poison and falsehood and serve life's desires. If trapped in this region, they can never escape matter and time. But some, who hold 'Truth's image in the sheltered heart', can move forwards. Savitri proceeds, and reaches 'a brilliant ordered space'. Here there is no wildness, but the rule of law and reason. Life is well managed and ordered, but the spirit's freedom is absent. Religion has fixed rules, ethics imposes limits. 'Even meditation mused on a narrow seat; / And worship turned to an exclusive God'. There are prayers to the universal, but the doors to the universe are shut. There is no love, in this rational, dry religion. The sacred book lay on 'the sanctified desk', but its true knowledge was lost.

Savitri proceeds further and reaches a road with a horde of gods, goddesses and other beings, proceeding towards the world to save it. She asks for the road to 'Find the birthplace of the Occult Fire, / And the deep mansion of my secret soul.' The gods tell her they come from her own hidden soul, to help mankind. 'We are thy will and all men's will towards Light'. She should proceed through the winding highway of the world to the source. Savitri follows the road that leads to a narrow path, where she feels 'the silent nearness of the soul'.[38]

The fourth canto describes the triple forces of the soul and their counterparts. Proceeding, Savitri sees a woman in 'a pale lustrous robe', who is 'A spirit touched by the grief of all that lives'. She knows the pangs of the earth and the stars, of death and life. She is Savitri's secret soul. She is every person and animal that suffers, though she has no power to save. 'God gave me love, he gave me not his force', she says. She brings love and sympathy, and many have felt her compassion. She is always with the sufferer and is one with them. Even while watching God's indifference, she has not turned against the cosmic law, only hoping and praying for change. Then, like a growl of thunder, the Man of Sorrows speaks: 'I am the Man of Sorrows, I am he / Who is nailed on the wide cross of the universe; / To enjoy my agony God built the earth, / My passion he has made his drama's theme.' In his long speech he goes on to say, 'I am the seeker who can never find, / I am the fighter who can never win'. His suffering gives him evil thoughts, and he is full of hate.

Savitri tells the being of pity, that she is a portion of her soul. It is because of her that the wretched can still hope, but she could only bring solace, she could not save. Savitri says she will return one day as a bringer of strength. Then there will always be peace and joy.

Her spirit continues upward, and she comes across a woman 'in gold and purple sheen', seated on a boulder shaped like a throne. She holds a trident and a thunderbolt, and her feet are on a 'couchant lion'. She is the embodiment of courage and strength, the Mother of Might. She tells Savitri she is her secret soul, in the world to help the unfortunate and save the doomed. Without fear of heaven or hell, she guides people on the path to the Divine. But there is too much crookedness and evil, too many hostile powers. Some that she guides pass onward towards the light, the mass fall back unsaved, but her work continues, and 'Slowly the world progresses on God's road'. But then another voice came into Savitri's mind, 'Of the dwarf –Titan, the deformed chained god', the ego of the world of desire, who wants the whole world for himself, and believes he is God unevolved in human form. He will complete what god has left imperfect, eliminate his sin and error. 'He was the first creator, I am the last. / I have found the atoms from which he built the worlds.' Whatever humans have achieved he now lists, and says that after conquering earth, he will conquer heaven.

But Savitri turns instead to the being of power, addressing her as 'Madonna of might, mother of works and force'. She too is part of her soul, put forth to help mankind. She had given men strength but could not give wisdom. She says she will return bringing light, and then, 'Thy wisdom shall be as vast as their power'. Hate, fear, and weakness will leave people's hearts, and the cry of the Ego, represented by the lion's roar, will be hushed.

Savitri continues upwards and comes to a harmonious and happy space, with a sweet fragrance, birdsong and the murmur of bees. Here a woman sits, in a clear, crystal light. Her floating voice is like music, and she tells Savitri, 'I am thy secret soul'. She has come to heal the desolate earth, to bring peace, strength and solace. She is charity and silence, knowledge and light, the power that 'labours for the best'. She makes even sin and error steppingstones, and all move towards the light. God grows in men in different forms. 'He is the God for which men fight and die, / He is the war of Right with Titan wrong.' There are many more forms of god. He is wisdom, 'the glad resignation of the saint', the voice of the prophet, beauty, truth, immortality. 'These powers are mine and at my call they come. / Thus slowly I lift man's soul nearer the light.' But human minds cling to ignorance. She says, 'I shall save earth, if earth consents to be saved.'

In response, a warped echo rises, from the human mind bound to its senses. This warped human thinks he knows all and makes a speech about his achievements. 'I am the mind of God's ignorant world', he proclaims. He has so much knowledge, about the earth, life, matter, evolution, the mind, the methods of ant and ape. All that humans have discovered is laid forth by him. But still, he admits, he does not know the cause of things, the hidden power. Maybe it is just better to remain human, within the limits of nature, for 'How can man grow immortal and divine?'

Savitri hears the warped answer but turns away to speak to the being of light, approaching her with the words, 'Madonna of light, Mother of joy and peace.' This Being tells her that she too is a part of her own self, put forward to raise the spirit to its forgotten heights. Because of her, she says, the soul draws nearer to God, and love grows in spite of hate. The hunger for the eternal has to be nursed. One day she will return, she says, his hand in hers, 'Then shall the holy marriage be achieved, / Then shall the divine family be born, / There shall be light and peace in all the worlds.'[39]

Savitri moves forward, seeking that 'mystic cave' of the soul. She finds herself in total darkness, in the night of God, in which nothing but God exists. Her knowledge, power and thoughts have disappeared, she has only 'the simple purity of emptiness'. She is in this spaceless vastness, but then again finds her inner self. Dawn comes with great beauty and an imperishable lustre. She sees 'the mystic cavern' in a great hill, where her secret soul dwells. In the holy stillness are great rock doors, with two golden serpents on the lintel, an eagle covering it with wide wings and doves nesting in the cornices. Entering, she sees giant stone gods, who live without breath, and various shapes on the walls, reflecting aspects of life. There is no sound, nothing breathes, but all the worlds and God are there, and as she moves through the rooms, she finds the various gods and goddesses, Brahma, and the Master and Mother of all life, Krishna and Radha in their eternal embrace. Then through the last tunnel, there is a deathless sun, a house of flame and light, a wall of fire, and crossing this, she finds her secret soul. There an immortal and infinite being stands who looks on the finite world, his tranquil happiness undisturbed. This is the secret deity, which is her own self. She has chosen to put a small part of herself to live on earth. She merges with the immortal self, and then returns to the earth.

Then, the lotus of her heart opens, a flaming serpent is aroused, touching her inner centres it reaches her head. There sits the Mother, a part of the original power, and Savitri is transformed.[40]

The last rains have ended, and Savitri's life is full of joy. Her own light and bliss pervade the lives of others. But then comes a nameless fear and formless dread. The voice of Night and Death informs her that happiness in this world is impossible, and death is the terrible Mother, the black Kali, that removes the will to live and destroys joy. But this is followed by the voice of Heaven and Light, which asks her to proceed further without fear. It reminds her that she has not come for herself, but to help the struggling world. Her life has to be a bridge between earth and heaven. To save the world one has to share its pain, or one would not understand how to guide mortals to transcend it. 'He who would save the world must be one with the world, / All suffering things contain in his heart's space / And bear the grief and joy of all that lives.' Then she looks into herself again and sees the origin of the world, and how life grew and evolved. God, nature, the centres of consciousness, the inner lotuses, are all revealed to her. She looks beyond thought, sees infinite nothingness and knows there is a sign within it, and feels everlasting peace.[41]

In the little hermitage in the forest life continues, outwardly peacefully, but there is an inner change in Savitri, a stillness. One night while Satyavan sleeps, a voice speaks 'from her own heart'. The voice is not hers, but as it speaks, everything is transformed and she experiences truth and reality in her own self and in the Self of all, as she unites with the universal self. She is everything, she is beyond time and space, in the Superconscient, looking out of eternity, at Time.[42]

On the fateful day, Savitri and Satyavan go into the forest together, where he starts cutting wood. Suddenly he feels ill and full of pain. He holds on to Savitri but dies. At this moment, Savitri realizes that Death is standing there.[43]

Part 3

Book 9: The Book of Eternal Night

Satyavan is dead, and Savitri is alone in the huge forest, holding his lifeless body. Then, as sometimes happens in a great crisis, her mind and thoughts recede, and a calm power enters her. She turns to meet the god of death. She places Satyavan on the ground, and a luminous form of him arises from his dead body. The form moves forwards, with Death behind him, and Savitri following. It is very difficult for her to follow, but her passionate spirit carries on, while she is in a trance. They reach the giant rock gates beyond which a living being cannot cross, and Death asks her to return. But Savitri arises like 'a shaft of fire and light'.[44]

It is a 'chill dreadful edge of Night', and all wait. The darkness hangs around her like 'a curtain of impenetrable dread'. There is no past, present or future, the mind cannot think, the soul cannot feel itself. Love, knowledge and heart's delight are unknown. But Savitri, 'armoured with light', moves on into this unknown world. There is no path, no end, no goal, she could not see Satyavan either. She is 'Lost in a blindness of extinguished souls', but she is still alive. Then, ahead she sees a gleam of light, and as it grows, Savitri awakes to her lost self. She sees Satyavan as 'a luminous shade'. Again, Death speaks to her and asks her to return. Satyavan is now in a different world, he says, while those on earth are full of pain. But, he adds, her strength deserves a reward, hence she can choose her prize on earth. Savitri replies that she does not bow to Death, she has a flaming will that can even influence matter, yet as Death has offered, she makes a demand, that whatever Satyavan dreamed or desired in the forest, should be granted. Death replies that based on those dreams, he would return Satyavan's father to power, and restore his kingdom and his friends. Though these things were not worthwhile, he would restore them if 'the deluded soul' preferred. And then again, he requests Savitri to return. But Savitri responds with powerful words. She is an equal spirit, she says. 'My will too is a law, my strength a god. / I am immortal in my mortality.' She again asks that Satyavan be returned. Death responds with scorn. Has she forgotten her mortal role? He is the creator out of the void and the destroyer too. But Savitri asserts that her God is will and love and sweetness, and love will remake Death's universe. They continue travelling through the blind night. Death finally questions her, what does she hope for? Only he is eternal, timeless and illimitable. All come to him for rest and peace, death is the refuge of the soul. Even the gods he says, come from his imaginations. Death has assumed a form, but in the changeless void neither Satyavan nor Savitri was visible.

Savitri replies that she is love. Love is in the heart of every being and knows the truth of all. She knows the one calm and silent Lord of all, and thus she who could conquer Death was born. Death remains silent and the three of them still move on through the gloom.[45]

Book 10: The Book of the Double Twilight

They walk onwards in the darkness: 'A walk to nowhere in a land of Nought'. Is Savitri condemned to wander in darkness because she believes she is equal to heaven and a living fire of God? Or is she atoning for all since the first act of breaking through the Inconscient? The world is created through an occult truth, the Inconscient is nothing but the sleeping Superconscient. Death walks beside us, but is just a stair to climb, a doorway to be crossed, and eternal night merely the shadow of eternal day. Sri Aurobindo explains that there is infinite potential in every aspect of life, even when it appears to be dark. Gradually, a light begins to glow, and Savitri enters a twilight world of vague, indistinct and temporary beings. There is a floating atmosphere, with evanescent colours and lights, and an elusive presence of purity, beauty and delight that cannot be grasped. It is a dream happiness, but Savitri does not lose herself, she still possesses her soul.[46]

Then Death speaks again, explaining that this is the unsubstantial world from which hopes come. Thoughts, dreams and yearnings create this world, but nothing in it is real. Visions create all this, there is no ideal in heaven or earth. Love is just a desire of the body, seeking in its loneliness 'a human prop'. There is no eternity in perishable beings, only the Alone is permanent. The gorgeous ideal has no reality, truth does not shine in the falsehood of the world. Even the avatars lived and died in vain, the words of sages and prophets had no effect. The earth remains as it was. If Satyavan had lived, he said, their love would have died, but now that he is dead it would live for a while in her sad breast, then memories would fade. Even in heaven there is a snake, and in the heart of a rose lives a worm. He explains in detail the different ways in which love between two souls ends, the clash of egos, dull indifference, the compromise of routine, an uneasy union that continues. In fact, Death presents a realistic account of how love dies within a marriage! But, he says, that Satyavan's death has saved their love. Savitri had only been following an unreal dream, and now she should return. But Savitri replies that Death is creating 'a dangerous music' mixing truth and falsehood. Their love did not conform to anything he described, as she and Satyavan are twin souls, 'born from one undying fire'. Death does not give up. Her thoughts are just a hallucination, he responds. She should open her eyes and see the reality. He had created the world with atoms and gas but thought and memory intervened, and these have no reality. Love is 'no gleaming angel from the sky' but actually a poison in the breast.[47]

Savitri replies that Death has veiled reality, imposing his own idea on it. It is God who made the world of matter, in order to imbue it with the divine spirit. Gradually, living forms emerged from the void, the soul is a secret presence in them, as humans evolved, they understood and conquered many of the powers and forces of the world, and glimpsed the unknown. The material world is still incomplete and imperfect, and Savitri tells Death that he is seeing this half-finished work as if it were the whole. The world actually is made for joy not sorrow. The thinking soul seeks the eternal, and finally there is bliss on earth. Savitri requests Death to return Satyavan, because it is for god's work on earth, the two of them were born to heal the unhappiness of the world with love and bliss. But Death again responds that these are just thoughts, ideals and dreams. The conversation continues on these lines. Death then offers her earthly joys, but Savitri affirms she wants Satyavan, nothing else. Then Death offers her daughters and heroic sons, there would be many to love her if she returned to earth. Savitri insists she wants only Satyavan. The three walk on.[48]

They come to a downward slope, where thoughts fell to a lower level. The twilight still floats around 'a less delightful dream'. She sees plains, mountains, streams, cities, harbours and ships, but the shapes are all shadowy. There are fragments of human thoughts and hopes, of arts and philosophies, of old creeds, religions and voices of prophets, poems, crafts, systems, sciences, that were lost and then reborn, but these were all dreams, repetitive cycles in the revolving world. Death speaks and points out these cycles of life, stating that immortality is only through him. Death asks her to leave her life behind, die and enter the path to immortality. However, Savitri responds that she cannot seek eternal rest and peace. The world is far from truth and perfection, but truth and the Divine exist there. The world is the body of God, and she would work to reveal this. Death seemed to be listening, though he requests her not to challenge the ancient laws. Savitri responds that no laws are inviolate.

Finally, the goddess form of Savitri takes her place. The goddess Savitri praises Death as her shadow and instrument but asks him to stand aside and return Satyavan. As Death resists, Light envelops him, and he flees. Thus, in that dream twilight of the symbolic world, the shadow of Death retreated.

Savitri and Satyavan are alone now, but still, there is a translucent wall separating them.[49]

Book 11: The Book of Everlasting Day

God's everlasting day surrounds Savitri. Her soul stands close to the infinite and she feels its delight. She is aware of worlds of light and joy, of the triple mystic heavens, and seven immortal earths, the lowest of which is still a heaven. The beauty of these worlds is described, the creator is the same as the one who created earth and death. The creator speaks, telling her that heaven and earth are two powers born from one, they are divided but will one day be rejoined. Till then she and Satyavan have to work within the dual law. But if she wishes, they can leave the earth, and both can rise to heaven. The offer is made several times, but Savitri simultaneously hears the cry of a million sorrowful beings and chooses to remain on earth. She requests that love, joy and sweetness descend on earth. The great being speaks, and allows her to descend to earth with Satyavan, to continue his work, so that life on earth becomes divine.[50]

Book 12: Epilogue

Awakening from a deep trance, Savitri finds herself on earth, holding Satyavan, who is alive again. She finds a new power, life and joy within her. Together they will work to bring joy and light to the world. They leave the forest and meet Dyumatsena and the queen. His sight and kingdom have been restored, but he asks what took them so long to return. Satyavan says he is in Savitri's hands, and as they look at her, a light emanates from Savitri. A sage and priest ask her how the earth will change, how this will lead to a happier age. Savitri replies that when one begins 'to feel love and oneness', 'a golden change' would ensue.

A greater dawn would await them.[51]

9
The Mother

Mirra Alfassa, or the Mother, was the most important person in Sri Aurobindo's life, and carried forward his work following his death. Some aspects of her life in association with Sri Aurobindo are offered here, though even this cannot do justice to her life. Seventeen volumes consisting of the collected works of the Mother have been compiled, including her own writings, her comments on Sri Aurobindo's writings, and collections of her answers to questions. Many of the Mother's works are originally in French, but have been translated into English. Apart from these, there are thirteen volumes of conversations recorded by her disciple Satprem, titled *The Mother's Agenda*, also originally in French. Satprem was a Frenchman whose original name was Bernard Enginger (1923–2007). As a member of the French resistance during the Second World War, he had been captured and spent a year and a half in a concentration camp. In 1949, he arrived in Pondicherry, where he became the secretary to the governor for a short period. During this time, he met Sri Aurobindo and the Mother. He then travelled to various places, including Brazil and Africa, but returned to Pondicherry and joined the ashram in 1953. Even after that, he left several times on his travels, and gradually became close to the Mother and understood her experiments. He noted down and, from 1964, recorded his conversations with her, as he recognized their importance to the world. Some extracts were published while the Mother was alive, but after she left her body, he put these together in thirteen volumes in French, titled *L'agende de Mere*, which were later translated into English. These provide an invaluable account of her life and experiences, particularly from 1960–73. They also shed light on the earlier years, as the Mother recounted aspects of these too in their conversations.

Mirra had spiritual and occult experiences from her childhood. According to her own accounts, by the age of thirteen she used to travel astrally at night, clothed in a golden robe. She recollected healing people of Paris with the power of this expanding, voluminous, robe.[1] Through her spiritual experiences, she also saw that union with the Divine, and a divine life on earth, was possible. In her sleep she met many teachers, one of whom she referred to as Krishna.

Even while her occult experiences continued, she also focused on her studies. In 1893, after graduating from school, she studied art and developed as a talented painter. She married the famous painter François Henri Morriset on 13 October 1897. She knew many great artists, including Rodin and Matisse, and helped Henri in creating murals in the Church of St James in Pau, in southern France. Their son, André, was born in 1898. Though always aware of a divine presence, she had no interest in a Christian traditional God. She recounted that between the ages of eighteen and twenty, she had attained a constant awareness of the divine presence, and had done this on her own, without help or guidance.[2] Later she came upon a book on raja yoga written by Swami Vivekananda, and this helped her realize in a few months what would otherwise have taken her years.[3] At age twenty or twenty-one, she read a French translation of the Bhagavad Gita, and even though this was not a good translation, it was a transformative experience.[4] She continued reading various texts on spirituality, but at the same time was also aware of the industrial revolution, and the scientific and philosophical works of the times, as well as the political upheavals in France and Russia. Soon she met Louis Thémanlys (1874–1943), the head of the occult group, Cosmic Movement in Paris, who was in charge of publishing the *Revue Cosmique*. He handed over this charge to her, and thus she came to know of the author of most of the articles, Max Théon, who was also the founder of the movement. Max wrote in English and the articles were being poorly translated into French, but when Mirra took over she checked and corrected the French versions. She supervised the publication and distribution of the *Revue Cosmique* for five years. She continued to see a guide and guru in her inner visions, the one to whom she had given the name 'Krishna'. Her serious occult work began around 1903–04, when she constructed 'a protective path' between the terrestrial and other worlds. It took months to prepare this path which allowed for a safe crossing after death.[5] In 1905 Mirra finally met Max Théon, who was a mysterious person, probably of Polish origin, said to know Sanskrit, to have received a spiritual initiation in India, and to have been with Madame Blavatsky in Egypt.[6] Max was married to Mary, who was known as Alma, and who was also adept in the occult. Max and Alma lived in Tlemchen in Algeria, but Mirra first met him when he visited Paris. Théon's group was one of many such spiritual groups popular in those days. Mirra then visited the Théons in Tlemchen in July 1906 and Henri joined them in August, both returning to Paris in October. In Tlemcen,

Mirra had found that Max and Alma were adept occultists who could command material forces, and she learnt a lot from them. Even their dog, known as Little Boy, had occult powers! She developed a deep admiration for Alma. The Théons believed that in occult tradition there were seven successive universes, and this was the seventh and last. Like Sri Aurobindo, they also believed in the further evolution of the human being, towards a greater perfection. Mirra again visited the Théons in Tlemcen in July 1907, stayed for two months, and further developed her occult powers. In the occult world she also learnt of the tradition of the four great asuras, representing falsehood, darkness, death and sorrow, the counterparts of four gods or emanations of Truth, Light, Life and Bliss. In occult beliefs, both groups are creations of the Great Universal Mother, to provide freedom of will to all beings. But the divine being has also placed love in the inconscient, that can overcome all evil forces. These Asuras were immortal but could transform themselves if they agreed to Incarnate in a body. Mirra had met the Asura of the Dark Lucifer in Tlemcen, and also believed that Théon was the Asura of Death. When she met Paul Richard, she felt he was the Asura of Falsehood, an Asura who called himself Lord of the Nations. Soon she had the experience of uniting with her psychic being, a term they used for the soul.[7] Francois and Mirra divorced in March 1908. After her divorce she became close to Paul Richard, also part of the occult group, who had stayed with the Théon in Tlemcen for one month in early 1907. They married on 5 May 1911 even though Mirra still believed that Richard was the Asura of Falsehood. According to her, the marriage was for two reasons. Paul, having divorced his first wife, could not get custody of his three children without marrying again so Mirra agreed to the marriage as she was 'indifferent'.[8] It seems her main aim, though, was to convert him from his demonic or Asuric nature.

Before meeting Sri Aurobindo, she had already realized her inner divinity by the end of 1911 [9] and aimed for a bodily union with the Divine, and of realizing a divine life on earth. She also soon attained union with her Psychic, a term used by Théon for the personal soul. The Psychic was the soul that incarnated and went through various experiences, different from the eternal soul. It was a spark of the Divine within each human. Later Aurobindo used the term in the same way. These early years are documented in her book *Words of Long Ago* (or *Paroles d'autrefois*),[10] and partly recounted to Satprem, published in the *Agenda*. These show that her philosophical ideas were fully developed before she met Aurobindo. Her work, 'Conversations: Questions and Answers', based on the questions posed to her by students and disciples, was only an elaboration of these early ideas.[11] During these early years Mirra also met other spiritual people. She was friendly with Alexandra David-Neel, a Theosophist, practicing Buddhist, and intrepid traveller across the world, and was impressed by Inayat Khan (1882–1927), the Sufi mystic and musician, who had travelled to Britain and France. She also knew Abdul Baha (1844–1921), the son of Bahaullah, the founder of the Bahá'í religion.

An amusing story is about how, in Tlemcen, she had met the 'King of cats' and learnt how to communicate with cats at a deeper level. In general, the belief is that animals go through many incarnations before their evolving souls took on a human body. She now believed that in some circumstances a cat can evolve directly to a human body and was testing this out. It is interesting that Charles W. Leadbeater, a noted Theosophist and occultist, also vouched for this. This partly accounted for the care she gave to the many ashram cats later in India. According to the Mother, one of the cats wanted to become a human, and therefore had an untimely death, and its psychic and a portion of its vital entered a human being. But the Mother also had a deep fondness for cats, and has provided many descriptions of the cats she knew.[12]

In 1953, commenting on her early work, she said by 1912 she had already foreseen and formulated Sri Aurobindo's programme for bringing the Divine on earth.[13] As seen in chapter 2, Paul, this time accompanied by Mirra, again came to Pondicherry for the French elections in 1914, intending to stand as a candidate. They travelled by ship, reaching Pondicherry via Colombo on 29 March. That same afternoon, she met Aurobindo for the first time, and realized he was the Krishna she had seen in dreams.

The Mother always identified herself with the Universal Mother, and in 1914 was totally convinced of this and Sri Aurobindo also knew this, she said.[14] The Universal Mother is the creative power of the Divine and Sri Aurobindo wrote about the divine mother, describing her powers. It seems he also identified Mirra with the divine mother. Soon after the first meeting, Mirra experienced a profound peace that permeated her entire being, as she opened herself and surrendered to the Divine in the presence of Sri Aurobindo. This peace had earlier been experienced by Sri Aurobindo when he meditated with guru Vishnu Bhaskar Lele. This peace was an essential background to all their activities. After this first meeting, her kundalini too was awakened, and the energy fixed itself above her head.[15] Sri Aurobindo had a similar experience earlier.

Mirra fully supported Paul in his attempts to get elected, but fraud prevented the election. Did Sri Aurobindo also feel that Paul was an Asura? As pointed out in chapter 2, there is no evidence of this in the early years, though Georges van

Vrekham, a Belgian journalist and follower of Sri Aurobindo and the Mother, believes he must have done so.[16]

Paul Richard had also repeatedly praised Aurobindo.[17] He wrote two books while in Japan, *To the Nations* and *Lord of the Nations*. The first consists of a series of essays predicting the downfall of capitalism after the first world war and the liberation of India, along with a critique of nationalism. This was translated into English by Sri Aurobindo, and Rabindranath Tagore added an introduction, in which he commented on Richard as, 'This solitary young Frenchman, unknown to fame, his face beaming with the lights of the new dawn and his voice vibrating with the message of new life'.[18] Mirra got Spanish flu in Japan at the beginning of 1919. Through an occult experience, she wrote, 'I had understood that the illness originated from beings who had been thrown violently out of their bodies', i.e., in the war. They were not conscious that they were dead and became vampires.[19]

After Mirra settled in Pondicherry, Sri Aurobindo confided in her that he was not proceeding, he reached a point but then regressed. Mirra conveyed what she had learnt from Théon, that the light had to descend into matter, into the body. Then Sri Aurobindo stopped writing in *Arya* as he descended into the vital, and further into matter. On 15 August 1924, Sri Aurobindo said he was in the process of bringing the Supermind into the physical consciousness.[20] Transforming the physical was the first step to that of the vital and mental. The descent had to go below matter to the subconscient and inconscient, and the Mother had a role in all this.

The Mother always knew she represented the Universal Mother, both she and Sri Aurobindo revealed that four powers of the divine mother. Maheshwari, Mahakali, Mahalakshmi and Mahasarasvati, were in her. These powers had descended into her probably in 1946, though she did not remember the exact date, but they could not be used unless there was a certain receptivity of those around her.[21]

After Sri Aurobindo's death on 5 December 1950, for a short time, the Mother was devastated but then she recovered and continued Sri Aurobindo's spiritual quest. Sri Aurobindo left his body through his own choice, and had planned to do so, but had kept this a secret from the Mother, as she would otherwise have not allowed him to depart. It was initially a great shock to her. Though he remained in seclusion while she was active in the ashram, they were internally united in all the work that was done. He was the stable base against which all action took place. As she explained later, 'he was actually doing everything.'[22] Even after his death, his Supramental force remained within her, but his physical presence was absent. How would she live without him? Yet she had the task of bringing the Supramental down into the body, she had to continue with this. To do this she temporarily sealed off the deep psychic part of herself. As she said, 'I understood that I had the entire responsibility for all the work and for the sadhana – well, then I locked a part of me away, a deep psychic part that was living, beyond all responsibility in the ecstasy of the realization'.[23] If she had not done that, she would not have been able to live without him. Now she had to proceed alone, all responsibility was hers. After three days of seclusion, she had understood what had to be done, but all work was suspended for twelve days, before the ashram slowly limped back to normal.

Education was a major goal, and the following year a plan was made to establish an international university. The Sri Aurobindo International University Centre was inaugurated on 6 January 1952, the name later in 1959 being changed to Sri Aurobindo International Centre of Education. The centre included departments of science, technology, humanities, fine arts and a lot else. From 1950 to 1958 the mother devoted her time to the ashram, which now had about 1,000 members and about 500 students that attended the school and university. She visited the playgrounds and played tennis herself. Sri Aurobindo was keen on an education that taught students how to think, rather than memorizing things, and the Mother worked out the educational programme in detail. The aim was to encourage the students towards a divine life, and for this each aspect of the personality had to be cultivated. The physical body had to be perfected as far as possible, as this would infuse consciousness in the cells. Thus, gradually a gymnasium, a playground, a sports ground and a tennis ground were set up. Sometimes films were screened in the playground and here the Mother also held evening classes. Men and women lived together in the ashram, whereas in all other ashrams in India, and in many educational institutions they were segregated.

After focusing on the body, attention had to be given to the vital. The vital, as analysed by Sri Aurobindo and the Mother, was from where desires, emotions, passions and depressions emerged. If harnessed in the right way, everything could be accomplished. The vital contained life forces, and therefore through it other unseen forces could inadvertently be attracted. The lower vital, of unwanted desires, had to be controlled. A strong will, the ability to concentrate and hold one's attention, and an appreciation of beauty and harmony, would help to create a positive vital. If a concentrated will and aspiration was used, practically anything could be achieved or acquired.[24] Beauty and harmony in the surroundings is also a manifestation of the eternal and while Sri Aurobindo created beauty through poetry, the Mother did it through art. Eastern and Western music, classical dance, theatre, embroidery, marbling, were all cultivated in the ashram, along with other arts and crafts. All these enriched and perfected the vital. The mental too had to be perfected as the mind was the organizer and planner of action, which could be very powerful when developed. In the ashram school, all types of subjects were taught, but the Mother pointed out that all knowledge was linked with spiritual realities. Truth was in all these, and subjects had to be taught in a way that revealed this. The fourth component of the being is the Psychic, the evolving soul. The Psychic represents the spark of the Divine within, and one should aim to be conscious of it and this was the main aim of education in the ashram. Each child and individual had to be seen as unique and education had to be tailored accordingly, and the higher spirituality too had to be developed. The aim was to function through divine consciousness, and not through the Ego. The children of the ashram belonged to the future and the teacher was seen as a helper and guide, revealing the knowledge that is already within. Therefore, in the ashram teachers too were constantly learning. But as the Mother said, 'Religious teaching belongs to the past and halts progress. Spiritual teaching is the teaching of the future – it illumines the consciousness and prepares it for the future realization. Spiritual teaching is above religions and strives towards global truth.'[25]

The Mother did not speak much about her own work on the spiritual plane, and on the physical body and the cells, but this was her focus. Early in 1951, she spoke about changing the consciousness of the cells, something that had never yet been done.[26] Changing cell consciousness was extremely difficult as it was something that had a universal aspect and would affect all cells, not just those in her as an individual. It would create a new consciousness in the world, reducing calamities and atrocities.[27] This was the main task she set herself in succeeding years. The first step towards transformation was descending into the subconscious and below into the Inconscient, which is universal and not personal, and transforming the nature from there. Otherwise, the habits, tendencies etc., with which one is born, would remain. The next step is transforming the cells.

On 26 Feb 1951, talking in the playground, the Mother spoke of a gnostic consciousness, which has understood the elements of truth in all religions and beliefs, and knows the place of each. This is one of the results of Integral Yoga.[28] On 14 January 1954, she spoke of the experience of having another body, young and strong, into which she could enter at times.[29] The experience of transforming the cells continued, and she also described what the new Supramental body would be like. The new body would have no sexual attributes and the inner organs would be replaced by centres of different forces. There would no longer be animal procreation.[30]

*

On 15 August 1954, the de facto transfer of Pondicherry to India finally took place, though the legalities were only completed in 1962, after which it became a union territory. The Mother was a French citizen, but in 1954 she applied for dual citizenship, though India did not have any provisions for this. As prime minister, Jawaharlal Nehru, too, was not clear about the role of the Mother. In December 1952, Dilip Kumar Roy, Aurobindo's protégé, had actually visited Nehru and complained about the Mother, saying she was not in favour of Pondicherry uniting with India, and that she was very autocratic and controlling. Roy then founded his own ashram in Pune, with his friend and companion Indira Devi. After Sri Aurobindo's death, Roy had been quite depressed as seen from the exchange of his letters with

Shri Krishnaprem.[31] But when Nehru visited the ashram for the first time on 16 January 1955, he was favourably impressed, and came again in September and in June 1963. Both Sri Aurobindo and the Mother thought very highly of Nehru.

The Mother's collections of questions and answers form six volumes. These came about when she started taking French classes for the students, soon after Sri Aurobindo's death. Students and sadhaks were free to ask her anything they liked, as long as they phrased the questions in French. These classes, later termed Entretiens, can be considered her specific teachings. In tradition, the present universe was the seventh, which would again dissolve into pralaya, but the Mother, like Max Théon earlier, believed it was not so; this one was permanent. Among the matters she explained was that each atom had a divine spark, but the psychic being was only in humans. She commented on and explained innumerable other topics in these sessions.

At different times during her life, the Mother also recollected her beliefs regarding her many previous incarnations. Among them were those of Queen Hatsheput, Queen Tiy, mother of Amenhotep IV, later known as Akhenaton; Jeane d'arc Joan of Ark, Queen Elizabeth I (1533–1603); Queen Margaret of Valois (1553–1615); Queen Katarina Catherine II of Russia. She felt she was on earth at one time in four different bodies, Joan of Ark, Queen Elizabeth, Margaret of Valois and Mona Lisa. She stated that these were emanations of aspects of her, not full incarnations. According to her, this was the first time the divine mother had incarnated fully.[32]

She also said that Sri Aurobindo had been Leonardo da Vinci, Caesar Augustus and Louis XIV among others. Some of Nolini's incarnations too were known, he had been Yuyutsu of the Mahabharata. Questioned about him being Leonardo, Sri Aurobindo denied any knowledge of it.[33]

The Mother had been battling occult forces for quite some time, then on 29 February 1956, she affirmed that she had succeeded in bringing the Supramental consciousness down to earth. This happened in the evening in the playground. After reading a few passages from *The Synthesis of Yoga*, the lights were turned off, and in the dark silence this experience took place. The Mother reported that she had a huge form of living gold, and in this form, she shattered the golden door that separated the Divine from the world.[34] This was not a vision, but something concrete. The Supermind had been working in her ever since Sri Aurobindo left his body, and finally there was a breakthrough. This day came to be known as The Golden Day. She wondered if her mission on earth had ended, but she was given a sign that her work had to continue. Yet this Supramental descent was not noticed by others seated there, as they had not acquired the capacity to perceive it. The actual Superhuman was still a long way away and would be something entirely different from the human being of the time. After this the Supramental force was active on earth and a new world was being born, though it still could not be perceived. When the Supramental creation was realized, there would be no religions and no gods, but life would reveal itself in forms representing divine unity. The gods could participate in the new creation if they wished or could remain in their own world as friends.

To usher in the new world, one had to move forwards, leaving aside attachments to past conditions. There had to be enough people who could receive the force. On 3 February 1958, the Mother had another experience representing a training ground for the Supramental world. There was a luminous orange light, and a calm joyous atmosphere, as the first inhabitants of the Supramental world were preparing themselves for it. Everything there had one substance, transforming itself through hidden forces.[35] In April that year she took the mantra '*Om Namo Bhagavate*' as her own, realizing that it had for her a special transformative power. Still, she realized that the essential link between the Supramental world and the earth had yet to be built.

In 1958 she reported that this link was being built, and the Overman was present in her physical body. This transitional being would be able to produce new beings without using the old 'animal methods'. There would be a new and more refined, luminous physical body, and a sense of universality and oneness. The members of the ashram and even the children she interacted with, did not seem to change, and to see the reason for this the Mother entered their subconscious and further descended into the general Inconscient. Here in a crevice between two rocks, there was pitch darkness, but suddenly she was flooded with a golden light. This took place on 5 November 1958, and it was a rich experience, a recognition of the warm golden source of the Supramental creation, which was even the source of the Inconscient. This was a vivid experience that gave her a further incentive to proceed.[36] But soon another change took place, and she withdrew from her usual routine. By the end of 1958, she stopped her playground classes, games of tennis, and even excursions outside the ashram, unless it was essential, though she continued to meet people within the ashram. These could be sadhaks with specific problems or requests, those who had birthdays, heads of departments in the ashram to check that all was functioning smoothly, as well as visitors from outside. In December that year, she was faced with an attack of dark forces that left her ill. But on 24–25 July 1959, she had a new experience of the Supramental directly entering her physical body, flooding it with reddish-gold light.[37] At this time she also met Sri Aurobindo in the Supramental world. Though she had met him before, this was an actual, physical meeting, and therefore she reopened her inner Psyche that she had sealed off when he left his physical body. The two were now again united.

Her focus now was entirely on transforming the body and its cells and this process is extensively recorded by Satprem.

The Mother had two aspects. She was a person on earth, but behind that, both she and Sri Aurobindo knew that she was the divine mother and the consciousness of the Divine, though usually not revealed, was always within her. Her efforts in these later years were to transform the physical, such that the Divine could enter and be part of the physical body. If it could enter her body, the transformation of matter could begin. To enable this transformation, she had also surrendered her physical self to the Divine within.

The transformed body would be luminous and flexible, would need no food, and would function differently. It would not feel pain and would be immortal.[38] If this transformation could take place, it could speed up the transformation of others. The mind and vital were already Supramentalized, but the physical was a different matter. The transformation of matter was extraordinarily difficult, and the body began to lose its centre, and its usual way of functioning.

A notable day was 24 January 1961 when she noted that the full Supramental force entered her body. But again, following this she faced an attack in the form of filaria, caused by mosquito bites in which her legs swelled, and she could hardly move them. Towards the end of February 1962 this was miraculously cured, but in March 1962 a new crisis began, and a severe illness took hold. In fact, on 16 March, death was near, as even her heart stopped a few times, but then the severity of the crisis passed, though illness continued. On 3 April, she recorded that at night between 11 and 12, an Asuric being took the appearance of Sri Aurobindo and said she was not doing his work. She met this being three times who had only power and force, but not love, and between 12:15 and 2 a.m., met the true Aurobindo. She felt that a group was supporting the Asuric forces, and the attack had affected her heart. But soon after this she felt the manifestation of the Supreme Love, and a realization of the Supramental. It was a brief time of victory, before returning to the limitations of the body.[39] On 12–13 April, she had a near-death experience when the vital and mental elements left her body and only the physical remained to continue with the experiment of Supramentalization of the physical.[40] The old ways of body functioning began to break down, as new experiences began. Matter appeared multicoloured, and full of energy and vibrations. The changes in the cells were extraordinarily painful. She appeared ill to those who did not know what was going on, but as Satprem explained, this was a transformation in which she was fully conscious. She also remained aware and conscious of this and other worlds and could use the divine force to intervene in various unfortunate events. During the Indo-China war of 1962, the sudden cease-fire, she said, were because of her efforts. She saw the war being caused by the Asura, the Lord of Nations. In response, the Mother was bringing down forces of peace in the areas of battle.[41]

By 1962, 'the Supramental realization of earth had essentially been accomplished'.[42] That year she left her body but returned to it. She said, 'It was decided that I take up my body again, that I return into my body'.[43] The second stage was accomplished, but the transformation of the body continued after this. She stated that the cells had begun to change and the mental and vital had withdrawn.[44] Without an ego, the body was kept alive by the Supreme, by a higher will for a higher purpose. She felt that the cells of her body were being transformed and were being divinized. The cells which had functioned automatically for thousands of years, had to become conscious. This was very painful for her body. All avatars suffer to take humanity a step forward, but even while she suffered, the divine ananda was present. Satprem provided a record of these experiments, as he was very close to her.

She continued to be head of the ashram and to supervize everything. There were 1,300 residents and 700 in the ashram school and many kinds of people.[45] When she met them, she gave her blessings with two or three rose petals, 'charged with her force', as she had learned from Alma Théon many years ago. She was said to be in touch with all deities and secretly working on the world at night. 'Krishna walked with me, Shiva was present in this room.' She worked in the philosophical, religious and political structures of the world to integrate them with the process of transformation.[46] She did this at night while apparently asleep. She said she visited America, Europe and different places in India.

But she said, 'The Asura of Falsehood, alias the Lord of the Nations, was doing his utmost to bring about an apocalyptic destruction'.[47] After the Indo-China war of 1962, the Mother is said to have intervened in the Indo-Pak war of 1965. During the 1960s, structures in the world were changing from within. In 1968 there was the velvet revolution in Czech, the Vietnam war, and in Pondicherry, the foundation of Auroville.[48] Reviewing these events, the Mother said a terrestrial reorganization had begun. She had another near-death crisis, but while those around her thought she was near death, she was in other landscapes, other worlds. 'During several hours the landscapes were marvellous, of a perfect harmony.' There were 'visions of the interior of immense temples, of living godheads. Everything had a reason, a definite goal, to express non-metalized states of consciousness.' 'The vital and mental left her body, the psychic being remained.'

Terrace darshans had started, the first taking place on her eighty-fifth birthday on 21 February 1963. She now lived on the second floor, and this terrace opened out of the room where she received guests, which was also her music room, where she had a Wurlitzer organ that she sometimes played. For the five minutes on the balcony on darshan days, the streets below would be crowded as innumerable people sought her blessings.

Thus, life continued in the ashram with its ups and downs. On 11 February 1965, some buildings of the ashram in the town area were attacked in the context of anti-Hindi protests, with the feeling that those in the ashram were Hindi speakers, though they were mainly from Bengal and Gujarat and not the Hindi heartland. But it was another expression of the local people not liking or appreciating the outsiders in their midst. Why was this? The Mother herself commented on the problem and said that all who had a higher intelligence and culture welcomed the ashram and those who formed part of it, as it was not against any religion, government or social class, but stood for 'Light, Peace, Truth and Love'.[49]

Despite the ongoing work on the transformation of the cells, and the several illnesses faced by the Mother, her outer work too continued. She continued taking care of the ashram, seeing visitors when possible, and responding to letters, while internally her other work continued.

One of the Mother's dreams came true with the founding of Auroville, an international city. The idea behind it is expressed in the following words, 'There should be, somewhere upon the earth, a place that no nation could claim as its sole property, a place where all human beings of goodwill, sincere in their aspiration, could live freely as citizens of the world, obeying one single authority, that of the Supreme Truth …'[50]

She had thought of such a city even in the 1930s, but after Sri Aurobindo's death, gradually the thoughts and dreams crystallized into something concrete. The foundation stone of the city, ten kilometres north of Pondicherry, was laid on 8 February 1968. In 1968, Auroville was just beginning. The Mother guided its early years and was tolerant of the variety of people who came, some of whom decided to stay. The aim of this potential city was to put into practice Sri Aurobindo's ideal of human unity. Gradually groups of cottages were set up on the arid land, with gardens and natural surroundings. Separate pavilions represent different countries.

At the centre of Auroville is Matri Mandir, 'the temple of the Mother', representing the universal mother. It is a golden sphere, surrounded by gardens. Within is an inner chamber, completely white, with white marble walls, and in the centre a crystal globe. Through the apex of the sphere, sunlight is electronically guided to fall on the crystal. Here people meditate in silence. Matri Mandir is said to be beyond all religions, a meeting point of silence, in which the spiritual force is revealed.

Auroville, however, is not merely about meditation, but about ways to promote and live a harmonious and constructive life. It has research centres experimenting with local, eco-friendly construction material, with new varieties of crops, the development of natural insecticides, and other products. Fruit trees of various kinds are grown in large orchards. Workshops produce handmade paper, natural oils for aroma therapy, incense, candles and other items. There is an extensive library, a school which incorporates Aurobindo's philosophy, and a publishing unit. A medical centre integrates indigenous and Western systems of medicine.

The Mother did not live to see Auroville at its height. She was focusing on establishing Sri Aurobindo's concept of a perfect world which was not an escape from life and did not involve leaving the body. According to Satprem, based on his closeness and conversations with the Mother, the transformation of the cells and organs within her body was continuing, and the Supramental force was passing through her to the earth. But the results had not yet shown up in her physical body, which, as seen from surface perception, was growing old. She had heart problems, her hearing and eyesight deteriorated, and she had difficulty eating. She seemed to be ill and did not speak much, but she repeatedly told those around her that she was not ill, she was in the process of transformation. But among those close to her it was Satprem who continued to have an absolute belief in her. After midnight on 1 January 1969, she felt herself suffused with golden light, and saw that the consciousness of the Superman had descended into her. Would this consciousness form the Supramental body? In 1970 she began to see what the new body would look like, and on 24 March 1972, she actually saw the transitional body. It was slender, harmonious and neither man nor woman.[51] It would seem from the conversations recorded by Satprem, that the Mother now had a Supramental body, but it was still in the Supramental world. How and when would it manifest as a physical body?

The date of 15 August 1972 marked the hundredth anniversary of Sri Aurobindo's birth. Celebrations in the ashram began on the 14th at midnight, with great devotion and beauty, with chants of Sri Aurobindo's name and music that had been specially composed for the occasion. A full moon shone over the tomb. In the morning, the Mother provided a message, 'One more step towards eternity.'[52]

Her body was becoming frailer, and from April 1973, further illnesses crept on. Pranab Kumar Bhattacharya, the head of physical education, was among her close attendants and provided an account of it. She still carried on some work, receiving heads of ashrams and giving them instructions. But on 20 May things took a turn for the worse. After this she mostly remained in bed with her eyes closed. Her attendants were with her, and doctors attended on her regularly. On 10 November, her daily check-up by Dr Prabhat Sanyal indicated a failing heart and low blood pressure. By this time, she also had bedsores which must have been increasingly painful. By nighttime, she was repeatedly asking to be lifted from the bed, and Pranab and Champaklal did so, until she finally slept at 4 a.m. On 14 November she wanted to walk, but despite being held from both sides she could not and was laid back in bed. She again wanted to walk on the 15th, but her helpers refused, as they knew it was impossible, even though she was a little better that day. On the evening of 17th, at 7:25 p.m., she peacefully left her body. Her son André had visited her earlier in the evening as he usually did.

Initially no one was told about her death. At 11 p.m. she was washed and dressed and carried down to the main hall at 2 a.m. Senior ashramites and others were informed and over the next two days thousands filed past her body. The coffin was closed on the 20th, and she was laid in the tomb above Sri Aurobindo's.

Many had expected to see her in a new transformed body and were bewildered that this had not happened. But Nolini Kanta Gupta explained the death was only a precursor to the coming of the new body.[53] The actual physical transformation was postponed but was already there in the subtle physical. K. D. Sethna and other devotees began to accept this concept of 'postponement' but retained the belief that the Mother had promised a physical transformation. Yet as their understanding grew, they realized that the Mother had not promised that she would be transformed here on earth, but that the work of transformation she had undertaken, would permeate the whole world and hasten the Supramental descent.

But one person insisted that the physical transformation would have taken place, had the Mother not been placed in her tomb in an untimely manner. Satprem, the closest to her, who later put together the Agenda, had not been allowed to meet her from May 1973. He quoted a note dictated to him in 1967, given to five senior people in the ashram, stating that in the process of transformation, the body may go into a trance that would seem to be a cataleptic state. They should not call doctors or announce her death but keep her carefully sheltered from all possible harm and injuries. This could last days, weeks, or even longer, and they should be patient, she said.[54] Satprem believed the Mother had been buried while she was still alive.

Whatever the truth of these last days, it is undeniable that Sri Aurobindo had the greatest and widest intellect of anyone in India, and that the Mother had tremendous perception, occult sensibilities and a talent for organization. Both provided answers to eternal questions, and guidance to not only those who met them, but to millions of others through their writings.

Epilogue
A Vision of the Future

Sri Aurobindo presented a completely new and detailed vision of the future of the world and our role within it. As expressed in *Savitri*, he envisioned a time when there would be 'The sun-eyed children of a marvellous dawn'.[1] While he drew upon concepts from ancient India and some similarities can be observed with ideas proposed by Western philosophers, his work originated from his reasoning, intuition and personal experiences. He consistently emphasized that his philosophy was unrelated to any specific religion, including Hinduism or any other. Although he borrowed certain terminology from Hindu texts, the philosophy he developed was not derived from any sacred or other existing text.

In summary, Sri Aurobindo explains that the Divine permeates everything; there is no aspect of the world in which Brahman does not exist. This understanding aligns with what is known from the Upanishads and other ancient Indian texts, where Brahman is regarded as the Absolute, the uncreated and eternal source of all, without form or shape, and transcending space and time. At the same time, Brahman is within all. However, Sri Aurobindo diverges from traditional texts at this point. The goal of life is not moksha, or union with the Divine in the sense of merging with it, but rather the purpose of creation is to manifest a perfect world of harmony and unity, where each individual form is infused with divine consciousness. Sri Aurobindo delves into the process of how this transformation will occur. Proceeding from Brahman, the Ultimate and Absolute, emerges sat-chit-ananda: Being-Consciousness-Bliss. Sat represents the truth, and thus, sat is true being. Chit signifies not only consciousness but a conscious force. Ananda represents bliss and delight, which constitute the true nature of every living being. Next, we encounter Supramental consciousness or the Superconscient, which is reflected in the Supermind. The Supermind is a power of sat-chit-ananda. Beneath this lies the Overmind, the realm of the gods. The human mind is positioned below the Overmind, with the higher mind, illumined mind and intuitive mind situated between the two. The ordinary mind can be further divided into its physical, vital and mental aspects. The physical aspect pertains to the body, the vital aspect encompasses the energy of emotions and desires, while the mental aspect involves reason. Additionally, each individual possesses a psychic being, an individual soul. The Psychic represents the soul formed by a spark of the Divine, and the psychic being is the soul personality based on this spark. At times, the term Psychic may also refer to the embodied soul in its finer, divine aspects.

Below the level of the mind and body lies the subconscious or subconscient state, and beneath that is the Inconscient, which represents the universal subconscious. Through a process of involution, the divine light enters the Inconscient and gradually ascends or evolves through various forms of matter, progressing from plants to animal and bird forms, culminating in the current highest form, the human being. However, evolution does not cease there, continuing until it reaches the level of the Supermind. There, a new kind of being will emerge, possessing a new type of body and mind.

Integral Yoga can combine elements of devotion, action and knowledge. Although Sri Aurobindo did not present a universal path for all, he emphasized that each individual has to consecrate one's life to the Divine, be open to intuition and discover their own unique path. Furthermore, both Sri Aurobindo and the Mother explained that in the Supramental state, individual religions cease to exist.

Though his work has been compared with that of various other thinkers, there is something distinctly unique about it. Among the many from the East and the West who have written about Sri Aurobindo, Gavin Flood, editor of the Routledge Hindu Study Series, refers to him as 'India's forgotten philosopher'. Flood suggests that while Aurobindo's philosophy has its roots in India, his solution represents a fusion of Indian heritage with European philosophical ideas. Sri Aurobindo's work resolves the dichotomy between matter and spirit, incorporating not only elements of Advaita but also European romanticism. Flood considers Sri Aurobindo's ideas relevant today to contemporary philosophical and religious studies concerning transcendence, rationality and secularism.[2]

Author and professor Brainerd Prince explores Aurobindo and his integral philosophy, examining both their contemporary relevance and their significance in the 'academic study of religion'. Prince believes that Aurobindo's philosophy is best understood within the framework of the hermeneutical philosophy of religion. Further, he considers three of Sri Aurobindo's works as key texts, *The Life Divine*, *The Human Cycle* and *The Synthesis of Yoga*, which address metaphysics, history and action, respectively.[3]

In the present, there exist diverse new age groups who hold the belief that humanity is progressing towards a heightened state of existence. Writer David L. Johnson asserts that 'The most comprehensive understanding of the nature of life and the evolving universe is that articulated by Sri Aurobindo'.[4]

While Sri Aurobindo's work is not directly based on them, it does share some parallels with certain Vedantic philosophies, such as Vishishtadvaita, Dvaita and Shivadvaita, as well as with various Western philosophers. As explored earlier, his work also resonates with statements found in early Hindu texts, such as the Vedas and Upanishads, along with the philosophies of Vedanta, Samkhya, Yoga and Tantra. Additionally, there are similarities in the theories of the five koshas (bodies or sheaths), the chakras (energy centres) and the concept of yugas (successive ages), as discussed in chapter 5. Among the four yugas, the Satya Yuga bears resemblance to the supramental future envisioned by Sri Aurobindo and the Mother. However, the concept of yugas is cyclical, and the envisaged future represents an upward movement, avoiding a descent into a dark age once again.

Sri Aurobindo's theories have also often been compared to those of quantum physics.[5] In his paper on this subject, Indian scholar Nikhil Kumar highlights the comparison between Sri Aurobindo's theories and quantum physics. Kumar specifically focuses on Werner Heisenberg's 'Uncertainty principle', which introduces the concept of uncertainty in the transformation of particles into waves and vice versa. Most scientists accept Heisenberg's view, while others support Einstein, who saw quantum theory as a stage leading to a higher theory. Nikhil Kumar suggests that Sri Aurobindo, in both *The Life Divine* and in *Savitri*, rejects 'uncertainty' as he views matter and its components from a higher perspective.[6] Rod Hemsell, among others, has drawn comparisons between the growth of quantum theory and Sri Aurobindo's vision.[7]

If we look at the Mother's vision of the transformed, Supramental body (see chapter 9), we find similarities with the vision of American physicist and futurist, Michio Kaku. A professor of theoretical physics in New York, Kaku envisions a different kind of life in the future with a new type of human being, which would be the result of scientific advancements. But unlike the new human being of philosophers, this would be created by science. Science has made so many advances, he says, that in a hundred years we will possess powers that are attributed to gods today – not through magic wands or potions, but through nanotechnology, computers, artificial intelligence, biotechnology and quantum theory.[8] Sri Aurobindo, however, refused to predict what the future human would be like.

Various evolutionary theories continue to abound. Twelve of these were summarized by Huchzermeyer from a 2007 study entitled 'What is Enlightenment' in an American journal.[9] The list includes: the Neo-Darwinists, the Progressive Darwinists, the Collectivists, the Complexity Theorists, the Directionalists, the Transhumanists, the Intelligent Designers, the Theistic Evolutionists, the Esoteric Evolutionists, the Process Philosophers, the Conscious Evolutionists and the Integralists. The last category is of utmost importance to Sri Aurobindo, which calls him, Gebser and Pitirim Sorokin are mentioned as the pioneers. There are also several other New Age Evolutionary theorists, such as James Redfield, and the New Age concept of 'Indigo Children', who are born with special capacities.

But the philosophy of Sri Aurobindo is neither about Christianity, Hinduism or any other religion, nor about any existing philosophy. People from all religious backgrounds, who came to his ashram, dropped their past convictions and identities as they began to understand Integral Yoga. And together, he and the Mother envisaged a future in which the world had moved beyond religion, hopefully to a new universality.

Notes

Abbreviations

CWSA: *Complete Works of Sri Aurobindo*
CWTM: *Collected Works of the Mother*

Introduction

1. Sri Aurobindo, *On Himself* (Pondicherry: Sri Aurobindo Ashram, 2000), 483 (reprint).

2. Sri Aurobindo, *The Integral Yoga: Selected Letters of Sri Aurobindo* (Pondicherry: Sri Aurobindo Ashram, 1994), 5–6 (reprint).

3. Ibid., 6.

1. The Early Years

1. Sri Aurobindo used different spellings of his name: at first, Aravinda, as he was named by his father; later in India, Arvind, then Aurobindo; finally, it was crystallized as Sri Aurobindo. He uses this spelling for Acroyd, as his middle name, which he later dropped; but it is also spelt Ackroyd and Akroyd. 'Krishnadhan' is the spelling Sri Aurobindo used; it is alternatively spelt Krishna Dhun and Krishna Dhan. These spellings used in the text are those from 'Autobiographical Notes', *CWSA,* vol. 36, (Pondicherry: Sri Aurobindo Ashram, 2006, reprint).

2. Krishnadhan also had two sisters, Biraj Mohini and Tinkoti. The latter married Nabakumar Mitra. *See* 'Personalia / Krishna Dhan Ghose'. Available at sri-aurobindo.in.

3. The Brahmo Samaj is an organization for social and religious reform founded by Ram Mohan Roy in Calcutta on 20 August 1828. The Samaj went through several phases:

The first was closely linked to the ideals of its founder. Ram Mohan Roy was a great scholar, who had studied the Vedas and Upanishads, as well as the main ideas of Islam and Christianity. The Samaj presented the idea of one universal God and the equality of all, propagated the ideas of the Vedas and the Upanishads, and also advocated social reforms, including the abolition of Sati, child marriage and polygamy. It attempted to improve the position of women and took a stand against caste. After Ram Mohan Roy's departure for England in 1830 and his subsequent death there in 1833, the organization declined until it was revived by Debendranath Tagore – leading to the second phase. Debendranath was formally initiated into the Samaj in 1843. A new system of initiation and membership was started, which gave each Brahmo member a sense of belonging. Each member was to acknowledge the one absolute God, *Parabrahman*, creator, preserver, destroyer, giver of all good in this world, all-knowing, all-pervading, formless and beneficent. Only this Parabrahman, one without a second, was to be worshipped and revered without any image or ritual, though all sects and religions were to be respected. Keshab Chandra Sen joined the Sabha in 1857, and though he was very close to Debendranath initially, differences arose slowly. His aim was to create a Brahmo organization that would conduct its own inter-caste and community marriages. Sen also wanted to integrate the true spirit of Christ into the Brahmo movement and bring about a social revolution within Hinduism. Nevertheless, Debendranath and some other Brahmos could not accept his radical ideas.

In its third phase, by November 1866 the organization then split into two groups, with the Adi Brahmo Samaj under Debendranath and the Brahmo Samaj of India under Keshab Chandra Sen. The Adi Brahmo Samaj remained primarily a monotheistic Hindu organization. Debendranath retired from active work, and appointed Raj Narayan Bose (Swarnalata's father) as the president. Later, under the influence of Rabindranath Tagore, this section of the Samaj gained new life. The Brahmo Samaj of India began a new programme of spiritual and social reform. In 1868, Keshab Chandra laid the foundation stone for a new centre of worship, known as the Tabernacle of New Dispensation. In 1870 he went to England to spread the Brahmo message, and Krishnadhan Ghose, Sri Aurobindo's father, travelled with him, albeit for a different purpose.

In 1878, another split took place in the Brahmo Samaj of India, leading to the fourth phase, and the Sadharan Brahmo Samaj emerged under younger leaders. These included Sivnath Shastri (1847–1919), Shibchandra Deb (b. 1811) and Manmohan Ghosh, among others. They instituted a democratic constitution for the Samaj, while their other ideals were along the lines of Debendranath's views. They also organized other activities and set up a college and some schools and continued to spread Brahmo ideas in different areas.

Keshab Chandra's group would become known as the Nava Vidhan (New Dispensation), including elements of Christianity, Islam, Buddhism and Hinduism.

In the Fifth phase some attempts at unity were made with the founding of the Brahmo Sammilan Samaj in 1902. Chittaranjan Das (1870–1925) was one of the key people who organized this. By this time, the Brahmo Samaj and its offshoots had spread from Kolkata to various parts of India.

The three main branches of the Brahmo still exist. *See* Dalal, *Hinduism*, 84–85.

Though Sri Aurobindo did not appreciate Brahmo ideas, they may have had a subtle influence on him, especially as Raj Narayan Bose was his grandfather, and Keshab Chandra Sen and Manmohan Ghosh were friends of his father. His wife, Mrinalini, had a Brahmo background. And Chittaranjan Das had defended him in the Alipore Bomb case.

4. Annette Akroyd (1842–1929) knew several languages. In 1873, she started a boarding school for women in Calcutta, the Hindu Mahila Vidyalaya. After her marriage to Beveridge in March 1876, the school was closed, but reopened in June as Banga Mahila Vidyalaya. She later translated the *Babur Nama* and the *Humayun Nama* into English.

5. The cause of malaria, which was transmitted by the Anopheles mosquito, was discovered in 1897.

6. For the ICS, a new system of recruitment was initiated in 1876, lowering the age limit to nineteen. *See* Bradford Spangenberg, 'The Problem of Recruitment for the Indian Civil Service During the Late Nineteenth Century', *The Journal of Asian Studies*, vol. 30 (2), February 1971 issue (Cambridge University Press, 23 March 2011), 341–60.

7. 'Krishnadhan Ghose's letter to Jogendranath Bose', 2 December 1890. Available at http://overmanfoundation.org/krishnadhan-ghoses-letter-to-jogendranath-bose/.

8. A saveloy was a type of sausage. Sri Aurobindo, *On Himself* (Pondicherry: Sri Aurobindo Ashram, 2000), 2.

9. 'Making Britain', The Open University. Available at https://www.open.ac.uk /arts/ research/asianbritain/making-britai.

10. The details are found in 'Personalia / Krishna Dhan Ghose'. Available at sri-aurobindo.co.in.

11. 'Autobiographical Notes', *CWSA*, vol. 36 (Pondicherry: Sri Aurobindo Ashram, 2006), 31. In a late discussion on 12 December 1940, Aurobindo said that he intentionally did not appear for the riding test, as he did not want to be part of the British government, and 'had a strong dislike for the British'. He appeared for the ICS exam only because his father wanted him to. *See* Nirodbaran, *Talks with Sri Aurobindo*, vol. 2 (Pondicherry: Sri Aurobindo Ashram, 1973), 466.

12. Interview in Empire, 8 May 1909, reprinted in Bengali, 9 May 1909. Quoted from Peter Heehs, *The Lives of Sri Aurobindo* (Columbia University Press, 2008), 32.

13. 'Autobiographical Notes', *CWSA*,149 (reprint).

14. Brajendranath De, 'Reminiscences of an Indian Member of the Indian Civil Service', *The Calcutta Review*, vol. 132 (3), September 1954, 181.

15. The British ship *SS Roumania*, travelling towards Bombay, sank on the night between 27 and 28 October 1892. It hit a sandbank near Foz de Arelho on the Portuguese coast. Two passengers and seven lascars survived. Available at www.fozdoarelho.net and wrecksite.eu.

16. De, 'Reminiscences of an Indian Member of the Indian Civil Service', 181. *See also* Nirodbaran, *Talks with Sri Aurobindo*, vol. 2 (Pondicherry: Sri Aurobindo Ashram, 1973), 466.

17. After Maharaja Khanderao Gaekwar died, there was a brief and terrible rule by his brother Malharrao, who was then deposed by the British. Various relatives were invited to meet the Maharani, who chose Gopal Rao, renamed Sayaji Rao Gaekwar III (b. 1863, ruled 1875–1939). He took over as ruler in 1881, at the age of eighteen.

18. Raj Narayan's (7 September 1826–18 September 1899) favourite texts were the Upanishads, but among his other readings were the works of Hafiz and the medieval French mystic Jeanne Guyon (1648–1717). He was a Brahmo traditionalist. Sri Aurobindo would comment, saying, 'My grandfather started by being a Brahmo and ended by writing a book on Hinduism and proclaiming it as the best religion in the world'. A. B. Purani, *Evening Talks* (2018), 708–9.

19. 'Letter of 24 August 1894' in 'Autobiographical Notes', *CWSA*, 123.

20 Ibid., 568.

21. This was first published in Bengali in the journal *Sahitya* in 1911–12, and as a book titled *Aurobindo Prasanga* in 1923, and finally brought out in English by Aurobindo Ashram. Dinendra Kumar Roy, *With Aurobindo in Baroda* (Pondicherry: Sri Aurobindo Ashram, 2006), 5.

22. Ibid., 12, 16–17, 23.

23. Questioned about why he married, Sri Aurobindo is said to have told his friend Charu Dutt that he was at that time under a 'spell of despair.' If he was just going to be a pedagogue, why not marry? But he also commented on why Buddha or Confucius had chosen to marry. He said:

'They marry before they change, then the change comes, and the marriage belongs to the past life.' 'Nirodbaran, Memorable Contacts: Mrinalini Devi, A Talk on the Occasion of Her Birth Anniversary'. Available at sri-aurobindo.co.in.

24. B. Ghose, *Sri Aurobindo*, 13.

25. 'Early Cultural Writings', *CWSA*, vol. 1 (Pondicherry: Sri Aurobindo Ashram, 2003), 116–17.

26. In his corrections to the King's College Register, he states that from February 1893 to 1905, he was professor of English and Vice principal, Baroda College. During that time, he performed other work, though there wasn't any formal appointment. (*See* 'Autobiographical Notes', *CWSA*, 21, 42). However, official records state he was appointed acting secretary from May–September 1903, and assistant Huzur Kamdar from the end of 1903–September 1904, and he puts the official title Huzur Kamdar under his name in one of his letters. Ibid., 183, 568.

27 *On Himself*, 23.

28. Ibid., 21.

29. Jatindranath Banerjee (19 November 1877–5 September 1930) was born in Channa village, in District Burdwan. Interested in fighting for independence, he wanted to join the army to learn martial arts, but could not do so, as Bengalis had the British label of a 'non-martial race'. He was devoted to the Goddess Bisalakshi, whose temple was there, and, though married to Hiranmoyee, later became a disciple of Soham Swami and was given the name Niralamba Swami. He set up an ashram in the village, and his wife joined him there. Their only daughter had died. (Bagha Jatin is Jatindranath Mukherji and is not the same as Jatindrananth Banerjee).

30. Sister Nivedita, originally Margaret Noble, was at first a disciple of Vivekananda. She was also influenced by Peter Kropotkin (9 December 1842–8 February 1921), a Russian historian, philosopher and socialist, and Okakura Kakuzo, a Japanese nationalist, who visited Kolkata in 1901. There were others in Bengal involved in physical training for an actual revolution. Among them was Sarla Devi Ghosal, a granddaughter of Devendranath Tagaore.

31. The Bhawani Mandir idea lapsed on its own. 'Autobiographical Notes', *CWSA*, 74

32. 'Autobiographical Notes', *CWSA*, 91, 95, 110; Nirodbaran, *Talks with Sri Aurobindo*, 105–6.

33. Nirodbaran, *Talks with Sri Aurobindo*, 107.

34. 'Autobiographical Notes', *CWSA*, vol. 6–7 (Pondicherry: Sri Aurobindo Ashram, 2002), 263–303. His writings in *Bande Mataram*

are extensive and cover a variety of topics with the underlying theme of nationalism. They cannot be summarized here but are (and should be) analysed for any history of the national movement.

35. 'Speeches, 1907–1908', in *Bande Mataram*, *CWSA*, vol. 6–7, 828.

36 Ibid., 828; *See* 213–23, where Sri Aurobindo analyses incidents in Bengal and feels the British encouraged Muslim fanatics, whom they previously feared, in order to counter the Swadeshi movement.

37. Ibid., 370.

38. J. Ramsay MacDonald, *The Awakening of India* (Hodder and Stoughton, 1909), 49; 'Autobiographical Notes', *CWSA*, 96.

39. 'Karmayogin', *CWSA*, vol. 8; *The Ideal of the Karmayogin* (Pondicherry: Sri Aurobindo Ashram, 1909), 26.

40. 'Swaraj and the Musalmans', in 'Karmayogin', *CWSA*, vol. 8, 31.

41. Benoy married Umarani in 1913. They had nine children. He died on 1 October 1947.

42. A. B. Purani, *Life of Sri Aurobindo* (Pondicherry: Sri Aurobindo Ashram, 1977), 92.

43. Sri Aurobindo, *Letters to His Wife Mrinalini Devi* (Auro e-books, 2014), 6–7. Available at www.auro-ebooks.com.

44. Ibid., 10–15.

45. Ibid., 20–21.

46. Ibid., 21–22.

47. 'Autobiographical Notes', *CWSA*, vol. 36, 74.

48. 'Uttarpara Speech, 30 May 1909' in 'Karmayogin', 6–7.

49. 'Kena and Other Upanishads', *CWSA*, vol. 18 (Pondicherry: Sri Aurobindo Ashram, 2001), 339.

50. Sri Aurobindo wrote several essays on the works of Kalidasa. *See* 'Early Cultural Writings', *CWSA*, vol. 1 (Pondicherry: Sri Aurobindo Ashram, 2003), 151–264. His translations of Kalidasa can be found in 'Translations', *CWSA*, vol. 5 (Pondicherry: Sri Aurobindo Ashram, 2003), 12–309.

51. 'Karmayogin', *CWSA*.

52. 'Perseus the Deliverer' was first published in *Bande Mataram*, June to October 1907. 'Complete Plays and Stories', *CWSA*, vol. 3–4.

2. Pondicherry (1910–50)

1. Peter Heehs, *The Lives of Sri Aurobindo* (Columbia University Press, 2008), 217.

2. For an account of the early years, *see* Nolini Kanta Gupta, *Reminiscences* (Pondicherry: Sri Aurobindo Ashram, 2015).

3. Georges van Vrekham, *The Mother: The Story of Her Life* (New Delhi: Rupa & Co, 2011), 78.

4. For more on Richard and the Mother, *see* chapter 9.

5. Michel Paul Richard, *Without Passport: The Life and Work of Paul Richard* (American University Studies: Peter Lang Publishing, 1987). This presents an account of his life up to 1919. 'Autobiographical Notes', *CWSA*, 266–270, 582.

6. 'Autobiographical Notes', *CWSA*, 177.

7. *See* Nolini Kanta Gupta, *Reminiscences* (Pondicherry: Sri Aurobindo Ashram, 2015), 53, 89 (reprint).

8. Purani, *Life of Sri Aurobindo*, 154–55.

9. Once when he was writing on poetry, he quoted the Latin maxim, '*nihil humani alienum*', [nothing human is alien to me], and seemed to apply it in those early years. Of course, his focus always remained reading and studying, what he meant was that yoga or spirituality should permeate all aspects of a normal life. 'The Future Poetry', *CWSA*, vol. 26 (Pondicherry: Sri Aurobindo Ashram, 1997), 70.

10. 'Record of Yoga', *CWSA*, vol. 10–11, 13–23. *See* Synthesis of Yoga, chapter 10.

11. Ibid.

12. 'Autobiographical Notes', *CWSA*, vol. 36, 195–96.

13. 'Prayers and Meditations', *CWTM*, vol. 1 (Pondicherry: Sri Aurobindo Ashram, 2003, second edition), 294, 295.

14. Nilima Das and K. D. Sethna, *Glimpses of the Mother's Life* (Pondicherry: Sri Aurobindo Ashram, 1978), 162.

15. Georges van Vrekham, *The Mother: The Story of Her Life* (New Delhi: Rupa & Co, 2011), 167.

16. Sri Aurobindo.in / personalities.

17. Reminiscences of Bhupal Chandra Bose, in Sri Aurobindo, *Letters to His Wife Mrinalini Devi* (Auro e-books, 2014). Available at www.auro-ebooks.com 31; aurobindo/the incarnate word (online).

18. Letter of Mrinalini's sister. *See also* the account of Ila Sen, who knew her in Shillong. *Sri Aurobindo's Wife Mrinalini Devi: A Reminiscence by Ila Sen* (Overman Foundation).

19. 'Autobiographical Notes', *CWSA*, 148.

20. M. P. Pandit, ed., enlarged by Roshan, 'Part 4: Letters to Barindra Kumar Ghose', *Champaklal's Treasures* (Pondicherry: Sri Aurobindo Ashram, 2008), 170–76.

21. Ibid.

22. Barindra Kumar Ghose, *Sri Aurobindo*.

23. Nirodbaran, *Talks with Sri Aurobindo*, vol. 1 (Pondicherry: Sri Aurobindo Ashram, 1973), 115. However, Sri Aurobindo also remarked that it was because of Richard's suggestion that he put together his synthesis of his experiments with Yoga. Ibid., 170. In May 1940, Sri Aurobindo commented on Paul Richard's Lord of the Nations. He said Richard was in communication with this being, and the plans and methods he wrote about were what was happening in Germany at the time. Hitler and his army were destroying civilization wherever they went. *Talks*, vol. 2, 143–4; He also commented on Gandhi's statement that there was little difference between imperialism and fascism, saying there was a big difference, and Gandhi would not even be able to make such a statement in a Fascist regime. Ibid., 146. *See* Nirodbaran, *Twelve Years with Sri Aurobindo* (Pondicherry: Sri Aurobindo Ashram, 1973), 99.

24. In the Himalaya, Richard lived like a sannyasi and also wrote three short books during that period: *To India: The Message of the Himalayas*, *Messages from the Future*, and *New Asia*. It seems he was asked to write the last book by Mahatma Gandhi. He returned to France and remarried, but he always believed in the greatness of Sri Aurobindo and his vision. He later became a professor in the US and wrote other books, including *The Seven Steps to the New Age*. For more on Paul Richard, See 'A Rare Interview', 10 August 2013. Available at https://

overmanfoundation.wordpress.com: A meeting with Paul Richard', 29 April 1967. Available at www.srichinmoylibrary.com.

25. Dilip Kumar Roy's interviews with Paul Richard, 2 April 2012. Available at https://overmanfoundation.wordpress.com.

26. Nolini Kanta Gupta, *Reminiscences* (Pondicherry: Sri Aurobindo Ashram, 2015), 91–92.

27. Ibid.

28. Ibid., 113–114.

29. 'Despair on the Staircase, 'Collected Poems', *CWSA*, vol. 2, (Pondicherry: Sri Aurobindo Ashram, 2009), 639.

30. M. P. Pandit, ed., *Breath of Grace* (Pondicherry: Sri Aurobindo Ashram, 1973), 79.

31. Purani, *Evening Talks with Sri Aurobindo,* 534.

32. 'Prayers and Meditations', *CWTM*, vol. 1 (Pondicherry: Sri Aurobindo Ashram, 2003, second edition).

33. Pandit, ed., enlarged by Roshan, 'Part 4: Letters to Barindra Kumar Ghose', 176–77.

34. 'Autobiographical Notes', *CWSA*, 260–61.

35. Purani, *Evening Talks with Sri Aurobindo*, 57.

On January 2, 1934, Mahatma Gandhi wrote to Sri Aurobindo that he would visit Pondicherry and wanted to request a meeting. However, Sri Aurobindo declined the meeting, as he was committed to maintaining his seclusion and could not break away from it. 'Autobiographical Notes', *CWSA*, 442.

36. Letter of 30 August 1920; 'Autobiographical Notes', *CWSA*, 257–59.

37. Das unfortunately died in 1925, and his party lost its importance, though it survived till 1935 and then again merged with the Congress.

38 *On Himself,* 281.

39. 'The Mother, with Letters on the Mother', *CWSA*, vol. 32 (Pondicherry: Sri Aurobindo Ashram, 2012), 32. The entire book is relevant; *see* particularly 31.

40. Purani, *Evening Talks with Sri Aurobindo*, 367, 590.

41. 'The Mother, with Letters on the Mother', *CWSA*, vol. 32 (Pondicherry: Sri Aurobindo Ashram, 2012), 32.

42. Purani, *Life of Sri Aurobindo*, 216–17.

43. 'Letters on Himself and the Ashram', *CWSA*, vol. 35 (Pondicherry: Sri Aurobindo Ashram, 2011), 270–273.

44. *Glimpses of the Mother's Life*, vol. 2 (Pondicherry: Sri Aurobindo Ashram, 2000), 17.

45. Narayan Prasad, *Life in the Sri Aurobindo Ashram* (Habra-Prafullanagar: Sri Aurobindo Karmi Sangha Trust, 2010), 64.

46. 'Letters on Himself and the Ashram', *CWSA*, vol. 281.

47. Rabindranath Tagore, *Aurobindo Ghosh*, 58–60.

48. Letter from Tagore, 30 November 1919. It is not clear to whom the letter was written.

49. See particularly, *CWSA*, vol. 27–32 (Pondicherry: Sri Aurobindo Ashram).

50. Letter of 17 June 1933; *On Himself*, 186.

51. Purani, *Evening Talks with Sri Aurobindo*, 580.

52. van Vrekham, *The Mother*, 218.

53. Dilip Kumar Roy: Sri Aurobindo came to me. Ibid., 219.

54. van Vrekham, *The Mother*, 235.

55. Aurobindo had inspired Barin to pursue a spiritual path after his release from prison. With Sri Aurobindo living in seclusion, Barin was unable to meet him regularly and therefore did not want to stay on.

56. For accounts of the ashram, *see* Pandit, ed., 'Part 4: Letters to Barindra Kumar Ghose'.

57. van Vrekham, *The Mother*, 259.

58 Purani, *Evening Talks with Sri Aurobindo*,137.

59. Golconde was carefully designed to reflect both spirituality and beauty. It was first used as a dormitory before it became a guest house. It was completed in 1945, as construction was delayed by the Second World War.

60. *See* Nirodbaran, *Twelve Years with Sri Aurobindo*, for a detailed account.

61. 'Autobiographical Notes', *CWSA*. *See* 453–68, on the Second World War.

62. Ibid., 103–4.

63. Ibid., 66.

64. van Vrekham, *The Mother*, 298.

65. 'Autobiographical Notes', *CWSA*, 84.

66. Nirodbaran, *Twelve Years with Sri Aurobindo*, 156.

67. 'Autobiographical Notes', *CWSA*, 469–74. This section also describes Aurobindo's subsequent response to the Wavell Plan of 1945 and the Cabinet Mission proposals.

68. For details of his life and the care he required during these years, *see* Nirodbaran, *Twelve Years with Sri Aurobindo*.

69. 'Autobiographical Notes', *CWSA*, 474–80.

70. Ibid., 494.

71. Ibid., 497.

72. Sri Aurobindo did not revise the Death and Epilogue sections of Savitri. Savitri was completed two weeks before the darshan on 24 November 1950, and other works too came to an end. Nirodbaran, *Twelve Years with Sri Aurobindo*, 188.

73. Heehs, *The Lives of Sri Aurobindo*, 382. *See also* chapter 5.

74. 'Letters on Himself and the Ashram', *CWSA*, 71.

75. He told Nirodbaran to 'Take up Savitri, I want to finish it soon.' It was the first time he had ever said something like this. Nirodbaran, *Twelve Years with Sri Aurobindo*, 187.

76. Ibid., 192.

77. Ibid., 194.

78. 'Notes on the Way', *CWTM*, vol. 11 (Pondicherry: Sri Aurobindo Ashram, 2002, second edition), 328; K. D. Sethna, *The Vision and work of Sri Aurobindo*, 105.

3. A New Analysis of Ancient Texts

1. *See* Roshen Dalal, *The Vedas: An Introduction to Hinduism's Sacred Texts* (New Delhi: Penguin India, 2014).

2. 'The Secret of the Veda', *CWSA*, vol. 15 (Pondicherry: Sri Aurobindo Ashram, 1998); 'Hymns to the Mystic Fire', *CWSA*, vol. 17 (Pondicherry: Sri Aurobindo Ashram, 2013).

3. 'Vedic and Philological Studies', *CWSA*, vol. 14 (Pondicherry: Sri Aurobindo Ashram, 2016).

4. 'The Secret of the Veda', *CWSA*, vol. 15, 4.
5. Ibid., 8.
6. Ibid.
7. Ibid., 5.
8. Ibid., 10.
9. Ibid., 11.
10. Ibid.
11. Ibid., 15.
12. Ibid., 19.
13. Ibid., 23.
14. Ibid.
15. Ibid., 24.
16. Ibid., 26.
17. Ibid., 27.
18. Ibid., 32.
19. Ibid., 58–69; 79–90.
20. Ibid., 90, 91–108.
21. Ibid., 108–158.
22. Ibid., 43.
23. Ibid., 44.
24. Ibid., 159–86.
25. Ibid., 187–210.
26. Ibid., 56.
27. Ibid.
28. Ibid., 211–22.
29. Ibid., 232.
30. Ibid., 247.
31. Ibid., 274.
32. Ibid., 277.
33. Ibid., 288.
34. Ibid., 289.
35. Ibid., 363.
36. Ibid., 368.
37. Ibid., 369.
38. Ibid., 370.

39. Ibid., 378–79.

40. Ibid., 379.

41. Ibid., 387–92.

42. Ibid., 603.

43. 'Hymns to the Mystic Fire', *CWSA*, vol. 17 (Pondicherry: Sri Aurobindo Ashram, 2013), 3–23.

44. Ibid., 24.

45. Ibid., 30.

46. Vijaya Rajiva raises a question in his comment: 'He does not explain the paradox of having a ritual in order for it to be symbolic.' *See* 'A critical examination of Sri Aurobindo's Secret of the Veda', bharatabharati.in.

47. 'Isha Upanishad', *CWSA*, vol. 17; 'Kena and Other Upanishads', *CWSA*, vol. 18, 18; Sri Aurobindo, *The Upanishads* (Pondicherry: Sri Aurobindo Ashram, 1996).

48. Sri Aurobindo, *The Upanishads*, 1.

49. Ibid., 2.

50. Ibid., 3.

51. Roshen Dalal, *The 108 Upanishads* (New Delhi: Penguin Random House India, 2019).

52. 'Isha Upanishad', *CWSA*, vol. 17, 30.

53. Ibid., 31–39.

54. Ibid., 40–91.

55. 'Kena and Other Upanishads', *CWSA*, vol. 18.

56. Ibid., 319.

57. Roshen Dalal, *Hinduism*, 62–63.

58. Sri Aurobindo, *The Message of the Gita* (Pondicherry: Sri Aurobindo Ashram, 1938).

59. Ibid., xvi.

60. Ibid.

61. Ibid., xvii.

62. Ibid., xviii.

63. Ibid., xviii.

64. Ibid., xix.

65. Ibid., 1–12.

66. Ibid., 15.

67. Ibid., 18.

68. Ibid., 19–20.

69. Ibid., 21. Though he says the state of consciousness is the same after death, but as there is no material universe or physical body, there and perhaps a limited memory of the former life, it could not be quite the same, but according to him, the same consciousness we had on earth, survives after death.

70. Sri Aurobindo, *The Message of the Gita*, 25–32.

71. Ibid., 35.

72. Ibid., 38.

73. Ibid., 97.

74. Ibid., 107.

75. Ibid., 108.

76. Ibid., 281.

4. Early Historical and Political Works

1. 'The Human Cycle', *CWSA*, vol. 25, 41.

2. Ibid., 12.

3. Ibid., *See* chapter 2: The age of Individualism and Reason, 15–25.

4. Ibid., 26–27.

5. Ibid., 27.

6. Ibid., 29.

7. Ibid., 31.

8. Ibid., 35.

9. Ibid., 41.

10. Ibid., 41. Treitschke.

11. Ibid., 42.

12. Ibid.

13. Ibid., 48.

14. Ibid., 50.

15. Ibid.

16. Ibid., 55–62.

17. Ibid., 63.

18. Ibid., 65.

19. Ibid., 63–72.

20. Ibid., 73.

21. Ibid., 148.

22. 'The Ideal of Human Unity' in 'The Human Cycle', *CWSA*, vol. 25, 553.

23. Ibid., 554.

24. Ibid.

25. Ibid., 555.

26. Sri Aurobindo, 'War and Self-determination' in 'The Human Cycle', *CWSA*, vol. 25, 599–605.

27. Ibid., 602.

28. The Passing of War in 'War and self Determination' in 'The Human Cycle', *CWSA*, vol. 25, 606–11.

29. 'The Unseen power, War and Self-determination' in 'The Human Cycle', *CWSA*, vol. 25, 612–22.

30. Ibid., 619.

31. Ibid., 621.

32. 'Self-determination, War and Self-determination' in 'The Human Cycle', *CWSA*, vol. 25, 623–34.

33. Ibid., 625.

34. Ibid., 626.

35. Ibid., 633.

36. League of Nations' in 'War and Self-determination' in 'The Human Cycle', *CWSA*, vol. 25, 634–63.

37. Ibid., 663.

38. '1919, in War and Self-determination' in 'The Human Cycle', *CWSA*, vol. 25, 664–67.

39. Ibid., 667.

40. 'After the war' in 'War and Self-determination', 'The Human Cycle', *CWSA*, vol. 25, 668.

41. Ibid., 668–81.

42. 'The Renaissance in India', *CWSA*, vol. 20.

43. Ibid., 3–42.

44. Ibid., 33.

45. Ibid., 43–52.

46. ibid., 53–94.

47. Ibid., 87.

48. Ibid., 97–384.

49. Ibid., 100–01.

50. Ibid., 441–44.

5. Philosophical Backgrounds: The East and the West

1. C. Sharma, *The Advaita tradition in Indian Philosophy* (Delhi: Motilal Banarsidass, 2007).

2. Srinivasadasa, Swami Adidevananda, trans., *Yatindramatidipika: A Handbook on the Philosophy of Ramanuja* (Madras: Sri Ramakrishna Math).

3. Swami Tapasyananda, *Sri Madhvacarya: His Life, Religion and Philosophy* (Madras: Sri Ramakrishna Math); B. N. K. Sharma, *History of the Dvaita school of Vedanta and Its Literature* (Delhi: Motilal Banarsidass, 2000, revised edition).

4. S. Radhakrishnan, *History of Indian Philosophy*, vol. 2 (New Delhi: Oxford University Press, 2002), 751–56.

5. Appaya Dikshitar of the sixteenth century was among those who contributed to the Shivadvaita philosophy. *See* Roshen Dalal, *Hinduism: An Alphabetical Guide* (New Delhi: Penguin India, 2010), 35.

6. S. Radhakrishnan, *History of Indian Philosophy*, 670–71.

7. Ibid., 756–60.

8. A good description of Samkhya can be found in Surendranath Dasgupta, *A History of Indian Philosophy*, vol. 1 (Delhi: Motilal Banarsidass, 1997), 208–58.

9. Swami Venkatesananda, *Yoga Sutras of Patanjali* (Shivanandanagar: The Divine Life Society, second edition, 2001).

10. Surendranath Dasgupta, *A History of Indian Philosophy*, vol. 1 (Delhi: Motilal Banarsidass, 1997), 367–404.

11. Ibid., 274–365.

12. J. C. Chatterji, *Kashmir Shaivism* (State University of New York Press, 1986).

13. Teun Goudriaan and Sanjukta Gupta, *Hindu Tantric and Sakta Literature* (Weisbaden: Harrassowitz, 1981).

14. There are a number of books on Tantra. *See* Agehananda Bharati, *The Tantric Tradition* (New Delhi: B.I. Publications, 1983); N. N. Bhattacharya, *History of the Tantric Religion* (New Delhi: Manohar, 1999); N. N. Bhattacharya, *Tantrabhidhana: A Tantric Lexicon* (New Delhi: Manohar, 2002).

15. Dalal, *Hinduism*, 206.

16. Ibid., 475.

17. Ibid., 224.

18. The *Manusmriti* states that anyone who accepts gifts from a greedy king who is not ruling according to prescribed laws, goes to twenty-one narakas or hells in succession, and then proceeds to list these. (*Manusmriti* 4. 87–90) The Puranas provide more descriptions and varying figures of twenty-eight or more hells. Dalal, *Hinduism*, 274.

19. Dalal, *The 108 Upanishads*, 137–38.

20. The best descriptions of the chakras and Kundalini are found in John Woodroffe, *The Serpent Power* (Madras: Ganesh & Co., 1992).

21. Dalal, *Hinduism*, 151, 410.

22. 'Letters on Yoga', *CWSA*, vol. 28 (Pondicherry: Sri Aurobindo Ashram, 2012).

Discussing Brahman and Moksha, Sri Aurobindo explains the difference between the active and passive Brahman but affirms that in the end both unite. Moksha leads to the silent, passive Brahman. The atman refers to the universal self, it is not born, and does not change. (Ibid., 30–31). The soul is born from the Divine and evolves as the psychic being. He equates the jivatman with the atman and follows the Samkhya concept of the Self or atman being inactive, and activity being a result of Prakriti or Shakti.

Interpreting some Upanishadic and Puranic terms, he refers to the seven lokas, and equates them with his own system, thus Bhu is the physical world, Bhuvar, the vital, and svara the mental. Only the first has a material existence. (Ibid., 38–39).

He writes most extensively on the Samkhya system (Ibid., 40–41), and also uses the Samkhya principles extensively in his writing particularly in Savitri.

He affirms that the jiva is essentially the same in all, but in manifestation has its own svabhava. (Ibid., 56) and explains the psychic being in the context of traditional terminology, describing the mind, vital and physical consciousness. (Ibid., 55–68; 102–24). He also explains the chakras (Ibid., 229–44), as well as asuras, hostile forces and avataras.

He looks at the ten avatars of Vishnu as 'a parable of evolution' (Ibid., 487) but does not take into consideration the many different versions of the avatars in the Puranas which vary from 10–39. He discusses the different attributes of the ten avataras. The avatara, he says, does not have to perform extraordinary acts, but the acts must have a profound significance, and relevance. (Ibid., 490).

He points out that spiritual teachers, prophets, and even intellectuals are vibhutis, not avataras. He comments on Rebirth (Ibid., 532–55).

The succeeding volumes of letters (vol. 2–4) are mainly guidance on aspects of Integral yoga, though there are also passages on other aspects.

23. 'Essays in Philosophy and Yoga', *CWSA*, vol. 13 (Pondicherry: Sri Aurobindo Ashram, 1998), 465–68.

24. S. K. Maitra, *The Meeting of the East and the West in Aurobindo's Philosophy* (Pondicherry: Sri Aurobindo Ashram, 1968), 49.

25. 'Essays in Philosophy and Yoga', *CWSA*, vol. 13 (Pondicherry: Sri Aurobindo Ashram, 1998), 215.

26. K. D. Sethna, *Sri Aurobindo and Greece* (Pondicherry, Sri Aurobindo Ashram, 1998).

27. Maitra, *The Meeting of the East and the West in Aurobindo's Philosophy*.

28. 'The Renaissance in India', *CWSA*, vol. 20, 330.

29. 'Letters on Poetry and Art', *CWSA*, vol. 27, 522.

30. 'Early Cultural Writings', *CWSA*, vol. 1, 629.

31. 'The Human Cycle', *CWSA*, vol. 25, 41.

32. 'Autobiographical Notes', *CWSA*, vol. 36, 112.

33. 'Letters on Himself and the Ashram', *CWSA*, vol.

34. As in Maitra, *The Meeting of the East and the West in Aurobindo's Philosophy*, 170.

35. Steve Odin, 'Sri Aurobindo and Hegel on the Involution-Evolution of Absolute Spirit', *Philosophy East and West*, vol. 31 (2), April 1981, 179–191.

36. 'The Superman' in 'Essays in Philosophy and Yoga', *CWSA*, vol. 13, 151.

37. 'The Human Cycle', *CWSA*, vol. 25, 41.

38. Wilfried Huchzermeyer, *Sri Aurobindo and European philosophy* (Auroville: Prisma, 2018). *See* chapter 7.

39. 'Early Cultural Writings', *CWSA*, vol. 1 (Pondicherry: Sri Aurobindo Ashram, 2003), 518–521.

40. 'Letters on Yoga', *CWSA*, vol. 28, 374; *The Renaissance in India*, *CWSA*, vol. 20, 27.

41. Maitra, *The Meeting of the East and the West in Aurobindo's Philosophy*, 48, 67; For an overview of Western philosophy, *see* Will Durant.

42. 'Early Cultural Writings', *CWSA*, vol. 1, 585–89.

43. David T. Johnston, *Jung's Global Vision: Western Psyche Eastern Mind: With references to Sri Aurobindo* (Stratton Press, 2019).

44. Huchzermeyer, *Sri Aurobindo and European Philosophy* (Auroville: Prisma, 2018). *See* Chapter 5, 48.

45. K. D. Sethna, *The Spirituality of the Future* (Fairleigh Dickinson University Press, 1981), 257.

46. Including K. D. Sethna, *Teilhard de Chardin and Our Time* (Pondicherry: Sri Aurobindo Ashram, 2000); R. C. Zaehner, *Evolution in Religion: A Study in Sri Aurobindo and Pierre Teilhard De Chardin* (Oxford University Press, 1971).

47. Huchzermeyer, *Sri Aurobindo and European Philosophy*. *See* Chapter 10.

48. Maitra, *The Meeting of the East and the West in Aurobindo's Philosophy*, 288–315.

49. For instance, Satya Prakash Singh, *Nature of God: A Comparative Study in Sri Aurobindo and Whitehead* (Aadyaa ebooks).

50. Prema Nandakumar, *Dante and Sri Aurobindo: A Comparative Study of the Divine Comedy and Savitri* (Humanities Pr., 1982); Brenda Deen Schildgen, *Dante in India: Sri Aurobindo and Savitri*, Dante Studies, with the Annual Report of the Dante Society, no. 20 (John Hopkis University Press, 2002), 83–98. IAS Sri Aurobindo told Nolini, he began learning Italian by reading Dante. Nolini Kanta Gupta, *Reminiscences* (Pondicherry: Sri Aurobindo Ashram, 2015), 90. Sri Aurobindo himself

saw Dante and Shakespeare as the greatest writers. Nirodbaran, *Talks with Sri Aurobindo*, vol. 1 (Pondicherry: Sri Aurobindo Ashram, 1973), 417.

51. K. A. Martin, 'A comparative study of the mystical elements in Sri Aurobindo's *Savitri*: A legend and a symbol, and Kazantzakis' *Odyssey*, A modern sequel (2010)'. Thesis presented to Faculty of English and Foreign Language Name, The Gandhigram Rural Institute, available on Shodhganga.

52. Sri Aurobindo, *Letters on Savitri* (Pondicherry: Sri Aurobindo Ashram, 2000), 71.

53. First put forward by Madame Blavatsky, the theory was elaborated on by C. W. Leadbeater and Annie Besant. Adyar, Annie Besant, *Man: Whence, How and Whither, a Record of Clairvoyant Investigation* (Madras: Theosophical Publishing House, 1913).

54. 'Is India civilised?' in 'The Renaissance in India', *CWSA*, vol. 20, 70–71.

55. Nirodbaran, *Talks with Sri Aurobindo*, vol. 2 (Pondicherry: Sri Aurobindo Ashram, 1973), 17.

6. A Life Divine

1. *The Life Divine* was published in serial form in *Arya* between August 1914 and January 1919. It was later revised by Sri Aurobindo, with Book 1 being published in November 1939, and Book 2 in July 1940. The second part was extensively revised before publication, with some chapters that appeared in Arya being deleted, and new ones taking their place. The book was first published in 1939–40, and the fifth edition in 1970, which is the version used here. It is also available in 'Early Cultural Writings', *CWSA*, vol. 21–22 (Pondicherry: Sri Aurobindo Ashram, 2003).

2. Sri Aurobindo, *The Life Divine* (Pondicherry: Sri Aurobindo Ashram, 1970), 1.

3. Ibid., 3.

4. Ibid., 6–24.

5. Ibid., 24.

6. Ibid., 27.

7. Ibid., 31–32.

8. Ibid., 36.

9. Ibid., 37.
10. Ibid., 40.
11. Ibid., 46.
12. Ibid., 48.
13. Ibid., 49.
14. Ibid., 52.
15. Ibid., 65.
16. Ibid., 71.
17. Ibid., 80–90.
18. Ibid., 93.
19. Ibid., 96.
20. Ibid., 98.
21. Ibid., 132.
22. Ibid., 142.
23. Ibid., 144.
24. Ibid., 147.
25. Ibid., 150–58.
26. Ibid., 170.
27. Ibid., 173–87.
28. Ibid., 188–97.
29. Ibid., 198–206.
30. Ibid., 207–17.
31. Ibid., 231–39.
32. Ibid., 240–61.
33. Ibid., 262–70.
34. Ibid., 278–79.
35. Ibid., Book 2: The Knowledge and the Ignorance: The Spiritual Evolution.
36. Ibid., 295.
37. Ibid., 302.
38. Ibid., 311.
39. Ibid., 295–321.
40. Ibid., 412–38.
41. Ibid., 501–10.
42. Ibid., 511–632.

43. Ibid., 633–56.
44. Ibid., 657–82.
45. Ibid., 683–725.
46. Ibid., 726–41.
47. Ibid., 749–50.
48. Ibid., 750.
49. Ibid., 761.
50. Ibid., 762.
51. Ibid., 742–64.
52. Ibid., 765–92.
53. Ibid., 805.
54. Ibid.
55. Ibid., 805–6.
56. Ibid., 806.
57. Ibid., 808.
58. Ibid., 811.
59. Ibid., 812.
60. Ibid., 815.
61. Ibid., 818.
62. Ibid., 821.
63. Ibid., 823.
64. Ibid., 824.
65. Ibid., 853.
66. Ibid., 848–88.
67. Ibid., 964–1014.

7. The Synthesis of Yoga

1. Sri Aurobindo, *Synthesis of Yoga* (Pondicherry: Sri Aurobindo Ashram, 1998), 2.
2. Ibid., 15.
3. Ibid., 16.
4. Ibid., Introduction, 1–46.
5. Ibid., 47.
6. Ibid., 51.

7. Ibid., 72.
8. Ibid., 80.
9. Ibid., 93.
10. Ibid., 97.
11. Ibid., Part 1, 47–270.
12. Ibid., 274.
13. Ibid., 305.
14. Ibid., 335.
15. Ibid., 358.
16. Ibid., Part 2, 273–520.
17. Ibid., 521.
18. Ibid., 527.
19. Ibid., 521–82.
20. Ibid., 586.
21. Ibid., 599.
22. Ibid., 627.
23. Ibid., 633.
24. Ibid., 634.
25. Ibid., 646.
26. Ibid., 661.
27. Ibid., 669.
28. Ibid., 693.
29. Ibid., *see* Part 4, Chapter 13, 693–700.
30. Ibid., Part 4, 583–872.

8. *Savitri*

1. Author's note at the beginning of the text.

2. Nirodbaran, *Twelve Years with Sri Aurobindo*, 179. The Mother told Mona Sarkar that Savitri described not only Sri Aurobinso's experiences, but hers too, even though she had not narrated them to him. Mona Sarkar, *Sweet Mother I* (Pondicherry: Sri Aurobindo Ashram, 2009), 26.

3. His comments on the poem and answers to queries and criticisms have been put together in Letters. Sri Aurobindo, *Letters on Savitri* (Auro e-Books), 9. Available at www.auro-ebooks.com.

4. Ibid., 10–11.

5. Sri Aurobindo, 'Book 1: The Book of Beginnings', *Savitri* (Pondicherry: Sri Aurobindo Ashram, 1994) 1–10, 12–21.

6. Ibid., 22–45.

7. Ibid., 46–73.

8. Ibid., 74–91.

9. Sri Aurobindo, 'Book 2: The Book of the Traveller of the Worlds', *Savitri*, 95–102.

10. Ibid., 103–15.

11. Ibid.,116–31.

12. Ibid., 114–50.

13. Ananke is a Greek goddess, personification of inevitability, compulsion and necessity. Usually depicted holding a spindle.

14. Sri Aurobindo, 'Book 2: The Book of the Traveller of the Worlds', *Savitri*, 141–72.

15. Ibid., 173–201.

16. Ibid., 202–19.

17. Ibid., 220–32.

18. Ibid., 233–37.

19. Ibid., 238–59.

20. Ibid., 260–76.

21. Ibid., 277–82.

22. Ibid., 283–88.

23. Ibid., 289–96.

24. Ibid., 297–302.

25. Sri Aurobindo, 'Book 3: The Book of the Divine Mother', *Savitri*, 305–09.

26. Ibid., 309–16.

27. Ibid., 317–33.

28. Ibid., 334–48.

29. Sri Aurobindo, 'Part II, Book 4: The Book of Birth and Quest', *Savitri*, 349–58.

30. Savitri can be seen as one of the avatars or prophets.

31. Sri Aurobindo, 'Part II, Book 4: The Book of Birth and Quest', *Savitri*, 359–68.

32. Ibid., 369–376, 377–86.

33. Sri Aurobindo, 'Book 5: The Book of Love', *Savitri*, 389–412.

34. Sri Aurobindo, 'Book 6: The Book of Fate', *Savitri*, 415–36.

35. Ibid., 437–62.

36. Sri Aurobindo, 'Book 7: The Book of Yoga', *Savitri*, 465–73.

37. Ibid., 474–87.

38. Ibid., 488–502.

39. Ibid., 503–21.

40. Ibid., 522–31.

41. Ibid., 532–50.

42. Ibid., 551–57.

43. Sri Aurobindo, 'Book 8: The Book of Death', *Savitri* has just one short Canto, Canto 3: Death in the Forest. In an early version of Savitri this formed Canto 3 of a shorter text with only six cantos, hence this is retained here. Minor revisions were later made to it (561–66).

44. Sri Aurobindo, 'Part III, Book 9: The Book of Eternal Night', *Savitri*, 571–81.

45. Ibid., 582–95.

46. Sri Aurobindo, 'Book 10: The Book of the Double Twilight', *Savitri*, 599–606.

47. Ibid., 607–20.

48. Ibid., 621–40.

49. Ibid., 641–68.

50. Sri Aurobindo, 'Book 11: The Book of Everlasting Day', *Savitri*, 671–712.

51. Sri Aurobindo, 'Book 12: Epilogue: The Return to Earth', *Savitri*, 715–24.

9. The Mother

1. 'Prayers and Meditations', *CWTM*, vol. 1 (Pondicherry: Sri Aurobindo Ashram, 2003, second edition), 81; Georges van Vrekham, *The Mother: The Story of Her Life* (New Delhi: Rupa & Co, 2011), 24.

2. Satprem, *Mother's Agenda* (Paris: Institut de Recherches Evolutes, 1977–1981), 19.

3. Ibid.

4. Ibid.

5. Georges van Vrekham, *The Mother: The Story of Her Life* (New Delhi: Rupa & Co, 2011), 47; Satprem, *Mother's Agenda*, 176.

6. van Vrekham, *The* Mother, 51.

7. Sri Aurobindo affirmed that the Mother was spiritual from childhood, and above the normal human even before she reached Pondicherry. *See* 'Prayers and Meditations', *CWTM*, vol. 1, (Pondicherry: Sri Aurobindo Ashram, 2003, second edition), 383–85.

8. Georges van Vrekham, *The Mother: The Story of Her Life* (New Delhi: Rupa & Co, 2011), 84.

9. Satprem, *Mother's Agenda*, 193.

10. 'Words of Long ago', *CWTM*, vol. 2.

11. van Vrekham, *The* Mother, 88; with commentaries on the Dhammapada in 'Questions and Answers 1929–1931', *CWTM*, vol. 3, 3–9.

12. 'Questions and Answers 1955', *CWTM*, vol. 7, 100; Satprem, *Mother's Agenda*,113–116, 462.

13. 'Questions and Answers 1953', *CWTM*, vol. 5, 355.

14. La Mère, *Glimpses of the Mother's Life*, vol. I (Pondicherry: Sri Aurobindo Ashram, 2000), 154.

15. Satprem, *Mother's Agenda*, 16 or 3103; van Vrekham, *The* Mother, 87.

16. van Vrekham, *The* Mother, 143; Nirodbaran, *Twelve Years with Sri Aurobindo*. On the Lord of the Nations who was behind the rise of Hitler *see* 225.

17. La Mère, *Glimpses of the Mother's Life*, vol. 1, 144. K R. Srinivasa Iyengar has also written a biography of The Mother.

18. Paul Richards, With an Introduction by Rabindranath Tagore, *To the Nations* (Madras: Ganesh & Co., 1921).

19. 'Questions and Answers 1953', *CWTM*, vol. 5, 182.

20. Purani, *Life of Sri Aurobindo*, 484.

21. Satprem, *Mother's Agenda*, 17; Questions and Answers 1954, *CWTM*, vol. 6 (Pondicherry: Sri Aurobindo Ashram, 2003, second edition), 291.

22. Kireet Joshi, *Sri Aurobindo and the Mothe*r (Motilal Banarsidass Publishers, 1 January 1996), 118.

23. Ibid.

24. 'Questions and Answers 1950–51', *CWTM*, vol. 4, 244.

25. van Vrekham, *The* Mother, 168.

26. 'Words of the Mother III', *CWTM*, vol. 15, 315.

27. Ibid., 316.

28. 'Questions and Answers 1950–51', *CWTM*, vol. 4, 157.

29. 'Words of the Mother I', *CWTM*, vol. 13, 56.

30. 'Words of the Mother III', *CWTM*, vol. 15, 298.

31. Dilip Kumar Roy, *Yogi Sri Krishnaprem* (Bombay: Bharatiya Vidya Bhavan, 1992), 260.

32. Satprem, *Mother's Agenda,* 151, 833.

33. 'Letters on Himself and the Ashram', *CWSA*, vol. 35, 57.

34. 'Words of the Mother III', *CWTM*, vol. 15, 102.

35. Ibid.

36. Ibid., 387.

37. Pandit, ed., revised by Roshan, *Champaklal Speaks* (Pondicherry: Sri Aurobindo Ashram, 2002), 107.

38. Mona Sarkar, *Sweet Mother II* (Pondicherry: Sri Aurobindo Ashram, 2009), 19.

39. Georges van Vrekham, *Beyond Man: The Life and Work of Sri Aurobindo and the Mother* (New Delhi: Rupa & Co., 1997), 373–74.

40. van Vrekham, *The* Mother, 467.

41. Satprem, *Mother's Agenda*, 277–296 – (978 of whole).

42. van Vrekham, *Beyond Man*, 378.

43. Statement made on 7 August 1963. Ibid., 379.

44. Ibid.

45. van Vrekham, *Beyond Man*, 390–91, 392.

46. Ibid., 395.

47. van Vrekham, *Beyond* Man, 398.

48. Ibid., 400.

49. 'Words of the Mother I', *CWTM*, vol. 13, 129.

50. van Vrekham, *Beyond* Man, 403. The Auroville charter was created on 28 February 1968, and Auroville was founded.

51. van Vrekham, *Beyond Man*, 472.

52. Ibid., 474.

53. Ibid., 479.

54. Satprem, *The Mind of the Cells* (Paris and Mysore: Institut De Recherches Evolution & Mira Aditi, 199), 212. (Translated from French by Jennifer Low and Michel Danino).

Epilogue: A Vision of the Future

1. *See* Sri Aurobindo, Part 3, Book 4, *Savitri* (Pondicherry: Sri Aurobindo Ashram, 1994).

2. Gavin Flood, series editor, in his foreword to Brainerd Prince, *The Integral Philosophy of Aurobindo: Hermeneutics and the Study of Religion*, Routledge Hindu Study Series, (London and New York: Routledge, 2017). calls him 'India's forgotten philosopher'. He says that Aurobindo's philosophy stems from that of India, but his solution is 'a fusion of that heritage with European philosophical ideas'. The dichotomy between matter and spirit is resolved, and one can see traces not just of Advaita but of European romanticism. He finds him relevant today to 'contemporary concerns in philosophy and the study of religions about transcendence, rationality and secularism'.

3. Brainerd Prince, *The Integral Philosophy of Aurobindo.*

4. David T. Johnston, *Jung's Global Vision: Western Psyche Eastern Mind: With references to Sri Aurobindo* (Stratton Press, 2019).

5. *See* for instance, Shelli Joye, *Sri Aurobindo, Quantum Physics and consciousness* (Independently published, 2018).

6. Nikhil Kumar, 'Culmination of the Quantum Theory in Sri Aurobindo's Poetic consciousness', *International Journal of Physical Sciences* (9 May 2013), vol. 8 (17), 717–727. Available at http: / / www. academicjournals.org.

7. Rod Hemsell, 'Sri Aurobindo's Vision and the 20th Century: Physics and the Philosophy of Evolution' (Auroville: ISSEI workshop evolution, Program Malta, 2006).

8. Michio Kaku, *Physics of the Future* (India: Allen Lane, Penguin Books, 2011).

9. Huchzermeyer, *Sri Aurobindo and European philosophy* (Auroville: Prisma, 2018), 157.

Acknowledgements

The idea for a book on Sri Aurobindo had been germinating for thirty years. Reading his works and visiting the Sri Aurobindo Ashram in New Delhi provided further inspiration.

Many thanks to Mrs Devi Wahi and Madhu Anjali of the Sri Aurobindo Society, Dehradun, who shared their knowledge and thoughts and who have created a peaceful and aesthetic venue where it is possible to reflect on and discuss his ideas. Thanks also to Geeta Singh for her insights and to Chanda Rani Akhouri, with whom I discussed the book at every stage.

Special thanks are due to Prasun Chatterjee for believing in this book, Teesta Guha Sarkar for her valuable suggestions and Isha Banerji for her expert editing, as well as others at Pan Macmillan India involved in design and production.

Index